ESSAYS ON HOUSING POLICY

ESSAYS ON HOUSING POLICY
THE BRITISH SCENE

J. B. Cullingworth
Professor of Urban and Regional Planning, University of Toronto

London
GEORGE ALLEN & UNWIN
Boston   Sydney

GEORGE ALLEN & UNWIN LTD
40 Museum Street, London WC1A 1LU

© George Allen & Unwin (Publishers) Ltd, 1979

British Library Cataloguing in Publication Data

Cullingworth, John Barry
   Essays on housing policy.
   1. Housing policy – Great Britain
   I. Title
   301.5'4'0941   HD7333.A3   78–40958

ISBN 0–04–350054–4
ISBN 0–04–350055–2 Pbk

Typeset in 10 on 11 point Times by Bedford Typesetters Ltd
and printed in Great Britain
by Billing and Sons Ltd, Guildford, London and Worcester

Preface

My involvement over the last decade with the Central Housing Advisory
Committee, the Advisory Committee on Rent Rebates and Rent
Allowances, the Scottish Housing Advisory Committee and the English
and Scottish Housing Policy Reviews prompted me to attempt a wide-
ranging analysis of British housing policy (within an extensive historical
framework), while at the same time revising and extending the now outdated *Housing and Local Government* (Allen & Unwin, 1966). My
unexpected move to the University of Toronto made this impracticable,
and the result is a far less comprehensive work than I had envisaged:
hence the use of the term 'essays' in the title. This excuse is not entirely
convincing: a truly comprehensive book would have been a major, if
not impossible, undertaking. As I embarked upon this in the period
immediately prior to my move, I became more and more alarmed at the
daunting prospect. Following the move I was tempted to abandon the
project entirely, particularly since my initiation into the different
complex of Canadian housing problems and policies immediately confused such clarity of thought as I naively felt I had attained in relation
to the British situation.

But the book had been started, and an early draft brought encouraging
responses. As a result the attraction of redesigning it in the form of a
series of essays was too great to resist. My main stimulant was the dismay at the outcome of the housing policy review – a dismay which was
shared by colleagues who contributed far more to it than I had done.
Those of us who were stimulated by the original enthusiasm of the late
Tony Crosland (and who did not have to carry this over the political
hurdles facing Peter Shore, his successor as Secretary of State for the
Environment) were distressed that the huge effort on the part of those
within and outside government should have produced such a poor
creature as the 'consultative document' for England and Wales. The
Scottish product is somewhat less disappointing (as anyone who has a
feeling for the different housing and political complexion of that
country will know); but the major directions were set south of the
border.

It was these personal feelings, together with my experience in working
with the very able civil servants and their politically attuned ministers
in both countries, which have made me reflect on the nature of policy
making within British government and gave me some awareness
(denied to most academics) of 'the art of the possible' which I have tried
to communicate in these essays. A wider understanding of this may contribute to a more useful debate on the future course of housing policy.

The essay form is a convenient one for an author who disclaims the goal of being comprehensive but, since a major theme throughout this book is that comprehensive policies are unattainable, there is more than an excuse. At times I despaired of achieving the comprehensible, let alone the comprehensive. Both the selection of issues and the way in which they were to be treated presented me with acute problems and, like any good research worker, I have jettisoned more than I have retained. The final outcome reflects my personal judgement in February 1978: nothing more is claimed, though it is hoped that the essays may make a small contribution to the continuing debate. Hopefully, also, the arbitrary has not become the idiosyncratic.

I dedicate these essays to my good friends in the Department of the Environment and the Scottish Development Department who have taught me so much. It is my immodest hope that the essays will assist in furthering the public debate without which even minor reforms in housing policy will be unattainable. Without this debate their political masters will be powerless to make more effective use of their services.

J. B. Cullingworth
Toronto
February 1978

Contents

Introduction

Housing policies can only be divorced from economic
reality as long as there are alternative resources to mask
the gap.[1]

These essays attempt to review the scope and purpose of housing
policies within a predominantly British context. The objective is to
explore the labyrinth of issues which are relevant to the formulation of
policy in relation to housing. This is more difficult than appears at first
sight – as successive governments, to their dismay have found. Even a
narrow approach involves a consideration of national economic issues
(what the nation can afford); of standards, costs, personal incomes
and subsidies (what individuals can afford); of the state of the construction and building materials industries (what is physically possible);
of the financial position of the Exchequer, of local authorities and of
building societies (what can be financed); of the capacity of the bureaucracies of local and central government (what is administratively
feasible), of land availability – and of water, sewerage and other services
(what is practicable in terms of land supply); and so forth. Then there
are questions of estimating needs; of determining consumer requirements in terms of space, design, location and internal and external
amenities; of striking the 'right' balance between new building to
increase the stock, redevelopment and rehabilitation; of determining
the total investment in housing in relation to investment in other
environmental services. Such questions lead to even wider issues
such as the relationship between housing finance and policies for incomes, income redistribution, income maintenance and tax reliefs;
the relationship between housing policies and planning policies for the
control of urban growth, the safeguarding of agricultural land and the
promotion (or restriction) of employment growth; the relationship
between policies for house building (and house allocation) and policies
for promoting domiciliary health care in contrast to institutional care.

Changing economic, social and political circumstances have a major
impact on the creation, recognition and definition of problems. Rampant
inflation destroys the basis of carefully laid plans for the 'reform' of
housing finance and leads to counter-inflation policies which may hold
down incomes and housing costs, but at the same time increase subsidies to a level which is unmanageable – thus leading in turn to cut-

backs in building programmes. Soaring land prices may present
problems which are politically insoluble in terms of land policies, and
result in the easier policy of increasing subsidies. Changed perceptions
of the role of tax reliefs can lead to new arguments on equity between
tenants and house purchasers. Slum clearance – once regarded as a
means of ridding the country of an 'unmitigated evil' – comes to be
viewed as a destroyer of inner city communities. Problems faced by
coloured immigrants may be so politically confusing or delicate that
new policies are forged to deal with 'deprived areas'. Action in relation
to deprived areas leads to reassessments of deprivation and the extent
to which housing policies are of relevance. Community development
programmes of 'urban aid' raise questions of 'the structure of society'
and the limits to which the alleviation of poverty can go in the absence
of 'structural change'. An energy crisis leads to new questions being
asked on housing design. Rising transport costs lead to new (or, to
be more exact, renewed) arguments on densities. Increases in the recorded incidence of homelessness raises doubts about the measurement
of housing need and the allocation systems of local housing authorities.
And – a hardy perennial – attempts are made to design a 'cheaper house':
usually in vain, but with exceptions which can have disastrous results
for a following generation.

Such issues – and there are many more – make 'housing policy'
a matter for intense and wide-ranging political argument (and, on
occasion, paralysis). Experts – appointed and self-styled – wrestle with
bits and pieces of the complex web of inter-related issues (such as rent
control, or 'equity sharing', or land supply, or mortgage stabilisation).
Newly appointed ministers quickly learn the difficulties which have faced
their predecessors. But the political process naturally tends to simplify
the issues, and debate is concentrated on such unanswerable questions
as 'how many new houses are needed to meet the housing shortage?'.
This is terminology with which politicians and the electorate find it easy
to cope; and they react strongly to what is seen as obfuscation by the
cognoscenti (though not in these words). The temptation to talk
in terms of discrete problems which can be 'solved' by 'programmes'
cannot be resisted. Thus in 1973, as in 1961 and 1933, 'the problem of
the slums' was to be solved by a clearance programme which would
be 'completed' within a fixed time-scale (five years from 1933, ten years
from 1961, nine years from 1973). Similarly, 'the housing shortage' was
to be 'met' by building 350,000 houses a year for ten years (1963), or
500,000 a year for an unspecified period (1965).

Even in the mid-seventies, when it was becoming clear that the housing
situation was no longer characterised by overall shortages, the major
debate was still focused on the number of new houses being built, and
the government were under constant attack for their poor 'record'. Yet
it was arguable, to say the least, that the country could not afford to

build houses on the scale that was needed, let alone on a scale that was not. Unfortunately, the issues here were too complex for popular debate, and few politicians – and no ministers – dared to state publicly that the situation required a low level of house building. Their actions spoke differently and, in consequence, public credibility was shaken and the political process debased.

There are several reasons why this happened, of which two are of particular relevance to these essays. First, political rivalries coupled with the absence of budgetary constraints on voters have led to election auctions, with politicians bidding against each other for electoral support. (At the 1974 election, the Conservatives promised reductions in mortgage interest, and Labour promised rent freezes; currently – February 1978 – a pre-election competition is developing between the two parties on 'the prizes that will be available to the thrifty' first-time house buyers.)[2] This flight from reality has been possible only only because of a second, more basic, problem: this is the lack of general understanding about the nature of housing problems and their relationship to other problems. Political heat has taken the place of factual light.

It is the author's hope that these essays will assist in increasing the latter at the expense of the former. Nevertheless, by the very nature of the issues involved, a wide field of political judgement will always remain. There can never be any question of 'taking housing out of politics'; but one can hope that the political debate can be better informed and placed on a more sophisticated level than has been the case in recent years.

It follows, of course, that the author's own judgements and views will become clear to the reader. Where this is equally apparent to the author, an attempt will be made to set out other interpretations and attitudes. But all is neither black nor white; and housing policy decisions frequently have to be taken on the basis of a crude balancing of costs and benefits. Objectivity is elusive even for those who try hard to achieve it.

The personal statement made in the last essay makes no claim to any such objectivity: it is explicitly political but, though one party might find more to its liking than another, it is not a party political statement.

These essays are not intended to provide a comprehensive coverage of all the issues with which housing policy is, or should be, concerned. That would be a daunting task which, in any case, would require a tome of huge dimensions. Instead, several important issues are selected for discussion. The selection is inevitably somewhat arbitrary, but the intention is to illustrate the nature of the problems with which housing policy is concerned and the extreme difficulty of devising sensitive policies which meet predetermined objectives while, at the same time, avoiding unwelcome repercussions. The difficulty is exacerbated by the fact that problems change; predetermined objectives become less relevant; new problems arise in relation to which existing policies are not only irrelevant, but also positively harmful; and policies pile up on top of each other to create a general confusion which governments find difficult to rationalise. After a century of housing policies the position has become so complex and counter-productive that a radical reorientation becomes imperative. Yet the cumulative effect of a succession of policies has the result of conferring substantial benefits on large sections of the electorate which they will not give up without a struggle. And since the struggle has powerful implications for the security of governments there is a strong incentive for them to take the easy way out and to abandon the hope of replacing outdated policies with effective and relevant alternatives. In this they find further support in the uncertainty and unpredictability of measures of reform, and the over-riding importance of non-housing issues which impinge on housing policy. Of these the present crisis of inflation is paramount.

There are no easy answers, and these essays do not purport to offer any, but it is hoped that an academic analysis may assist in promoting a fuller understanding of what the issues are, and the directions in which policy ought to be geared.

The first essay illustrates the range of institutions through which housing policies operate. These institutions are subject to varying degrees of governmental control, but few are (or could be) direct, efficient and effective instruments of centrally determined policy even if this could be elaborated in clear, unambiguous and consistent terms. In fact, as already indicated, 'housing policy' cannot be conceived in this way, and thus attempts to design a 'comprehensive' policy will always fail. The elusiveness of a 'comprehensive' housing policy is thus due not only to the difficulty of harmonising the conflicting interests of different institutions; though the institutions take on a life of their own and thus complicate the tasks facing government, they also reflect the differing interests of their constituents. Even if it were possible by some magic feat of institutional nationalisation to effect an amalgamation into an 'all-purpose' housing agency, major clashes of interest would remain. In large part these stem from history – which has led to a distribution of 'housing benefits' which (as is demonstrated later) are irrational, indefensible and in conflict with both social and economic policy objectives. Governments therefore wrestle with the issue of redistributing benefits. Their problem is exacerbated not only by the inherent political difficulties of redistribution, but also by the sheer impracticability of unravelling the knots tied by their predecessors.

The first of the difficulties is that of comprehending what the current situation is. 'An immense amount of government time is spent in trying to understand, not what will happen in the future, but what has already happened in the recent past. It is hard to go from here to there when we do not know the "here" as well as the "there".'[3] The difficulties of determining 'need' and 'demand', which are outlined in the second essay, are illustrative. Only a few of the relevant issues are discussed, but it is abundantly clear that the problem facing governments is not that of getting their arithmetic correct: it is one of establishing what the real issues are. Government influences on both need and demand (and the particular characteristics of each) are pervasive but sadly this does not mean that policies can be welded into a coherent and forceful whole. The issues are too complex and too inter-related with other 'non-housing' problems to be susceptible to such management. Thus governments are forced to manipulate bits and pieces of housing policy separately. The third essay, on council housing finance, demonstrates the obstacles to, and the difficulties of, comprehensive policies.

It is not too much of an exaggeration to say that one of the major hurdles facing housing policy reformers is that the majority of the electorate are well housed and receive considerable financial benefits from the existing situation. For this majority, any change could be a change for the worse, at least in the short run. The fact that it is virtually impossible (both conceptually and pragmatically) to calculate the real costs and benefits to individual households increases the difficulty.

It is in this context that policies in relation to the existing stock of housing assume such crucial importance. Though typically the focus of political argument may be on the house-building programme, this is only the tip of the housing policy iceberg. For the foreseeable future most people will live in 'existing' houses and benefit (or otherwise) from the accrued advantages (or disadvantages) attaching to these. New building can affect the situation only marginally – both within the foreseeable future and (even more so) within the likely lifetime of any government. New construction adds at most 2 per cent each year to the housing stock. It follows that a major part of housing policy has to be concerned with existing houses – their condition, their cost, their utilisation and their 'accessibility'.

This, indeed, was the origin of housing policy: historically, action in relation to the existing stock predated policies for new building. In fact British housing policy has developed in large part from nineteenth-century sanitary policies – and much the greater part of housing legislation reflects this.

The relationship between 'stock' and new building policies is a crucial one. If inadequate resources are devoted to the maintenance of existing houses, the result will be accelerated deterioration and an increase in the need for replacement building. If the prices charged for existing houses are artificially reduced there will be pressure for subsidising the prices charged for the new. If the higher standard new houses are subsidised there will be enhanced demand for these and reduced demand for poorer older houses. If subsidies are provided for slum clearance and replacement but not for improvement (or vice versa), the one will be encouraged and the other discouraged. If improvement subsidies are made more attractive to owner-occupiers than to private landlords there will be an incentive to transfer of ownership and a reduction in the supply of privately rented accommodation: this in turn may lead to an increase in the 'need' for public authority housing.

Examples could easily be multiplied, but the point is clear. The housing market is a complex web of inter-related sectors. Policies directed towards the problems of individual sectors will have repercussions throughout the system as a whole. Indeed, the repercussions may well give rise to even more serious problems than those which initially prompted governmental action. This is particularly the case where temporary measures are taken to deal with short-term problems. The classic case of this is rent control which is discussed in the fourth essay. There were forty years of rent control before it was explicitly accepted that this was not a temporary measure which could be abandoned once 'normality' had returned; and then it proved difficult to devise an adequate policy for stemming the rapid decline of the privately rented sector which the control had accelerated. Even the wide-ranging housing policy review failed to come to grips with the issues and they were hived off for separate inquiry.

Rent control was never conceived as a 'housing' policy, but the houses to which it related were predominantly old and, as standards rose, increasingly became 'in need of improvement'. The fact that this was financially impracticable within the context of rent controls was one major reason why a programme of grant aided improvements became necessary. This, together with slum clearance, is discussed in the fifth essay. The legacy of the industrial revolution which came so early to Britain (when incomes and housing standards were low) demanded forceful action in relation to both. The extraordinary achievements in these two areas are discussed in this essay, as are the changing nature and perception of the problems for which a 'sanitary policy' was for so long the appropriate one.

Housing is distinguished from other goods in its durability, its immobility and its cost. Each of these features has implications for housing finance, of which cost is the most important. The capital cost of a new house is, on average, three to four times annual adult male earnings. It follows that systems have to be devised for raising investment capital and for spreading the costs to the occupier over a lengthy period of time.

In the nineteenth century the normal way of doing this was by way of local investment markets. Investment in rented housing was easy and safe: hence the expression (which lives on despite its contemporary absurdity) 'as safe as houses'. The procedure was simple and, as long as the demand for housing was increasing, or remained stable, there was little risk involved: bad payers could always be evicted. For those who wished, management was direct, personal and tangible: it was not necessarily dependent upon the efficiency of some remote third party. Furthermore, 'the man of property' was a man of substance – who thereby acquired some local social standing.

Being extremely durable, housing could be a long-term investment, and it was popularly used by small investors as a means of providing security for old age. On the death of the owner the houses passed to the children who either sold them to other investors or retained them to provide their own 'pension'.[4]

One interesting feature of this system was that the investment was a permanent one. Investors were content with the weekly income: they did not expect capital repayment as well. The finance of owner-occupation was quite different: here a loan was being made to specific individuals and, like loans for other purposes, involved the eventual repayment of the loan as well as the interest charges. In the absence of a financial institution designed for the purpose of housing loans, private mortgages were of short duration and were given more on the basis of the 'safety' of the borrower than that of the house. Hence the possibility of a loan for house purchase was limited to the small numbers who were sufficiently credit-worthy and well connected.

The nineteenth-century system was thus essentially geared to the finance of rented houses. It was profitable to the investor and simple for the occupier. It was, however (in Bowley's words), a 'primitive' local market system:

The investor put his eggs in one basket, in the form of a small or large group of houses in a particular area. Any decline in the rents of one house was likely to be accompanied by declines in the rents of the rest of his houses, and, of course, vice versa. The possibility of realising his investment, even in favourable circumstances, depended on the existence of other local investors willing to buy them. There was no nationally organised market such as that for stocks and shares or government securities, and the units of investment were inconveniently large compared to shares. The organisation of the market in equity of houses was thus primitive and out of line with other investment markets. Its survival probably depended on the belief that it was possible to know all about the local market, but not about the other opportunities of investment. Socially it had the grave disadvantage that the supply of houses in any place depended mainly on the local supply of capital. Sooner or later it might be expected to die out like other primitive institutions.[5]

Several factors helped its decline, including the increasing standards of new building and maintenance imposed by the state, the growth of more attractive indirect investment opportunities, unfavourable taxation provisions, the imposition of rent controls and, probably, the simple fact that as the bulk of rented houses aged their costs of management rose.

The decline of this nineteenth-century financial system took place at the same time that a new system was gaining strength (and itself hastened the withdrawal of private investment from the rental market). This was the building society movement which, from modest 'self-help' beginnings, grew into a major housing finance institution.[6]

In effect a building society pools investments and makes them available for those wishing to buy a house. It provides the investor with a good security (avoiding all the risks and bother involved in rented housing), and it provides the house purchaser with a simple system of borrowing and instalment repayments. The building societies have 'effectively ousted the private landlord from the middle income residential market' and, on one view,[7] 'the only reason why the societies have not utterly routed the private landlord from all sectors of the market is their refusal to give 100 per cent mortgages, which effectively debars a great many families from owner-occupation'.

Some aspects of owner-occupation are examined in the sixth essay where it is argued that the political attractions of espousing its further growth need to be considered in the context of its relevance to a wide range of differing issues. Yet owner-occupation has now become so financially attractive to those who can get into it, that it seems likely that governments will be swept along by political tides to continue extending its benefits to more and more 'marginal' groups. There are alternatives, however, the most important of which involves a radical reform of housing finance. But it is politically more attractive to promote 'alternative' forms of tenure.

For the best part of half a century local authority and owner-occupied housing have been virtually the only new forms of housing provided. The costs to the public purse have assumed astronomical proportions in recent years, and the promotion of an alternative (through housing associations) proved viable only when equally huge subsidies were made available. Following an examination of this in the seventh essay, the discussion turns to the first attempt to 'harmonise' some aspects of policy in relation to the public and private rented sectors. This was the national scheme of housing allowances introduced in 1972. Born amid acute political controversy about the accompanying rent increases of council houses, it had latent promise of being a major innovation in social policy. But herein lies the problem: are housing allowances a part of housing policy or an aspect of broader policies relating to income maintenance? Much broader issues were thereby raised and, to date, remain unresolved.

Governments are continually faced with the difficulty of devising firm policies on shifting sands. Only when the overall housing situation is characterised by an acute and widespread shortage can policy be defined in simple terms of building more houses. This was the case for relatively short periods following the cessation of building during the two World Wars. As the general position improved, new and more intricate problems arose (or, to be more precise, came to the fore). In the 1950s a major one of these was that of the decaying stock of houses built during the industrial revolution. The enormity of this problem was masked by ignorance, but the development of better sources of information revealed its extent and character. Yet, by this time it was changing in significant ways, above all by the transfer of ownership from landlords to owner-occupiers. In the phraseology of stereotypes, the relatively easy political task of dispossessing the unpitying and unpitied landlord was increasingly replaced by the public theft of the assets of the upstanding owner-occupier. Attitudes also began to change in the face of mounting opposition to the 'destruction of communities' and disillusionment with the sanitary products of the new high-density era – itself an outcome of attempts to accelerate progress in the elimination of a previously defined problem. At the same time new perceptions arose – of who was getting what, and of the difficulties being experienced by 'ineligible' households whose housing choices were being significantly reduced by the decline of the private rental market (accelerated if not caused by rent control).

Governments have responded to the changing situation by *ad hoc* measures which have led to a financial commitment of huge proportions. In the final essay it is argued that this is neither necessary nor desirable. Limitations of space preclude an exhaustive analysis, and the discussion focuses on the inadequacies of the housing finance system. Until this is reformed, housing policy will inevitably lurch from crisis to crisis. Unfortunately there is no easy way out. Housing cannot be treated in isolation: it is inextricably inter-related with broader issues of inflation, incomes policy and income maintenance, inner city decline and a perplexing range of difficult social and economic trends. Nevertheless, it is suggested that the most hopeful way forward is through a reorganised housing allowance scheme (at the national level) and the operation of 'housing plans' (at the local level).

The conclusion is not an encouraging one, but hopefully the analysis may assist in widening the debate on the nature and scope of housing policy. An electorate increasingly concerned with public participation needs to be more sophisticated than was seen to be appropriate when housing policy was devoted to 'the housing of the working classes'. Consensus may not be the relevant objective, but at least the debate should be conducted on the basis of a consideration of what the problems are. This will inevitably underline the conflicts of interest which contemporary inequalities create. If all this makes it more difficult for governments to shirk their responsibilities – as was done in the housing policy review – so much the better.

1 The Institutional Framework

Faith in machinery is, I said, our besetting danger.
Matthew Arnold

Many institutions operate in the field of housing policy. Indeed, they are so numerous that a major problem of policy is to ensure that they operate in harmony – or at least with the minimum of conflict. National housing policies (to the extent that there are such things) are the responsibility of central government, but execution is the responsibility of a multiplicity of agencies: 460 independent political entities of local government (and, in Northern Ireland, the Housing Executive); development agencies such as the new town development corporations and the Commission for the New Towns, the Scottish Special Housing Association, and some 2,000 housing associations; finance institutions such as the Public Works Loans Board, the Housing Corporation and 380 building societies, as well as the joint stock banks and the insurance companies; an unknown number of private landlords, ranging from major companies to (more typically) individuals owning a very small number of houses or simply letting part of their own dwelling; and some 88,000 building and contracting firms.

These are the instruments of housing policy, and the control which central government exercises over them varies greatly. Absolute control applies only over the tiny number of houses built by government departments (1,259 in 1975) and, even here, the 'control' is operated by each of the departments concerned and their ministers (not the minister responsible for housing).[1]

The execution of policies is also affected by independent bodies such as the Parliamentary Commissioner for Administration (the 'ombudsman'), the Commissioner for Local Administration (the 'local authority ombudsman'), the Commission for Racial Equality, the Equal Opportunities Commission, the National Consumer Council, the district auditor and, in Scotland, the Commission for Local Authority Accounts. The powers and influence of these 'watchdogs' varies, but they are performing an increasingly significant role not only in protecting the citizen against maladministration, but also in promoting changes in both the operation and the character of 'policy'. In this they supplement the traditional if somewhat erratic role of the mass media.

Then there are the citizen and community groups which, in recent years, have adopted pressure tactics of a more strident and active character than that of the longer established professional and amenity organisations. Finally there is Parliament itself and the parliamentary institutions of the Expenditure Committee, the Public Accounts Committee, and the Comptroller and Auditor General.

None of these bodies is 'executive' but, in the same way that it is misleading to separate policy and administration, so it is inadequate to consider either in isolation from the wider range of institutions which bring their influence to bear on both.

In what follows, some of the more important institutions are selected for discussion. The objectives are to sketch the institutional framework and to illustrate problem areas of policy by reference to particular issues.

CENTRAL GOVERNMENT

Why, it can usefully be asked, do we talk in terms of *housing* policy? Would it not be more appropriate to consider housing as an aspect of broader policies relating, for example, to health or the environment, or economic development? Certainly, the changing names of the central government departments responsible for housing suggest that the question periodically arises. In England and Wales the central department was, from 1919 until 1951, the Ministry of Health. Since 1970 it has been the Department of the Environment. By contrast, Scotland (with its different and more intransigent economic problems) has the Scottish Development Department. Other countries align responsibilities differently: in the USA there is the Department of Housing and Urban Development, in Italy the Ministry of Public Works, and in Canada the Central Mortgage and Housing Corporation (together with the more recent Ministry of State for Urban Affairs).

Such comparisons are interesting and thought-provoking, but there are so many factors influencing the organisation of government that it is easy to read too much into the selected distribution of functions. In Britain, housing policy (like town and country planning policy) developed out of sanitary policies, and it was therefore natural that it should be the responsibility of the department concerned with 'the health of towns' problem – the Department of Health for Scotland, and the Ministry of Health in England and Wales. The Ministry of Health retained this function until 1951 (though it lost planning to a new Ministry of Town and Country Planning in 1943). The redistribution of functions which took place in 1951 was the result of two quite different forces: the pressure on the Ministry of Health created by the rapidly developing national health service, and the perceived need to bring housing and planning together. The result was the Ministry of Local Government and Planning. Its title, however, was changed in the same year following the return of a Conservative government which was unenthusiastic about planning but committed to a major expansion of the housing programme. Housing ousted planning and the name was changed to Ministry of Housing and Local Government. And so it remained until the beginning of the seventies when huge super-departments became the fashion.[2] Housing now became a part of a gargantuan department which for a time embraced the Ministries of Housing, Transport and Public Building and Works.

The need to bring road planning into closer relationship with town planning and housing development had long been recognised, but the merger also attempted to resolve 'the difficulty arising from the separation of the housing department's responsibilities from the responsibility for much public sector building and for relations with the construction industry, held by the Ministry of Public Building and Works'.[3] In line with current fashion, the new ministry was entitled the Department of the Environment. The name was considered (at least with hindsight) by a former senior Treasury official as being particularly relevant, 'for it has given a sign to give fresh illumination to a wide variety of tasks which were not formerly regarded as having anything in common'.[4]

The approach here was basically to bring together functions relating to the physical environment. The new department, in the words of the White Paper *The Reorganisation of Central Government:*

. . . will cover the planning of land – where people live, work, move and enjoy themselves. It will be responsible for the construction industries, including the housing programme, and for the transport industries, including programmes of support and development for the means of transport. There is a need to associate with these functions responsibility for other major environmental matters: the preservation of amenity, the protection of the coast and countryside, the preservation of historic towns and monuments, and the control of air, water and noise pollution . . . And it will have the leading responsibility for regional policy . . . and the particular responsibility of ensuring that people's rights are adequately protected wherever they are affected by the proposals of their neighbours or of public authorities.

The rationale was clear; and it reflected the growing concern for a better relationship between the many facets of environmental planning. Ironically, the change was made just at the time when concern for a different pattern of functional relationships was emerging – between housing policies and a wide range of social programmes for the relief of poverty, for helping coloured people to overcome the problems they faced in a white society and, more generally, for dealing with ill-defined problems of what came to be termed 'urban deprivation'. The introduction of a national housing allowance scheme in 1972 raised further questions on the relationship between rent rebates and supplementary benefits – a matter which became more problematic with the growth of the 'better off problem' and the 'poverty trap'. Later, a rise in the recorded rate of homelessness resulted in controversy over the allocation of responsibility between 'housing' and 'social services'.

Such issues – which are discussed later – raised some doubts about the logic of the new department. Though it provides a context for reviewing and elaborating new lines of housing policy, that very context might make it difficult to follow up radical changes in policy, for example, in promoting house production and improvement by tax incentives, or assisting low-income households with their housing costs by a social security, supplementary benefit or tax credit system.[5]

When such proposals arise they are dealt with at central government level by a host of interdepartmental committees. Following the establishment of the Cabinet Office Central Policy Review Staff, a new initiative was taken to design an effective 'joint framework for social policies'.[6] Among other features of this was the setting up of a study of 'the relationship between housing policy and other social policies'. At the same time, a major review of housing finance within the Department of the Environment developed into an even bigger review of housing policy. This rapidly found itself involved with bigger questions concerned with assistance to low-income families – questions which had to be passed on to an interdepartmental review of the relationship of means tested housing assistance to other social benefits.[7]

Incomes and prices policies added further complications and led to parliamentary pressure for a 'select committee to examine housing problems and the link between social security and the tax system and the incomes policy . . .'.[8] Finally (though it should be noted that this list is illustrative rather than comprehensive), concern for the 'inner city problem' which had been growing throughout the seventies developed into a political issue of significance, with an emphasis on the relationships between employment, incomes and housing. In the words of the Minister of Housing:

> . . . solutions to the problems of our inner cities . . . is not just a matter of applying major programmes and policies individually. They must be welded together in a co-ordinated and comprehensive approach. Housing and employment policies for example must work together and support each other to get a better match between people, jobs and homes. This could have major significance for the machinery at all levels.[9]

This recital of the changing context within which housing problems and policies are perceived underlines the difficulty of determining the 'best' allocation of functions between government departments. More to the immediate point, it demonstrates the many-faceted nature of 'housing'. Whatever administrative organisation is established, problems will always remain of finding the most effective framework for formulating policy. When the emphasis was on environmental issues a merger in a single department was logical. (Whether it has been effective is a different matter.) Now that the emphasis has shifted on to a broader social front – and additionally encompasses employment – no reallocation or merger can conceivably provide a logical solution.

In short, it is impossible to conceive of a central government department which would undertake responsibility for all the issues which are related to 'housing'. (A similar conclusion would emerge from a consideration of 'health' or 'education' or 'planning'.)[10]

This leaves a problem of crucial significance to a consideration of the formulation of housing policy: how can a basis be found for ensuring that housing policy adequately takes into account those relevant aspects which are the responsibility of other departments? It is difficult enough for a single department to co-ordinate all aspects of its work (and the bigger the department, the greater these difficulties are likely to be);[11] but once issues go beyond a single department, the difficulties grow enormously.

The difficulties are exacerbated by the natural tendency to departmentalism. Each department has its own framework for thought and action, its own methods of working, its own system of internal (and external) communication, and its own approach to the definition of those problems which fall within its area of responsibility. Like all organisations, individual departments develop particular styles of administration (which may be more easily felt than described), particular sets of loyalties, and a degree of isolationism which ministers all too frequently find themselves defending. Whatever ministers may say collectively, they are individually in competition with each other – for influence as well as resources. Interdepartmental co-operation tends to be alloyed by interdepartmental rivalry if not outright conflict; and the one leads easily into the other.

Exhortation to co-ordinate policies, to adopt a 'unified approach', or even to remove inconsistent practices leads to a host of difficulties. As was explicitly recognised in the White Paper *Policy for the Inner Cities*, though 'concerted action should have a greater impact' on the problems being addressed, 'the difficulties should not be underestimated: special efforts of co-ordination and joint working' are required 'which cut across established practices'. It is significant that the 'unified approach' which is seen to be required to deal with the problems of inner cities is to be restricted at first to a limited number of areas:

The powers and finances of central and local government will need to be used in a unified and coherent way. New forms of organisation and new methods of working may need to be tried. In the government's view, success is more likely to be achieved by concentrating special attention and the major part of urban aid on a few major areas initially.

Whether the achievements of this selective approach will be replicable over a wider area remains to be seen. Whatever success is attained in co-ordination in particular localities is hardly likely to be translatable to the national level. In the words of another CPRS report:

> . . . central government is, in fact, a federation of separate departments with their own ministers and their own policies. The aim of the Treasury and of the DoE in its capacity as the 'department of local government' often cut across those of the spending or service departments. They in turn compete with each other for scarce resources. The development of an interdepartmental view about a local authority service is a rare achievement.[12]

It has to be accepted that there is no satisfactory solution to these problems. The interconnections between policies are far too complex, and the effectiveness of particular programmes too uncertain. The Central Policy Review Staff have argued that:

> The treatment of social issues should, in principle, be related to some broad framework of social policy. In practice, there is an inevitable tendency for them to be dealt with individually as they come to the forefront. This can allow different departments to put different emphases on different major policy instruments – for example, means testing or helping the worst off through 'positive discrimination', rather than through general improvements in programmes.

To meet this and other related problems, the CPRS proposed that a group of senior ministers most closely concerned should meet *and think* (my italics) every six months or so in a 'strategic' capacity; that periodic 'forward looks' at likely forthcoming developments in the social field should be carried out by officials – here the major objective being 'to identify possible links and possible inconsistencies'; that 'social monitoring' should be improved; and that a programme of specific studies should be mounted, for example on financial poverty, central–local government relationships, social aspects of housing policy, housing the elderly and the handicapped, and the implications of a possible long-term decline in the birthrate.

How far all this would be effective is uncertain. Official 'studies', like academic research projects, tend to raise more questions than they answer; and the seemingly most important questions often prove unanswerable, ill conceived or even illegitimate.[13] Moreover, by the time a study is complete, the context within which it was conceived may have changed so dramatically that the questions posed are no longer relevant;[14] or, more simply, they may no longer be in the forefront of ministers' minds. 'A social problem which is given top priority in a particular week may look less significant when compared with other problems coming up for discussion in the following month; in the context of a full year it may seem quite insignificant.'[15] Improvements in 'social monitoring', statistical data and relevant research are certainly needed, but they again raise a host of new questions. They also inevitably meet technical (and conceptual) problems which may not be merely difficult but incapable of solution. At a more mundane level they can give rise to confusion and indigestion. Though a better 'data base' is always desirable, the effect can be to make decision taking more rather than less difficult.

Finally, the appealing idea of greater emphasis on 'the framework for policy' and on 'strategy' may well be delusive as well as elusive. What do the words really mean? Better 'co-ordination' of policies and greater 'coherence' in policy making? Improved 'understanding' of the nature of problems, and the implications and effectiveness of policies? A greater concern for the long run rather than for the immediate problems of the day? A more 'rational' ordering of priorities? All these are undoubtedly worthy objectives, and politicians and administrators yearn for ways of achieving them. Yet they partake of the nature of the philosopher's stone.

It is a difficult enough task for politicians and administrators to come to grips with immediate problems without being distracted by vague concepts of something better in the long run. The long run emerges from the short run and, in practice, much effort is (rightly) expended on attempting to comprehend the present and the recent past. (There is little point in attempting to predict the future pattern of housing requirements when there is bafflement about the current situation.) New policies emerge, not from high-level meetings on 'strategy', but from proposals set before ministers which appear politically appropriate. If 'strategy' means anything more than the general political approach it is the result of a series of decisions, not the justification for them. 'Strategies are simple-minded notions with which parties occasionally come into office, and historians sometimes attach as convenient labels for disparate happenings, but which never characterise the actual operations of any government.'[16]

None of this is to deny the importance of continued effort to improve the process of policy making, or the value of better data and research, or the benefit which ministers might gain from the occasional seminar.

It is, however, unrealistic to think that 'coherent strategies' can result from better data and hard thinking. The difficulties besetting the 1975–7 housing policy review are eloquent testimony to this in a relatively narrowly defined field. They are overwhelming in broader fields of social policy.

LOCAL AUTHORITIES

Local authorities are not, it should be noted, 'agents' of central government. They are independent statutory bodies, locally elected by the residents of each area – and at any one time a large proportion of them are of a different political complexion from that of the government of the day. They are 'citadels of local power'; and though central government may lay down national policies,

> . . . it is in the twists and emphases which councils give to central policies, and the degree of co-operation or unwillingness which they show, that their own power lies. They do not have the paper guarantees of local sovereignty which states in a federal system possess, but they have some of the reality of power which comes from being on the spot, knowing the special qualities and demands of the local people, and being costly and difficult to replace if the central government finds them unsatisfactory.[17]

Nevertheless, they are by no means autonomous bodies: though they have a wide measure of freedom to determine how they shall interpret and operate the powers entrusted to them, they are subject to several types of constraint – legal, financial and, increasingly, administrative. In the first place, since they are 'creatures of statute', they can do only those things for which they have specific statutory authority. Despite honest attempts by central government to give local authorities greater freedom (for example by the 1968 Town and Country Planning Act and the Transport Act of the same year), the course has been erratic, and much legislation has been restrictive. Acts of Parliament not only provide powers and duties but also embody central government policy. And the stream of legislation has been unceasing.

Particularly notorious was the 1972 Housing Finance Act, which removed from local authorities (in England and Wales, though not in Scotland) their freedom to determine rents. This gave rise to unprecedented controversy – and the infamous Clay Cross case. Though this particular Act was repealed by the Labour government of 1974, the issue of central control over rents remains at the forefront of political debate – inevitably so when (in 1974–5) Exchequer subsidies were running at a level in excess of £1,000m. a year.

Finance is, of course, the key issue, but it is not the only one, as the

Housing (Homeless Persons) Act of 1977 indicates. This Act, which imposes a *duty* on local authorities to assist certain classes of the homeless, is the first major intervention by central government in a traditional area of local authority discretion.

Nevertheless, the terms in which this 'duty' is expressed are significant. For example, local authorities are required 'to make inquiries' to satisfy themselves whether those who approach them for assistance are statutorily 'homeless', and if so whether they became homeless intentionally. Where the authority is satisfied on this score, it has to determine whether the household concerned falls within a given category of 'priority need'. If they are not in priority need, the local authority has the duty to provide advice and such assistance as it considers appropriate to help the household to obtain appropriate accommodation. If, on the other hand, they are judged to be in priority need (and have not become homeless intentionally), the local authority's duty is 'to secure that accommodation becomes available' for them.

The full provisions are long and even more complex than these extracts suggest, but the essential point is clear: the 'duty' is quite unenforceable. The Act confers no corresponding rights on those to whom the local authorities now have a duty. Indeed, it constitutes little more than a moral exhortation wrapped up in legalistic provisions (though the importance of this in influencing the policies of local authorities should not be underestimated). It is difficult to see how it could be otherwise.

Other housing duties are expressed in similarly vague (and unenforceable) terms. There is certainly no duty upon a local authority to provide housing, though there is a long list of needs which it has a duty to consider. These have been assembled over time as various new provisions have been added in successive Acts directed at particular problems.

The major legal obligation placed upon local authorities is 'to consider housing conditions in their district and the needs of the district with respect to the provision of further housing accommodation'. They are also required,

> . . . as often as occasion arises, or within three months after notice has been given to them by the minister, to prepare and submit to the minister proposals for the provision of new houses, distinguishing those houses which the authority proposes to provide for the purpose of rendering accommodation available for persons to be displaced by, or in consequence of, action taken by the authority under this Act.

As the latter part of this quotation implies, the provision was originally enacted in connection with slum clearance.

Similarly another 'duty', this time in connection with 'the abatement of overcrowding', dates from 1935:

If it appears to a local authority that occasion has arisen for a report
on overcrowding in their district . . . or the minister so directs, it shall
be the duty to cause a further inspection to be made and to prepare
and submit a report showing the result of the inspection and the
number of new houses required to abate overcrowding . . . and, unless
they are satisfied that the required number of new houses will be
otherwise provided, to prepare and submit to the minister proposals
for the provision thereof.

These provisions *prima facie* suggest that the duties are enforceable
by the minister, but the specific default powers of the original legislation
(which included the right of 'any four or more local government electors'
to lodge a complaint with the minister) were repealed on local government reorganisation.

Duties which seem to be more strongly enforceable were provided in
the 1969 Housing Act:

It shall be the duty of every local authority . . . to cause an inspection
of their district to be made from time to time with a view to determining what action to take in performance of their functions [under
various Housing Acts] and for the purpose of carrying out that
duty the authority and their officers shall comply with any directions
the minister may give and shall keep such records and supply him
with such information as he may specify.

This extends the 'housing survey' duties of local authorities in connection with lack of repair or maintenance, the sanitary condition of
dwellings, houses in multiple occupation, tenement blocks, and the
need for clearance, redevelopment and area improvement.

It is interesting to note the provision for compliance with ministerial
directions, which applies not only to the local authority but also to
its officers; but legal sanctions are again missing. Moreover the duty
relates specifically to 'inspection' of housing conditions, not the ameli-
oration of bad conditions.

The matter assumes a different perspective, however, when it is noted
that the 1957 Housing Act also imposes a duty on local authorities, in
exercising their powers, to 'have regard to the beauty of the landscape
or countryside and the other amenities of the locality, and the desirability of preserving existing works of architectural, historic or artistic
interest'. Again, they are required to 'comply with such directions, if
any, in that behalf as may be given to them by the minister'.

So far as allocating council houses is concerned local authorities have
virtually complete discretion. There is no statutory income limit or
residential qualification which authorities have to observe. They are
required to give 'a reasonable preference to persons who are occupying

insanitary or overcrowded houses, have large families or are living in unsatisfactory housing conditions', but obviously this is so wide as to constitute no restriction at all. Before 1949 the concern of local authorities was supposedly restricted to the 'working classes', but this was not defined. The 1949 Housing Act, which deleted reference to the working classes, merely gave statutory recognition to the current practice of selecting tenants according to their housing need. 'Housing need' is capable of widely differing interpretations and, in any case, the housing situation varies so markedly between different areas that no standardisation of selection procedures is possible – even if it were desirable. A family who might be considered by a local authority in a small provincial town as being in urgent need might not even be accepted on the waiting list of a big city.

Nevertheless there has been considerable criticism of the restrictions placed by some local authorities on certain types of need, particularly that of newcomers to an area. A succession of reports[18] has condemned the residential qualifications operated by local authorities, some of which require applicants to have lived in the area for many years before they will be accepted on the housing list. However, with one exception, central government has rested content with exhortation. The exception is interesting in that it demonstrates the difficulty of central control – and the ease with which it can be circumvented. It came with the London Government Act of 1963 which, while allocating the main housing responsibilities to the London boroughs, gave the Greater London Council powers for dealing with problems which were not capable of local solution.[19] The Greater London Council has a statutory duty to review the housing needs of Greater London as a whole while the boroughs are required to keep lists of applicants for council housing. The boroughs are statutorily required to accept and register all applications made to them from anyone resident in their area. This does not, however, mean the end of 'residential qualifications' since the boroughs can – and do – simply hold new registrations, and preclude them from active consideration, until the local residential qualification has been met. Typically, a minimum of five years' residence in Greater London and one year's residence in the borough is required before an applicant will be considered for a council house.[20]

It is difficult to see how central government could prevent such practices. Thus the proposal in the housing policy review that legislation might be passed 'to prohibit residential or other qualifications for entry to local authority lists'[21] would be purely symbolic.

Much 'housing policy' is therefore the responsibility of local government: central government provides the enabling framework, but the operation of policy lies at the local level. This is what local government is all about. Moreover, despite constant pressures on central government to control 'inadequate' local authorities, the essentially local character of housing markets demands a flexible national framework. This has become even more appropriate as over-riding 'national shortages' have given way to a great variability in the nature of local housing problems. In the words of the housing policy review, 'the key to the success of national housing policy now lies in the development of effective *local* housing strategies, planned and carried out by local authorities with the minimum of detailed intervention from the centre'.[22]

It is, however, in the area of financial control where central government has a legitimate and important interest, and where its power is seen most forcefully. There has always been a significant control by way of loan sanction:[23] no capital expenditure may be incurred by local authorities without this sanction (unless it is financed from revenue). Loan sanctions are given by the appropriate departments: the Department of Education and Science for school building, for instance. In respect of housing it is the Department of the Environment. This requirement gives the DoE considerable powers for controlling the cost, type and design of local authority house building. These powers have been well used. Moreover they have been instrumental in transforming advice and guidelines into mandatory requirements. Parker Morris standards, for instance, were originally 'commended' to local authorities, but in 1969 they became compulsory as a minimum provision. Similarly, 'housing cost yardsticks', though devised as 'an informal guide to housing costs', became 'a mandatory instrument setting a limit on grant and, subject to a small margin, on costs eligible for loan sanction'.[24] This extension of the use of loan sanction control (originally conceived as a safeguard against impropriety) has been effective in directing – or at least constraining – local authority housing policies; but increasingly it has been exercised as a means of controlling total capital investment. As the Layfield Report has shown, it is neither designed nor appropriate for this purpose.[25] It has been used simply because no better tool was to hand.

Nevertheless, too much can be made of this 'controlling' power of central government. It is significant that the illustrations given are all of central government imposing constraints on local authorities: it is much more difficult for central government to make them do something they have no wish to do – selling council houses, providing sites for gypsies, or increasing rents, for instance. Indeed, 'control' is not only too strong a word: it is an inappropriate one. In the words of a former permanent secretary of the ministry, 'housing legislation, though voluminous, gives the minister no effective powers of national direction . . .; his position is much like that of a mediaeval monarch grappling with a host of feudal barons'.[26] The relationships between local and central government are much more complex than the word suggests,[27] and these operate not only at the financial level, but also at political and professional levels. Moreover, the nature of the relationships varies markedly between different fields, and even between different issues in the same field. For example, there is far more 'control' over capital programmes than revenue programmes, and over building types than the allocation of council houses.

The boundaries are also constantly changing. Central influence on local authority rent policies was, until 1972, indirect and cautious, but in that year unprecedented controls were introduced by a Conservative government (which, in turn, were abandoned by the subsequent Labour government). No controls have ever been exercised over the selection of tenants (though there has been a constant stream of exhortations and a gradual extension of 'duties' in relation to specific categories of housing need). Acute problems on public expenditure have brought greater intervention, while the further extension of party politics in local government following reorganisation has increased the political resistance of local authorities to central controls. The rise of activist groups such as Shelter, the Disabled Living Foundation and the Child Poverty Action Group has introduced new elements into the situation.

The biggest influence in recent years, however, has been the public expenditure crisis. Clearly, in the interests of overall economic management, central government must control the total expenditure by local authorities (which amounts to over a quarter of total public expenditure). The means for doing this effectively and efficiently do not exist at present, though considerable effort is being exerted in finding ways of reconciling 'the need for control in aggregate with the need for local autonomy'.[28] If this is successful, there should be less confusion between the controls for the purpose of overall management of the economy and controls for the purpose of housing policy. How far central government will wish (and will be able) to control policies remains to be seen. Current thinking is in terms of giving local authorities greater freedom to deal with the particular problems of their areas within the context of approved investment plans. The rationale for this is partly a concern to allocate functions 'properly' between local and central government, and partly a recognition of the fact that *national* policies cannot cope with the wide variation in the character of the local housing problems of 460 areas.

This is hardly likely to be the end of the matter: 'all governments want to give local authorities more independence provided that the local authorities do what the government wants them to do'.[29] There are constant pressures on central government to force local authorities to act in line with national policies, whether these be on party political issues such as the sale of council houses or on the non-party political issues such as meeting the needs of the homeless.

There is here a clash of principle between enabling local authorities to act as truly local governments and ensuring that they meet national standards and follow nationally determined principles. The concern for inner cities raises this perennial issue again: the new 'partnership' between local and central government[30] implies a more direct role for the latter, and 'that might mean that councils in large conurbations would have to surrender some of their autonomy over how money was spent'.[31] In the words of the CPRS report, 'giving greater discretion to local authorities . . . is not easily reconciled with continuing attempts by central government to ensure that specific social problems are given high priority'.[32] As the Layfield Committee noted in their studies of local government abroad, 'a large measure of local autonomy is usually associated with greater variation in the provision of services than in this country, and a smaller and less precise redistribution between areas'.[33]

Nevertheless, there is nothing approaching a uniformity of provision by British local authorities, even in those services to which central government has attached particular importance. Indeed, the variety of provision (which seems inexplicable in terms of such factors as the size or resources of authorities) suggests that local government operates much more freely from effective central control than is customarily assumed. The truth of the matter is that individual local authorities are, in Stanyer's words, 'miniature political systems', in which differing 'interactions with their environment,' differing attitudes, differing calibre of members and officers, and a host of other local circumstances play an important role.[34] Central government may set 'the boundaries within which local authorities operate, but the divergence within those boundaries must be explained elsewhere'.[35]

Central government, which in any case tends to be schizophrenic[36] about its relationships with local authorities, thus faces real difficulties when it attempts to ensure that the policies which it favours are carried out. The problem is easier to tackle (or rather to avoid) when public expenditure is increasing. This allows 'priority' to be given to particular needs or particular areas simply by concentrating the additional expenditure there. When there is a 'no-growth' situation or cuts in expenditure (as at the time of writing), priorities can be attained only by reducing expenditure on non-priorities. This is more painful, but it is also more conducive to a thorough assessment of where priorities should lie.

NEW TOWN DEVELOPMENT CORPORATIONS

One way in which priority can be given to a policy is to establish an *ad hoc* agency for its execution. There are numerous examples of this device of which, in the field of housing, particular mention can be made of the new town development corporations.

The new town development corporations in Great Britain (and their successor body in England and Wales – the Commission for the New

Towns) have built over a quarter of a million houses during their life-time. Their function, however, has not been simply to build houses: local government is (usually) quite capable of fulfilling that purpose. The corporations have all had a superior purpose. With many of the earlier new towns this was to accommodate 'overspill' from London and other conurbations. The new towns of the sixties, on the other hand, were conceived as elements of regional policy, designed to stimulate economic growth and to house some of the large population increase which, at that time, was expected in the following decades. New towns were also established for other purposes, as at Peterlee, where the objective was to concentrate, in one urban area, development which would otherwise (under local authority control) have been scattered throughout a number of small mining villages, none of which could provide town facilities and amenities. Aycliffe, Cwmbran, Corby and Glenrothes were intended (initially at least) to serve or complement exist-ing or anticipated employment growth. As these illustrations show, the device of *ad hoc* agencies for new town development has been employed for varying purposes, all of which were thought to be beyond the com-petence of local government. Sometimes this was because the local authorities concerned were too small to undertake development on the scale envisaged; sometimes because it was thought to be unrealistic to expect them to give the required priority to 'strangers' from another area; sometimes because it was felt that local authorities would build 'housing estates' rather than 'new town communities'. Whatever the reason, it was judged that the best way of ensuring that central govern-ment policies were carried out was to set up an *ad hoc* government appointed and financed agency.

The corporations are thus direct instruments for the implementation of government policy. This does not mean, however, that they do not have a degree of independence. On the contrary, the nature of their tasks necessitates a fair degree of independence of action – what the Expenditure Committee have termed 'a distinctive style of operation . . . characterised by its speed and scale'.[37] At the same time, the central government departments have neither the capacity nor the skills to exercise complete control. As a result there has been concern that operation and control procedures have been inadequate 'to ensure that new towns meet their prescribed national policy objectives'. In the words of the Expenditure Committee:

Given a master plan, population and job targets, and the powers of development corporations to control and guide development with the singleminded approach that we have already noted, it is not surprising that the policies of certain new towns sometimes appear to be at variance with wider national policy objectives . . . the co-ordination and direction on these matters by DoE appears to be extremely weak.[38]

The development of a new town, however, is a complex undertaking. The speed of development, the problems of accommodating a large influx of population, of maintaining a balance between housing and jobs, of integration of new services with those of the local and other public authorities for the area, 'all combine to make expenditure planning and control in new towns a complex process'. Moreover, there are the inevitable uncertainties over the levels of expenditure which can be authorised by central government from year to year. There are also difficulties of co-ordinating the policies and programmes of different government departments. Indeed, the problem is more than one of 'co-ordination'. That term suggests that some kind of harmonisation can be achieved by administrative efficiency. Yet governments have conflicting objectives which are extremely difficult, and sometimes impossible, to 'harmonise'. Given a limited supply of mobile industry, there is an inevitable clash between the policy of giving maximum aid to the areas of high unemployment and that of promoting new town development in the south. More generally, the allocation of resources to new towns has to be judged in relation to the claims of the old towns.

These essentially political issues are the very stuff of 'policy'. Governments have continually to try to reconcile irreconcilables, to make compromises and to change direction as uncontrollable events buffet even the best-laid plans. And new towns throw up some special dilemmas for policy.

A major issue has been that of balancing house building with the growth of employment, while at the same time attracting workers who have the skills which are needed in the town as well as the housing need which the new towns were intended to relieve. At the same time the new towns have been concerned to establish a reasonable balance of tenure, with sufficient opportunities for owner-occupiers.

Each of these objectives presents problems for the others. Since a new town is, by definition, not a dormitory suburb, sufficient firms have to be attracted to provide jobs for those who move. (Indeed it has been the prospect of a house together with a job which has made the new towns so attractive to the 1 million people who have moved into them.) But, quite apart from the problems of competing for the limited supply of mobile industry, the new towns have had to ensure that they can obtain at least a high proportion of the needed employees from among the badly housed of the conurbations which they exist to serve.

Of course, it could be argued that anyone moving from London to a new town would provide a benefit to the London housing problem since he would vacate a house into which another family would move. In fact the situation is much more complex than this. Many of those moving to new towns (whether in 'official housing need' or not) had been sharing with relatives and, though their move had improved the living conditions both of themselves and of the family with whom they formerly lived, no vacancy was created for another family. Moreover, to the extent that whole dwellings were vacated, many were occupied by families from other parts of London and even from farther afield.[39] The direct benefit to any part of London was thus very small, and ingenious if cumbersome procedures were established to increase this.[40]

A parallel issue arose with the provision of houses for owner-occupiers in new towns. If these were to be earmarked (both on first purchase and on resale) to 'sponsored overspill' families – i.e. those in housing need who were obtaining a job in the new town) there would have been little demand. Recognition was given to this by allowing development corporations to sell at a discount and with right of pre-emption over a period of five years. But any major growth of owner-occupation was seen as a threat to the 'balance' of the town: the greater the proportion of owner-occupation, the greater the likely proportion of commuters. With such large parts of the town already developed by or planned for rented housing, there was little scope for extending owner-occupation except by the sale of rented houses. An officially sponsored study in 1968 concluded that there was a large potential demand for such sales at discounted prices.[41] and this was encouraged by the Labour government at the end of the sixties. In 1970–71, the Conservative government went further and instructed development corporations to make all their rented housing available for purchase by sitting tenants on concessionary terms, and also to ensure that private house builders made the maximum contribution to the new house-building programme which market conditions permitted.

This created some alarm among development corporations, some of whom were averse to 'pepperpot' sales (and preferred, for purposes of 'good estate management', to restrict sales to defined areas). Others were concerned that their rented stock would become so depleted that they would be unable to meet the demand for rented houses from new-comers to the growing employment in the town. In the two years 1972–3, over 23,000 rented houses were sold (raising £119m.) and in some new towns over 30 per cent of the corporations' rented stock had passed into private hands.[42]

This policy was proving too successful and it was greatly cut back. With the return of the Labour government in 1974 sales fell to a trickle.

The sale of public authority houses is an issue requiring discussion in a broader context than is appropriate at this juncture. The immediate point is that while local authorities can be *exhorted* to sell their houses, development corporations can be *directed* to do so. In 1973 less than half the local authorities in England and Wales sold any houses, while nearly all the new towns did so.[43]

Development corporations, however, have been noticeably less successful in responding to ministerial pressure to accommodate the most needy and the most disadvantaged, though this could be ascribed to the inherent difficulty of so doing and the general preoccupation with broader issues of developing the town, keeping houses and jobs in balance, and creating a 'generally balanced community'. It must be admitted, however, that the arguments on this issue are by no means always clear, and the statistical evidence is inadequate.[44] Nevertheless, it seems to be accepted that there is a weakness in policy here. The DoE consultation document on new towns[45] notes that:

> To avoid the tendency for those in greatest need in the cities to be left behind, the development corporations concerned will be asked to pay special attention in future to providing a proportion of their houses for those living in conditions of housing stress and to taking a proportion of individuals and families whose heads, perhaps because they are in special circumstances – e.g. single parents or disabled, do not need a job in the town to which they would like to move. The new towns must provide more direct help for people in such particular housing need.

The Expenditure Committee welcomed these sentiments but were concerned at the lack of any discussion as to how these wider housing opportunities were to become available. They called for an immediate review of the appropriate machinery.[46] The issue has now arisen in the context of enhanced interest in 'the inner city problem' and the role which might be played by development corporations in dealing with this.

At the secretary of state's request, the London new towns agreed, in 1976, to make 'special quota' allocations for 'families in special need'. Somewhat caustically a Greater London Council report commented that this additional help 'had been made possible by the ready availability of dwellings at some of the towns'.[47]

New town development corporations were established for specific purposes which local authorities were considered incompetent or inappropriate to fulfil. As these purposes were largely met (for the earlier new towns), a nice question arose as to the future of the corporations. Here the basic political question was that of deciding who was to benefit from their financial success, but there was a further significant issue of how far the new towns should be made a local authority responsibility (thus turning the local authorities into 'monopoly landlords'). The Conservative government of the fifties set up an *ad hoc* agency – the Commission for the New Towns – as a favoured alternative. The Labour government, in 1976, passed legislation to effect transfer of housing (but not the more profitable commercial and industrial legacy) to local authorities.[48] The debate on this issue has been heated and protracted over a period of some twenty years: indeed, ever since it became clear that many of the new towns would be profitable. So far as housing policy is concerned, however, the question was one of the extent to which the new towns should continue to meet non-local needs. As a DoE working party pointed out,

. . . development corporations and local authorities have different responsibilities and objectives, and these are reflected in their tenancy allocation policies. Local authorities have a duty to cater for the housing needs of their areas. In practice this means that people moving into the area from elsewhere are usually granted the lowest priority. Development corporations, on the other hand, are set up specifically to secure the development of a new town for a particular purpose, such as taking overspill from London or another con-urbation, or acting as a focus for economic growth, which means encouraging people to move into the town by making housing available to them. Local authorities and development corporations therefore quite properly adopt different priorities in allocating housing tenancies. Even in the furthest advanced towns there is still strong pressure from employers to maintain, and even increase, the number of tenancies made available for workers with particular skills wishing to move into the town.[49]

As so often happens, the debate continued until it no longer seemed important. By the time the 1976 legislation was passed there was more concern about the perceived role of the new towns in contributing to 'inner city decline' than about their role in attracting 'excess population' from 'congested conurbations'. The political pressure now upon them is 'to house an increasing proportion of the elderly and disadvantaged people who are willing to move from the inner cities'.[50] Such are the shifting sands of policy.

One issue which arose in the debate in the sixties on the future of housing in the new towns was the possibility of developing housing associations as an alternative to direct public authority ownership and management. There was much discussion of this in the new towns division of the ministry, but there was a limit to which the pace of changes in housing policy could be set by the particuliarities of the new towns. The discussion raised questions on which neither the housing division nor ministers were ready to pronounce. The opportunity – such as it was – was therefore lost; but the debate on a 'third arm' of housing policy continued. The term (indicating the mounting concern about the trend towards the ossification of the housing market into the two big 'arms' of owner-occupation and council housing) dropped out of use, possibly because it was difficult to visualise a body with three arms, but perhaps also because it invited the retort that the proposed development of hous-ing associations was more akin to a 'fifth wheel to the local authority bus'. More seriously, there was considerable anxiety and scepticism on the viability of an 'alternative form' of tenure.

The truth of the matter was that no alternative was viable until government made it so; and since none of the existing agencies could be expected to promote a competitor, the essential need was for the establishment of an *ad hoc* agency which, with government backing, would do precisely this. And so the Housing Corporation was born.

THE HOUSING CORPORATION

For much of the postwar period the major emphasis of policy in relation to new house building has been to provide for those wishing to become owner-occupiers or council tenants. However, it was increasingly realised during the fifties that, with the decline of the privately rented sector, something more was needed. Some attempt had been made to arrest the decay of the privately rented stock by way of easing rent controls and by making grants available for improvement, but a large proportion of landlords were small owners with little resources, skill or interest in either improving or expanding their holdings. The Labour Party policy at the time was 'municipalisation', but the Conservative government rejected this as a costly and unnecessary extension of the public sector. Nevertheless they had no positive alternatives. Discussions with major building contractors and with building societies strongly suggested that no significant revival of private landlordism was feasible. The only alternative was to stimulate action by non-profit-making housing associations. Accordingly, in 1961 an experimental scheme was promoted for the provision of housing association houses for letting at 'economic' rents (i.e. rents which covered 'costs' but which produced no 'profits'), or for co-operatives. The intention was 'to show the way to the investment of private capital in building houses to let'.[51]

These 'new-style' housing associations were to be distinguished from their 'traditional' predecessors in that they were to be neither charitable nor philanthropic though they were to be non-profit making. Since it was known that existing institutions would not provide the necessary capital for these new-style associations, £25m. of Exchequer loans were made available. This left the problem of establishing an agency for the administration of these. It was inappropriate in a 'pump-priming opera-tion' to set up a new body, so the services of an existing organisation – the National Federation of Housing Societies – were enlisted. This choice clearly indicated that the new provision was to be distinguished from owner-occupation (funded mainly by building societies) and from council housing. There was also the practical point that some local authorities were unsympathetic to the idea of housing associations.

The 'pump-priming' scheme was successful, at least to the extent that viable schemes were forthcoming. As a result the scheme was put on a permanent basis. However, since the intention (at this time) was essentially to provide a type of rental housing which would be different from council housing, it was considered important to attract private capital. As a result an *ad hoc* body was created: the Housing Corporation. The hope was that the new-style housing associations (now termed 'housing societies' to distinguish them from the 'traditional' associations) would be able to attract two-thirds of their required capital from building societies, while the Housing Corporation would provide the remainder as a second mortgage:

> This was seen by ministers at that time as a further step in the direction of getting housing society activity financed otherwise than directly through the Exchequer or local authority funds, and thus one got the development of two-thirds from the building societies and one-third from the Exchequer. It is convenient to have a Housing Corporation dealing with these things because as a separate body it can deal much more freely with the building societies on the one hand and the housing societies on the other.[52]

The expectation that building societies (and other private sources) would increasingly invest in housing societies was not realised. Most building societies were unenthusiastic about the scheme; or, at least, already had sufficient 'normal' demands for their limited funds. The hope that the role for Exchequer aid would gradually diminish proved in vain.[53]

Nevertheless, there was now an institution to hand which was specifically concerned with the development of housing societies, and which could be used as a basis for a different approach.

This came in 1974 when the Housing Act of that year transformed the role of the Housing Corporation and placed it in a dominating position in relation to the development and supervision of all types of housing association. A new (and generous) system of Exchequer subsidies was introduced and the Housing Corporation was empowered to borrow up to £750m. for lending to housing associations.

Since the 1974 Act (which was largely bi-partisan), major shifts in policy have taken place: with an expansion of the housing association movement, a change in the character of the provision (with a much greater emphasis on needy areas), and a wider range of experimentation with new forms of tenure. This was administratively possible because of the existence (and growing competence) of the Housing Corporation. The policies themselves are discussed in a later essay: here we note the importance to government of having to hand a creature of its own which could respond quickly to changes in policy.

THE SCOTTISH SPECIAL HOUSING ASSOCIATION

The Scottish Special Housing Association is a particularly interesting example of a government sponsored agency which has proved to be a successful instrument of central policy. It was originally established in 1937, as the Scottish Special Areas Housing Association, to supplement the activities of local authorities in the 'special areas' (previously termed 'distressed areas') of Scotland. Its role was to build houses, thus contributing to the relief of unemployment, and to relieve local authorities of the financial burden which council housing entailed. Since then its powers have been considerably extended. In 1938, the scope of its work was extended for experimental and demonstration purposes beyond the special areas, and the term 'areas' was dropped from its title. The background to this was the shortage of both bricks and skilled labour in Scotland, and the need for 'non-traditional' building systems.

In 1945, the association was empowered to build in any area which the secretary of state decided was an area of great need for housing or where assistance was required to supplement local authority building. In 1957, it was given a role in the provision of housing for Glasgow overspill in town development schemes. Here again its function was to supplement the operations of local authorities (in this case the 'receiving authorities') 'who, owing to limitations on their resources, would not find it practicable to make unaided the full contribution of which their district is capable'.[54]

The association was also given the major responsibility of building houses for miners transferring to developing mining areas: over 10,000 houses were built under this programme. In the mid-sixties this role was extended to more generally providing 'economic expansion housing' for letting to workers in incoming or expanding industries. (Some 17,500 houses have been provided under this programme over the last twelve years.) Additionally, when the policy of stimulating cost-rent housing was introduced in the early sixties, the association was empowered to build for 'economic letting' and also to convert or improve existing houses. The 1964 Housing Act (which provided for the establishment of the Housing Corporation) gave the association power to provide professional services to the Housing Corporation in Scotland. More recently the association has embarked on building programmes to assist those local authorities (such as Glasgow) who have large outstanding slum clearance programmes. The association also builds on an agency basis for government departments, health authorities and the prison service.

As this summary indicates, the association is, unlike local government, an executive agency of central government. Its functions are controlled by the secretary of state, and its policies can be changed quickly and effectively. Its governing body is appointed by the secretary of state, its capital finance is provided from the National Loans Fund, and any deficits are met by Exchequer 'deficiency payments'.

It should be noted, however, that the association *supplements* the work of local authorities: it does not replace them. It is used by central government to provide additional resources in areas of particular need and to carry out policies which are difficult for local authorities (or towards which local authorities are unenthusiastic – or even hostile). Above all it is, by its nature, much more amenable and flexible as an instrument of central government policy than could ever be expected on the part of independent local authorities.

It is not without difficulty, however, for both local and central government. This stems from the very fact of its being a centrally sponsored and financed institution which works alongside local government. A particularly intractable problem has been that of determining rents. The level of these cannot be allowed to get too far out of line with those of council houses, otherwise there will be consumer resistance (strongly articulated by the local authorities themselves). Yet central government has an obvious interest in containing Exchequer subsidies and, in any case, is loth to see its own creature setting rents at a level similar to that which it is pressing local authorities to increase. Local authorities, on the other hand, are not slow to appreciate the political mileage to be obtained from pressing for the association's rents to be set near their own level. To the extent that this is done, the case for a continued high level of Exchequer subsidies to council housing is strengthened. *Per contra*, the higher the level of association rents, the more eloquent is the political argument against the existence of this 'undemocratic' institution. Perversely, the greater the Exchequer subsidy, the stronger is the case for abolishing the association and transferring its financial liabilities to local government.

This is a political tightrope, and the balancing act is made all the more difficult because the association does not have the rate income which local authorities can use to keep rents down. The outcome has been a level of Exchequer subsidy far greater than would otherwise have been expected. The difficulties facing a 'centrally controlled' organisation are manifest.

A NATIONAL HOUSING CORPORATION?

The Estimates Committee were impressed by the activities of the Scottish Special Housing Association, and felt that similar organisations might be established in England and Wales 'in order to increase the number of house completions and to provide a balancing factor which would enable the government to ensure by direct administrative action that the number of houses built in any two-year period complies with what is required and what is in accordance with national economic policy'.[55]

In this the Estimates Committee were echoing the argument intermittently put forward over many years for a national housing corporation.[56] This has always been resisted on the grounds that it would be an unwarranted incursion into the field of responsibility of local government. The establishment of *ad hoc* housing agencies can be politically justified only where local government is accepted as being, in some way, inadequate to meet recognised needs – as was the case with the Scottish Special Housing Association (and its much smaller counterpart in the north of England, the North Eastern Housing Association, which was set up under the same 'special areas' policy). Similarly, the misleadingly entitled National Building Agency (which, like the building societies, does not build) was established in 1963 when industrialised building became the vogue, to assist local authorities and others to increase productivity in building.[57] Its role has been to act as an advisory and consultancy body to both public and private clients. It originally operated over a wide field but, following the return of the Labour government, its activities since 1967 have been restricted to housing.[58] It has had a somewhat chequered career and currently works in close co-operation with the Housing Corporation (with which it shares its chairman). Whether this is an indication of the flexibility of an *ad hoc* government sponsored agency or of the difficulty of retiring an institution which has outlived its original function is not clear. Nevertheless, there is a general issue here which is of importance. *Ad hoc* agencies (like committees) take on a life of their own and are not easily dispensed with even if they become redundant.[59]

One of the strengths of multi-purpose local authorities is that new functions can be added, and old ones allowed to wither away, without the agonies of institutional homicide. Similar agonies do, however, arise with local government reorganisation, as the turbulent postwar history of this amply demonstrates. But there has never been any serious suggestion that the responsibilities of local housing authorities would be better transferred to an *ad hoc* agency (as has happened, for example, with hospitals and water). There has been nothing equivalent to the Northern Ireland case where a Housing Executive was created to take over the responsibilities of the Province's local authorities in 1971, following mounting concern over their housing allocation policies.[60] Whatever the shortcomings of British housing authorities, they certainly do not justify any such draconian measures.

BUILDING SOCIETIES

Building societies are the main source of finance for house purchase yet they were curiously isolated from the mainstream of housing policy until the house price explosion of the early seventies. They operated in their traditional ways 'unobtrusively but effectively',[61] subject only to the legal framework of the Building Societies Acts and the supervision of the Chief Registrar of Friendly Societies. There was no control over their lending policies or their rates of interest. Government intervention was minimal (though increasing): the Exchequer advances under the House Purchase and Housing Act, 1959 to encourage building societies to lend on pre-1919 houses; the 'reference' to the National Board for Prices and Incomes in 1966 of the proposed increase in lending rates from $6\frac{3}{4}$ to $7\frac{1}{8}$ per cent;[62] the introduction of the option mortgage scheme (together with a new scheme for guaranteeing 100 per cent mortgages 'for persons of modest means');[63] and the attempt to peg interest rates at $9\frac{1}{2}$ per cent in 1973.

Despite the much greater concern now being shown by both the public and the government in building society affairs, there has been only one change of significance: the establishment of a joint advisory committee on mortgage finance consisting of the general managers of some of the leading societies and officials of the Treasury and DoE. Though it is difficult to assess how important this is, the experience of the government interventions in the period before it was established suggests that it should not be lightly dismissed.

Until the establishment of the joint advisory committee 'the building societies, managed by men who had come up through the ranks, knew little of the workings of central government' and 'by the same token, central government (of any hue) was equally ignorant about the operation of building societies'.[64] As a result government interventions were ill considered and ineffective. The first option mortgage scheme had to be 'virtually redrafted',[65] the low-start mortgage scheme found scarcely any takers, and the attempt to peg the mortgage interest rate at $9\frac{1}{2}$ per cent in early 1973 (with the help of a £15m. subsidy) failed – with the rate rising to 11 per cent by the end of the year.

It was the last of these which led to the setting up of the joint advisory committee and the much closer relationships (and mutual understanding) between government and the building societies. The cooperative measures taken since then are illustrated later, but first it is necessary to discuss briefly the operations of building societies and their role in the wider money market.

Building societies operate on a basis which offends a major principle of sound finance: they borrow short and lend long. That they are able to do this is a mark of the public confidence which they have acquired over their long history. By borrowing short they are inevitably subject to marked fluctuations in their income and hence in their ability to lend. Net receipts increased from £1,490m. in 1970 to £2,193m. in 1972; they then fell to £1,993m. in 1974, rose to £4,172m. in 1975, and dropped to £3,575m. in 1976. To partly offset the effect of these fluctuations on lending, societies vary their 'liquidity ratio' (the proportion of their funds which is retained in liquid investments such as government securities); and they also have a steadily growing income by way of repayments of mortgage loans (which grew steadily from £933m. in 1970 to £2,487m. in 1976). But this cannot iron out the fluctuations: gross advances in the four years 1973 to 1976 were £3,540m., £2,950m.,

£4,965m. and £6,134m. The numbers of loans made was as low as 433,000 in 1974 and as high as 715,000 in 1976.

The reason for all this volatility lies in the fact that, since the greater part of investment in building societies is short term, they are highly vulnerable to competing interest rates. They are also reluctant to change them, partly for administrative reasons (with some $4\frac{1}{2}$ million loans any change is a huge operation) and partly because they are even more sensitive to political reactions than they are to short-term market considerations. Governments cannot ignore the impact of increases in mortgage interest rates on the cost of living of millions of house purchasers and its effect in pricing many would-be buyers out of the market. On the other hand, if mortgage interest rates are held down, the related interest rate for investors becomes uncompetitive and leads to a 'mortgage famine'.

When market rates are falling, the competitive position of the building societies improves and leads to pressure for a reduction in the mortgage interest rate. Yet there is always the danger that the related reduction in their borrowing rate will result in a fall in investment, a shortage of funds for lending, and the need to increase borrowing rates again.

This inherent instability in the supply of building society funds has become markedly apparent in recent years following the introduction of competition and credit control in 1971, which ended interest fixing in the banking system and exposed the market to greater competition and more frequent variations in interest rates.

The importance of the volatility of building society activity lies in the fact that it has serious effects on the housing market and the house-building industry. A big increase in lending, such as took place between 1970 and 1972, has a major impact on house prices: the higher effective demand for houses cannot be met by an increase in supply and so prices rise. Indeed, in this particular case the rise began to feed upon itself: as purchasers grew confident that it would continue, they were prepared to offer more and they thus contributed to the expected rise. Though mortgage availability may not be the whole explanation, it goes far to account for the doubling of house prices between 1970 and 1973.

This upward surge was followed by a cut-back. Here the major effect was not a fall in prices (though the rate of increase fell) but a marked reduction in housing starts. While 228,000 new private houses were started in 1972 and 216,000 in 1973, the figure for 1974 was only 106,000.

The house price boom of the early seventies and the demand slump of 1974 were extreme (and exhibited features which are not easy to explain[66] – such as the small effect of the increased prices on housing starts in 1972 and the continued increase in house prices in 1973 despite the fall in mortgage availability). But it is eloquent testimony to the instability of the private housing market – of which the major feature is the instability of the mortgage market or, to be more precise, the volatility of the inflow of funds to building societies.

The societies have been criticised for their part in this, particularly their reluctance to adjust more readily to market conditions. It is argued that, were they to change both lending and borrowing rates in line with the money market, they could maintain a steady flow of funds. But neither they (nor the government) are willing to see too quick a rise in rates; and reductions are held back by competition between the societies.

The use of the plural noun, indeed, can be misleading. There are nearly 400 building societies and, though the largest statistically dominate the market, there is a degree of competition which militates against co-ordinated action, or even agreement. Most societies are members of the Building Societies Association, but this body merely recommends interest rates: there is no compulsion on member societies to follow recommendations.

One way of attempting a degree of stabilisation is by the expansion of local authority mortgage lending. This was one of the measures taken in the mortgage famine era of 1973–4. Local authority lending rose from £337m. in 1972 to £629m. in 1974 (and even higher to £856m. in 1975.[67] This, however, was an emergency measure which, in view of the public expenditure implications, is unpopular with government. Moreover, it is an inefficient use of administrative resources for local authorities to expand and contract their mortgage lending departments in a counter-cyclical way.

A further alternative is the establishment of a mortgage stabilisation system. This would involve a restraint on mortgage lending when the inflow of funds to the societies exceeded the amount needed to finance a previously determined lending requirement. Shortfalls could be met by Exchequer loans (as was done in an *ad hoc* way in 1974 when £500m. was lent to the building societies – all of which was repaid by July 1975).

The difficulty about a full stabilisation system is that, by protecting the mortgage market from general credit conditions, the management of the economy would become more difficult. On what grounds should housing be shielded from a cold climate? And if housing, why not hospitals or schools or roads? Government loans to building societies would also increase public sector borrowing. It is for these reasons (and possibly fears of a loss of independence on the part of the societies) that, though there has been much talk of stabilisation, little has been done.

To date, reliance has been placed on a voluntary scheme (agreed by the joint advisory committee) under which the societies adjust their lending (by adjustments to their liquidity ratio) to even out the effects of changes in interest rates on their flow of funds. The housing policy review expressed the government's 'belief' that 'an even greater degree of stability' could be achieved by developing these voluntary arrangements, possibly with Exchequer loans in exceptional conditions.[68]

The emphasis is clearly on pressing building societies to adapt to changing circumstances and to the requirements of government policy. Yet there is a clear warning that if building societies prove inadequate to the task (either of maintaining stability or of providing sufficient funds to meet the demands for house purchase loans) then some institutional device may have to be introduced. A 'special financial intermediary' is tentatively suggested as a vehicle for tapping the fresh sources of funds which might be required and for raising short-term loans to stabilise the flow of funds to the societies. This could be either a public or private body, 'but the building societies may prefer to develop any necessary machinery themselves'. If they do not, the agency could be established by the government, 'but this would clearly involve a greater degree of government involvement in building society borrowing and lending policies. If an intermediary proves to be the best solution, the government believe that the societies would themselves prefer to develop any necessary machinery.'[69]

This is a nice illustration of how governments attempt to influence agencies over which they have no formal powers of control. Behind the scenes the pressures may be more explicit, but it all seems a far cry from the prospect of nationalisation. This is a measure which is intermittently espoused[70] and which, though not seriously proposed by governments, is always in the background as a possibility. Yet there is perhaps too much truth in the cynic's comment that 'the government would never nationalise the building societies because it would lose control of them',[71] but it is unlikely that the bluff would be called.

THE MULTIPLICITY OF INSTITUTIONS

Sufficient has been said to illustrate the range of institutions which operate housing policy. There are, of course, many more – including estate agents, private developers, the building industry, fringe banks and private landlords. Each of these institutions has its distinctive history, its style of working, and its concept of its role in relation to 'housing policy'. Some, like local authorities, have well-developed channels of communication with central government. Others such as new town development corporations, the Housing Corporation and the Scottish Special Housing Association are creatures of central government, though the extent to which they act as an arm of the centre varies.

Some of the institutions have their own associations who are in constant or periodic contact with central government. Again, local authorities are the prime example (with half a dozen associations for the English and Welsh authorities and a single one for Scotland). The Building Societies Association is a relative newcomer to the machinery of consultation. Such bodies operate, with varying degrees of effectiveness, in the formulation of policy as well as in monitoring its progress.

Not all the institutions, however, have effective organisations or channels of communication with government, the most striking absence being that of a truly representative organ of private landlords. These form far too disparate a group to be able to appoint spokesmen. Such organisations as do exist in this field (such as the British Property Federation) have little locus in the consultative establishment: indeed, they are typically ignored because of their unrepresentative nature. An organisation like Shelter (which is a self-appointed representative of the underprivileged) is more effective than the landlords' organisations (with *all* political parties).

The case of Shelter is an interesting one in that it is one of the very few bodies which speak on behalf of consumers (though the National Consumer Council has recently moved into this field). But consumers – like private landlords – have insufficient community of interest to do little more than complain about grievances. Whether the development of tenant participation will alter this remains to be seen.

Housing, of course, is not alone in being a source of conflict, though there are few fields where divergent interests exist on such a large scale and so widely – within tenure sectors as well as between them; and between individual local authorities as well as between local and central government. A full list would be a lengthy one: it would include not merely differing interests between tenants and their landlords, but also between tenants as a whole and owner-occupiers, between recent and long-established house purchasers, between established residents and those seeking housing, and between the residents of rural and urban areas or growing and declining regions.

Representative bodies face major problems in acting in a representative way: witness the convolutions of the London Boroughs Association which can rarely obtain agreement between its constituents on important housing issues which inherently affect inner and outer London differently.

Professional organisations face similar problems even when, as in the following quotation from a housing report by the Royal Institution of Chartered Surveyors, they profess objectivity and neutrality:

The Royal Institution of Chartered Surveyors is perhaps better qualified than most to take a broad view, for amongst its membership may be found chartered surveyors in the public service as well as in private practice; members who act for tenants as well as members who act for landlords; members who manage housing departments of local authorities; members active in housing associations; and members covering a wide range of professional skills in planning, in housing finance, and in the economics of housing costs.[72]

Their recommendations were 'devised by men and women who have chosen to lead their professional lives dealing with housing problems, and they owe nothing to any predisposition to political ideology of the right or left'.

Perhaps so; but their forty recommendations are the very stuff of politics; and on one of them (relating to the determination of council house rents) there is actually a minority report.

Housing is not an issue which (in the words of the British Property Federation) can 'be taken out of the realm of party politics'.[73] The multiplicity of institutions is in part a reflection of the highly political nature of 'housing'.

Attempts to design a 'comprehensive' housing policy seem doomed to failure: because of this, because of the elusiveness of any operational concept of equity, because the issues of 'policy' involved are too complex to orchestrate, and because the instruments of 'administration' are too diverse to harmonise. As a study of the organisation of housing in London concluded, 'the distribution of organisational power' is so complex that the housing system could be better characterised as a 'disorganisation of housing'. As a result, housing opportunities vary greatly, 'not only according to the distribution of income, but also according to the constraints which differing geographical locations place upon organisations and people, and according to the varying ideologies of the agencies on which the government's policies depend for their implementation'.[74]

This is not a counsel of despair (though that might not infrequently be the state of mind to which ministers and housing reformers are reduced): it is the beginning of the wisdom necessary for the formulation of more effective housing policies. It is, of course, only a necessary prerequisite – not a sufficient one. What else is needed raises questions to which some answers will be attempted in subsequent essays.

2 Housing Need and Demand

> Talking once with a miner I asked him when the housing shortage became acute in his district; he answered 'when we were told about it', meaning that till recently people's standards were so low that they took almost any degree of overcrowding for granted.
>
> G. Orwell[1]

'The government's first objective is to afford a separate dwelling for every family which desires to have one.' So stated the 1945 housing White Paper.[2] Such political statements were commonplace in the euphoria of the early postwar years. The US Congress went even further and, in the preamble to the 1949 Housing Act, promulgated as the national housing goal 'a decent home and a suitable living environment for every American family'. Though such rhetoric still abounds in political debate, it is empty of meaning. The 'need' for housing, as with the 'need' for health services, or roads, or recreational facilities, is dependent upon the awareness, recognition and definition of 'problems': these in turn are dependent upon the standards of 'adequacy' adopted and the factors which are accepted as being relevant to them. All these constantly change: as one 'problem' is met, another emerges. A 'need' is a socially accepted aspiration, and the faster that one is met the faster do new aspirations arise.

Need, of course, is not the same as demand: it takes no account of price and ability to pay. But meeting a need involves costs, and if these cannot be afforded by those in need someone else has to pay. Thus subsidies become an important element not only in providing for needs but also in determining how far they can be met, and, indeed, in defining how great they are.

Once housing is subsidised, it can be argued (as it frequently is) that consumer preferences are 'distorted', and that more housing is 'consumed' than would otherwise be the case. In one sense, of course, this is not only a tautology but also the precise intention. It is the objective of a subsidy to encourage greater consumption of the subsidised good. The force of the argument, however, is that subsidies can have unintended effects such as under-occupation or inadequate maintenance or reduced mobility or a withdrawal of private investment in housing. Each of these distortions (the argument continues) leads to pressure for additional subsidies. Further distortions are created, subsidy bills mount, and it becomes increasingly difficult to establish 'real need'. With British housing subsidies and benefits currently running at an annual rate in excess of £2,000m. these arguments are not to be lightly dismissed.

On the other hand, as Needleman has pointed out, the distinction between demand and need is not as sharp as might be assumed:

> The choice of minimum socially acceptable standards is not com-pletely independent of the incomes and prices prevailing in the country concerned, while the same demographic factors that largely determine housing needs also strongly influence the effective demand for dwell-ing units.[3]

There is certainly some validity in this argument, though it is impossible to establish how much – which is why the issue is one of intense political debate. Certainly, subsidies can enable sharing households to occupy separate dwellings, but they can equally encourage the formation of separate households by groups and individuals who would otherwise be content to live as part of a family or in hostels or in other institutional accommodation. They may also affect the demand for second dwellings, particularly if (as was the case at one time) grants are available for improving rural cottages for this purpose and tax reliefs are available on second home mortgages.

In addition to their impact on quantitative demand, subsidies also affect the quality of dwellings demanded: the demand for particular sizes, locations, types and qualities of housing at subsidised prices may be very different from the demand at market prices and from 'need'. Again this may be intended, but the result can be the creation of new 'housing problems' or the intensification of old ones. For example, an area with a very low level of local authority rents and a large stock of substandard privately rented (and rent controlled) houses will find it difficult to secure a modernisation of this stock without massive sub-sidies, since the unsubsidised rent required to be charged for an im-proved house may be much higher than that charged for a new local authority house. The effect therefore will tend to be a heavy demand for continued local authority building and an acceleration in the deteriora-tion of the privately rented sector.

These financial and economic aspects are discussed more fully in other essays. They are mentioned here as a warning that the assessment of housing need or housing demand must have a price dimension, and (either explicitly or implicitly) assumptions have to be made about the level and incidence of subsidies.

Most British estimates, however, have been concerned with estimating 'need'. Typically this has been taken as the 'shortage' of dwellings as measured by the difference between the numbers of households and dwellings, plus the number of new dwellings required to replace inadequate ones. It is instructive to examine the problems to which this gives rise.[4]

PROBLEMS OF MEASUREMENT

The definition of the basic concepts of 'dwelling' and 'household' presents some baffling problems. At a time when there is a housing shortage, many persons who 'need' separate accommodation may be living as parts of other households: how are these 'hidden households' to be identified? Is a household consisting of a married couple and the parents of the wife to be counted as one or two units? Is a single person lodging with a household to be counted as a separate unit or as part of the main household? How are three students or businessmen 'sharing' a flat to be counted? And, since one is not generally concerned with what the census terms the 'institutional population' – those living in institutions, hotels, etc. (who form 3 per cent of the total population) – how is the line to be drawn between private households containing a number of lodgers and non-private households of the small boarding-house type?

So far as dwellings are concerned, is a large Victorian house adapted to provide a reasonable degree of privacy for several households to be counted as a shared dwelling or as several separate dwellings – and what is to be the definition of 'reasonable'? As the *Housing Report* of the 1951 census pointed out, 'it is easy to construct a definition of a structurally separate dwelling for the usual type of family house or flat originally constructed as such, but it is difficult to devise a form of words to cover every type of converted building in such a way as to provide, in a simple classification, a measure of the different degrees of separation which one dwelling space may have from another; on the justifiable grounds of simplicity the boundaries are inevitably made to appear more sharply defined than they really are'.[5] This raises a further issue: the more refined and elaborate are the definitions employed, the more difficult it becomes for them to be understood and applied by interviewers and the more unreliable and complex are the resulting tabulations. There is little to be said for devising a set of perfect definitions if few can understand what they really mean.

These definitional problems are not easily solved (and they become even more intractable in relation to qualitative issues) but, even if they were, the assessment of need would be only a snapshot picture of an essentially dynamic situation. Indeed, this is a major shortcoming of any analysis which is based on statistics relating to single point in time. They cannot reveal the social and economic forces which are at work in determining need.

Thus the early postwar estimates assumed that the majority of households would be family units, and there was little appreciation of the effect which socio-economic and demographic changes would have on 'non-family-type household formation'.[6] Insight into this important issue was gained by the use of the concept of 'headship rates'. This is a measure of the proportion of persons in each population group who head households. Thus, if there are (as there were in England and Wales in 1951) 4,043,000 married males aged under 40 and 3,187,000 of these head separate households, the headship rate is 78·8 per cent. Similarly, if there are (again as there were in 1951) 529,000 single males aged 40–59 and 142,000 of these form separate households, the headship rate is 26·8 per cent.[7]

These headship rates have increased markedly since the war. As a result, even if there had been no change in the structure of the population, the result would have been a major increase in the number of separate households. But, of course, there have also been significant changes in both the structure and the size of the population. The combined effect of all these changes has been dramatic. Between 1951 and 1971, though the population of Great Britain increased by about a tenth, the increase in households was about a quarter.

There is now available a greater wealth of statistical material than ever before. Unfortunately, though this helps us to understand what has happened in the past, it is of limited use for predicting the future. This applies particularly to the most important single aspect of future need: the total size of the population. In 1955 it was envisaged that the population of Great Britain would increase modestly from 50 million to around 52 million and remain at around that level. Ten years later the actual population was in excess of that number, and a revised projection was for a population increase from 53 million to 72·5 million by the end of the century. A further ten years later, in 1975, the projection had been revised downwards to an end-century figure of 58 million.[8]

Statistical work on household formation has now become highly sophisticated,[9] but there is a danger that this very sophistication may detract attention from the inevitable crudity of the assumptions which have to be made. Quite apart from the uncertainties connected with the population projections which form the basis of estimates, 'simple and rather crude adjustments' have to be made in order to translate 'households' (as defined in the census) into 'households requiring separate dwellings'. For example:

The number of households must be adjusted to allow for groups of people who can be said, in some sense, to need to live as a separate household in their own dwelling but are at present obliged to live as part of another household because of a lack of housing or other reasons. The most obvious case is the young married couple who live with in-laws until they can afford a home of their own. On the other hand some households, particularly one-person households, will not want a separate dwelling but while preserving their independence and catering for themselves will be quite happy to share a dwelling with another household. We therefore use the notion of 'potential households', their numbers being derived from actual households by adding married couples not heading a household and deducting three-quarters of those one-person households sharing a dwelling with another household.[10]

The inadequacy of such an arbitrary 'adjustment' is manifest, but it is difficult to suggest any alternative which is not equally arbitrary.

Apart from such difficulties, there is a real danger that official projections and estimates are taken as an indication of the housing shortage which can be 'met' by an equivalent provision of new dwellings. This would be so only if the provision were made in the localities in which the need arises, if those in 'need' were to benefit from the new provision, and if there were no increase in need in the meantime.

Some aspects of these three (inter-related) points are obvious. Clearly if new building were to be concentrated in areas of low need (because of effective demand or because of overestimates by the local authority) it would be of no benefit to those in the 'needy' areas. If the 'need' is for small dwellings for young single and elderly pensioner households, the provision of three- and four-bedroom houses will not be of much help; and similarly if the new supply is concentrated in the public sector while the 'need' is for more dwellings for owner-occupation (or vice versa).

More fundamentally, 'need' and 'supply' cannot be dealt with in the abstract: there has to be a translation into effective access. This means that any analysis of 'need' has to take into account market conditions (in the private sector) and 'eligibility' and 'allocation' policies (in the public sector). Indeed, it is quite possible to have a general surplus of housing accompanied by an acute need which market forces and public policies do not meet. This is not a hypothetical statement: it in fact represents the position in certain areas where there are both high vacancy rates and homelessness.

Yet surely, it may be argued, those in need will benefit indirectly from new building even if they are precluded from direct access to it? Here we encounter the concept of 'filtering'. This has been variously defined but typically refers to the 'trickling down' of vacated houses to lower income groups. There is no doubt that the concept has some validity, though there is considerable argument as to how much. The weight of evidence strongly suggests that it does not work effectively in relation to the most needy.[11]

These issues of access have come to the forefront of debate as the general housing position has improved. Indeed, it has become increasingly doubtful whether national (or regional) estimates of 'need' have much use. The only valid estimates are those which relate to housing market areas and which take account of local market factors.

HOUSING MARKETS

The major point arising in this discussion is the importance of relating the assessment of housing need to the public and private markets within which houses are obtained. Global estimates based on total dwellings and households may, as Holmans states, 'play an essential part in the determination of housing policy',[12] though this must be increasingly limited. In 1951 there were, in England and Wales, about 750,000 more households than dwellings, but by 1976 there were about 500,000 more dwellings than households.[13] Even in Greater London there was a small 'excess' in 1976,[14] though this is still unlikely to be the case in inner London.

These figures point to a continuing improvement in the general housing situation. Yet homelessness has become a problem of such importance that official statistics are now published.[15] The fact of this publication is of greater significance than the statistics themselves – which are of dubious validity. For what they are worth, they show that some 50,000 households a year apply to local authorities for assistance on the grounds of homelessness. About two-thirds are 'accepted' by local authorities and, of these, nearly three-quarters are rehoused in council-owned properties. The reasons for homelessness vary widely and range from family disputes (about a third of those accepted as homeless in the first half of 1976) to evictions for rent arrears or mortgage default.

There is considerable dispute about the meaning and adequacy of these figures. On the one hand it is argued that homelessness is essentially a 'social' rather than a 'housing' problem. On the other hand it is pointed out that, on a strict interpretation of the term, only those literally without a roof over their heads are counted and that, on a wider and more sensible definition, it should include those living in conditions of acute overcrowding or in severely substandard accommodation.

It is unlikely that this debate will ever be settled. As earlier studies have shown,[16] both the concept of homelessness and the reasons for it are issues for lengthy and typically inconclusive argument. Moreover, the very categories used for analysis (rent arrears, landlord requiring, family disputes, and such like) do not disentangle cause from effect.[17]

What is clear, in the words of a *Times* leader,[18] is that 'more new housing is not the simple answer. There are more empty houses than homeless households.' Yet, equally clearly, the homeless do not have easy access to available accommodation, and even if the causes of home-lessness were essentially 'social' rather than 'housing', its very existence by definition points to a particular housing shortage. A study under-taken in London in 1969 concluded that 'were it not for the shortage of rented housing in inner London many of the families who do not display conventional standards of behaviour would still find room in the housing stock. Were it not for rising rents – particularly in the expanding furnished sector – many of those evicted for rent arrears would still be paying their way.'[19]

In short, the fundamental issue is the structure and operation of the housing market. New house building (and estimates of the number of new houses 'needed') typically fail to take this into account. Homeless-ness is an extreme manifestation of the operation of the housing market (as is squatting),[20] but there are other less contentious issues which illustrate its importance. One of the most dramatic changes since the war has been the decline of the privately rented sector. In 1945 over a half of the total stock of dwellings was rented from private landlords. The proportion fell to a third in 1961, a quarter in 1966 and a fifth in 1971. Since then the decline has continued at the rate of around 100,000 a year. By 1977, the total number had fallen to around 3 million and formed less than 15 per cent of the total stock.

There are many reasons for this decline, of which rent control is only one (others include taxation arrangements and competition from tax-favoured owner-occupation and subsidised local authority housing.)[21] No postwar government has taken effective steps to reverse or even stem this decline, and there seems every likelihood that it will continue. Indeed, there is a strong body of opinion which holds that policy should be directed towards taking into 'social ownership' the remaining privately rented stock. This is proposed either for pragmatic reasons (to ensure that older houses are improved) or for political reasons ('the ownership of one man's home by another has always been repugnant').[22] The assumption here (as with global estimates of housing need) is that the functions of the privately rented sector can equally well be performed under different ownership.

This is not the case: the privately rented sector performs specific functions which other sectors either cannot or will not discharge. It caters particularly for the young, the student, the single and the mobile; it provides a stepping-stone to owner-occupation or the public sector; and it provides the most easy 'access' for newcomers to an area and those who require immediate accommodation.[23] For those who are not able to afford to buy or who are unable to obtain a mortgage, and those who are not 'eligible' for council housing, little alternative exists.

However unsatisfactory may be the housing provided by this sector and however inadequate its 'management', it manifests a flexibility in the housing market for which an effective substitute is difficult to envisage. Yet its decline demands a housing policy which provides precisely this: hence the emphasis laid on the necessity for 'broader' allocation systems on the part of local authorities:

> The huge decline in the privately rented sector has the important implication that the alternatives to a council house facing a household wishing to rent (or unable to buy) have declined greatly. The conclusion is that local authorities must take a wider responsibility for groups of people who at one time would have been housed in the private sector.[24]

Any estimate of housing need which ignores the extent to which the responsibility is in fact exercised will inevitably be inadequate.

The same point arises in a wider form in relation to the pattern of tenure as a whole. It is quite possible for an area to have 'sufficient' houses, but have 'needs' for which these houses cannot cater. Thus an area with a high proportion of owner-occupied houses may not have sufficient houses to meet the needs of those who cannot buy. Similarly an area of predominantly public sector housing may be unable to meet the effective demand for owner-occupation.

There can also be a mismatch between the types of houses available and the types which are needed. This is a common situation – with a 'surplus' of medium-size houses and a shortage of the small and the largest. And (at the risk of labouring the point) even if there is adequate provision of the type of houses required, this will not suffice unless those in need have access to them.

THE FUNCTION OF COUNCIL HOUSING[25]

Surely, it may be asked, it is precisely the function of the public housing sector to meet these varied needs? Does not this sector (council housing for short) provide just the flexibility which is needed? Unfortunately this is not so. Indeed, despite its numerical importance the function which council housing serves is by no means clear. Obviously, with nearly a third of the population living in council housing, its actual function is different today from what it was in the interwar years. Indeed, the very scale of council housing makes it more difficult to identify or determine its functions:

> In a very real sense the question of the priority to be attached to particular needy groups of people has been confused by the very extensive role now played by local authorities in the total provision of housing. In the evidence we received from local authorities, attention was focused on their wide range of responsibilities and the

categorisation of housing need. Little thought was given to vulnerable groups living in the private sector on the implicit grounds that their problems received fair priority within general policies directed towards meeting housing needs.[26]

The enormous change in the overall tenure pattern of British housing was a major reason why the Central Housing Advisory Committee report maintained that local authorities should take a wider responsibility for people who at one time would have been housed in the private sector. This applies both to 'general' needs and to rehousing from clearance areas. Increasingly, provision has to be made for 'non-traditional' needs such as those of single people, students, young mobile workers, unmarried professionals, and all those who traditionally have lived in bedsitter land. At the same time, more traditional needs must not be overlooked – particularly those of the large family, the low-income family and the homeless.

The CHAC report strongly supported the Seebohm recommendation that local authorities should 'take increased responsibility for housing the most vulnerable families'. In assessing need, it argued that account should be taken of two factors: the housing conditions in which a household was living and, secondly, the ability of the particular household to cope with those conditions.

If priorities were based on such a system, a high priority for public rehousing would be for households in bad conditions with which they are unable to cope, and where the potential ability to improve their own situation is low. Households in bad conditions, but able to help themselves, can be allocated council housing in turn or helped and advised on how to help themselves if there is likely to be a long wait for council housing due to local shortage.[27]

No recommendation of the committee has been more widely misinterpreted than this. It has even been suggested that the logical end result would be council estates forming ghettos of the poor and inadequate. The committee, however, were at pains to stress:

We are not suggesting that more affluent council tenants should be evicted or that council housing should be reserved for the poor. There are social advantages in having a broad spectrum of social classes living in a community and we certainly would not wish to see an official encouragement to a policy of income segregation. Our point is simply that in allocating council houses local authorities should give particular attention to those with incomes which are low in relation to their needs.[28]

With some 6½ million council houses, the notion of a low-income ghetto is difficult to conceive. (It could happen, of course, on particular estates and even more generally if there were a massive exodus from council housing, but these are very different issues, to which we return in the final essay.)

On this line of argument, local housing authorities have a very particular responsibility in relation to the poor. This function of council housing has tended to be submerged in the totality of its large-scale operations. Unfortunately, the truth of the matter is that local housing authorities, like sound business enterprises, tend to reject 'poor-risk' applicants: and, incredibly, social work departments often acquiesce in this. A quotation from Glastonbury's study of homelessness in south Wales and the west of England is illustrative. He reports a children's officer as saying:

> I wouldn't expect the housing manager to find houses for unsatisfactory tenants just because they had been requested by the welfare or children's department. It all depends on the causes of homelessness and who is to blame. You can't let these people jump the queue ahead of deserving tenants. Public opinion wouldn't stand for it. It's the length of time people have been on the waiting list and the standard of their previous tenancies that matters.[29]

Glastonbury entitles his book *Homeless Near a Thousand Homes* and he suggests that in many areas 'there were few difficulties over the shortage of tenancies and a great many difficulties resulting from the attitudes of housing managers'.

Clearly the distinction between the deserving poor and the undeserving poor is still with us. However, the reference to public opinion is a valid one. Public opinion can be relied upon to support discrimination against the loafers, the dirty, the unmarried mother, the newcomer and the coloured. But it is the task of a public authority to lead public opinion on these matters – not to follow it. On the other hand, the leaders cannot get too far ahead of public opinion: they will lose their seats at the next election if they do.

It would, however, be a gross error to equate 'problem' families with the 'housing poor'. The latter are simply those in poor housing conditions who face difficulties in improving their situation. In pressure areas (above all in inner London) this can give rise to homelessness: 'It is the lack of adequate and secure accommodation at rents that can be paid out of average and below-average earnings that renders most people homeless.'[30] However, the housing situation varies so significantly between different areas that generalisations are neither easy nor useful. What is clear is that local authorities need to know and understand the housing position of their areas if they are to devise intelligent and appropriate policies. It follows that whatever may be the function of council housing it is complementary to the functions of other housing providers in the same area, and that the responsibilities of local authorities extend well beyond the council house sector.

If local authorities are to have responsibility for the totality of the housing needs of their areas they will be concerned with far more than the provision of council houses: they will be ensuring that the demand is met for houses for purchase, for housing association accommodation, for furnished accommodation. Much of this provision can be made by agencies other than local authorities, and even where the actual house building is best undertaken by local authorities, ownership and management can often with benefit be transferred to others.

The reader will note a clear political judgement here, and it is appropriate to make it explicit: there are areas of the country where the scale of public ownership of housing is so large that questions must arise as to whether undesirable consequences follow. Quite apart from the important issue of concentration of power, there is the question of the effect of a very large public sector on private initiative. The position in Scotland is illustrative.

At present well over a half of the Scottish housing stock is publicly owned. Whatever problems have been solved by this scale of public activity (and the achievements are great) an unintended consequence has been the eclipse of private enterprise. As a result, public authorities have been compelled to do more and more in response to the huge and increasing dependence on them for the provision of decent housing.

The small scale of the owner-occupied sector implies a restricted market – one which is restricted even further by the differences in the price to the occupier of public authority and owner-occupied housing. Those moving into public authority housing in Clydeside pay on average substantially less than half those moving into owner-occupied housing.[31] As more older housing is demolished this gap is likely to widen. Those who wish to buy will need to have an income sufficient for the purchase of a modern house and the filtering process will be stemmed. Filtering is a very important (though inadequately documented) feature of the housing market. A large proportion of recent house purchasers have moved from owner-occupied houses: by selling their existing house they are able to improve their housing standards. At the same time the houses which they vacate are made available for other households who are 'behind' them in the filtering process.

If the cheaper houses are demolished the scope for filtering is restricted. Yet, in Clydeside, a large proportion of these cheaper houses probably need to be demolished anyway: thus, it is not easy to see how the situation can be improved, at least in the short run. What is needed is an increase in the supply of cheap satisfactory houses for owner-occupation. One way of achieving this is by the sale of older public

authority houses (discussed later). Another alternative is the purchase
and improvement of improvable old rented tenements, followed by sale
to owner-occupiers.

'GRADING' OF COUNCIL TENANTS

The situation in Clydeside is perhaps an extreme one, but the general
issue of the power of local housing authorities is not. In particular,
the widespread practice of 'grading' tenants according to their suit-
ability for particular standards of housing gives cause for concern.
This was expressed (in appropriately diplomatic language) in the CHAC
report. The committee had a

... feeling that there is a danger that applicants are graded according
to an interpretation of their desert; some housing authorities took up
a moralistic attitude towards applicants: the underlying philosophy
seemed to be that council tenancies were to be given only to those
who 'deserved' them, and that the 'most deserving' should get the best
houses. Thus, unmarried mothers, cohabitees, 'dirty' families and
'transients' tended to be grouped together as 'undesirable'. Moral
rectitude, social conformity, clean living and a 'clean' rent book on
occasion seemed to be essential qualifications for eligibility – at least
for new houses.[32]

As the committee's work progressed, they were increasingly led to the
view that grading was more related to the stock of housing than the
stock of applicants:

We have found considerable variation not only in the extent to which
local authorities 'grade' their tenants, but also in the reasons why
grading is thought to be necessary. On a very limited scale the
justification for grading is that some tenants will not take care of a new
house: at the extreme they may wreck it. It would not be sound policy
to allocate a high standard house to such an 'unsatisfactory tenant'.
But such families are very few in number, though they may pose
problems for the local authority out of all proportion to their
numbers. It is a far cry from allocating specially selected houses to
'unsatisfactory tenants' to grading all according to their 'fitness' for
particular types of houses. We were struck by the simple fact that the
approach of a number of local authorities to this seemed to vary
according to the range of house types they had available. A local
authority with a small range (e.g. all postwar houses) see no need for
careful grading. On the other hand, a local authority with a great
range tend to see a necessity for fine grading.[33]

What all this amounts to is that the bureaucracy of local housing
administration has developed procedures for distributing the housing

which it controls, and has tended to lose sight of its major objective: to provide for local housing needs. Fortunately, this attitude is beginning to crumble in the face of increasing consumer resistance – or what is known in housing circles (significantly) as the increasing 'choosiness' of council applicants. The implication is that local authorities need to review their housing stock and modernise (or even demolish) some of their 'less desirable' estates. However, the greater the proportion of a local housing stock which is owned and managed by a local authority, the less sensitive it may be to such an approach. Instead (as can be seen in the 'harder line' being taken by a number of authorities), rules may be elaborated to provide less choice: 'Applicants who refuse to accept a dwelling on perimeter estates shall forgo their priority and be relegated to a lower place on the list.'

The choice of housing should be the applicant's, not the local authority's: and the choice ought ideally to be one between houses of different standards and different rents. This is not a novel approach. Circular 41/67 of the Ministry of Housing and Local Government was based on this very principle: 'No family should be denied accommodation suited to its needs because of limited means, *but* tenants should so far as possible be offered a choice of accommodation at varying rent levels.'

The Central Housing Advisory Committee agreed and went further, but rapidly got into very deep water, and lamely beat a retreat, leaving the issue with the excuse that it took them beyond their terms of reference.[34] The truth of the matter is that there is a very difficult problem of reconciling a policy of giving real choice with a policy of giving the maximum financial assistance for housing. The dilemma is underlined by an extreme example. If housing were provided 'free', there would be a big demand for the best, and allocation would have to be essentially a matter of 'housing management'. At the other extreme, if housing were to be entirely a matter of market economics, the best would be the most expensive and the quality of a family's housing would depend upon their income and the way they were willing and able to spend it.

Part of the problem of housing management arises from what might be called the 'waiting list philosophy'. This has two very serious short comings. First, it implies that the local housing authority is concerned only with those who want, apply for and are considered eligible for council housing. Those who want other types of housing (or housing which the council does not provide), those who do not apply (perhaps because they think it is 'a waste of time' to do so), and those who are rejected as ineligible are ignored. The local authority thus has little or no idea how far it is meeting the needs of its area and, even less, how far the needs of its area are being met by other agencies of housing provision. Secondly, it implies that the role of the local authority is to actively meet the needs only of those at the 'top' of its list: the rest must wait.

All this stems from the way in which public authority housing has developed in Britain. Rather than being responsible for surveying the total needs of their areas and for ensuring that sufficient provision is made by all the appropriate agencies, local authorities have been predominantly concerned with the building and management of houses for those whose needs they recognise.

NEEDS, RIGHTS AND DUTIES

Despite a daunting labyrinth of law, no one has an enforceable right to good housing (or, indeed – with few exceptions, to any housing at all); and no authority has the duty to provide housing for those in need.

This may seem an exaggerated statement, but much confusion stems from the popular misconception that political statements and enunciations of policy somehow represent the legal position. Policy is one thing: legislation is another. So much is this the case that the British courts explicitly refuse to consider statements made by ministers as to the intention of legislation. The contrast with the USA is interesting:

> American experience shows that judges become much more important where there is a written constitution; they have to immerse themselves in major political questions; they see law as a positive instrument of national policy – the part played by the Supreme Court on racial desegregation over the years is an obvious example. On the contrary the British judge has trained himself as an umpire, avoiding clashes with the government of the day, cutting himself off from politics whenever possible, and divesting his judgements of social, economic and political references to the utmost.[35]

There are, of course, many rights which households have once they are in a house, but this does not extend to those who are without. Indeed, a move from a house – even on the part of owner-occupiers – may involve the reduction or even abandonment of certain rights. The old saying that 'possession is nine points of the law' has a particular validity in relation to housing.

Much of housing policy has been directed towards strengthening the rights of householders, but this has largely been confined to those who rent their dwellings from private landlords. Some protection has been accorded to mortgagors but, for the rest, governments have been content, in the main, to provide powers to local authorities. These powers are sometimes expressed as *duties*, but this is misleading, for two reasons. First, they are expressed in very broad terms; and secondly, there is no corresponding right on the part of the individual citizen to enforce a local authority to carry them out. The reasons for this are partly a matter of history and partly a matter of practicality.

The rights given to private tenants (and the corresponding duties placed on private landlords) are not mirrored in the public sector:

this stems in part from a belief that, unlike private owners, public authorities can be trusted to act fairly, but also in part from the political nature of central–local government relationships and the lack of strong pressure to change the *status quo*.

A significant feature of the typical allocation system, however, is the waiting list – a reflection of the British faith in the fairness of queueing. Partly this is because it is a very simple and understandable way of ordering priorities. It involves no elaborate system for allocating 'points' for varying degrees of hardship or need. It minimises bureaucracy, and it avoids giving discretion to administrators. It also avoids some particular difficulties which arise with more sophisticated schemes. For instance, 'applicants who improve their circumstances by . . . obtaining better accommodation after application are not penalised'; and 'applicants who limit the size of their families have an equal opportunity of housing'.[36]

Where there is little by way of a real housing problem, a queue system (or 'date order' system as it is more usually termed) has some clear advantages, though it will always be necessary to provide for 'exceptional needs' separately. Local authorities sometimes find it attractive to use this system for special categories of dwellings – higher standard high-rent houses, for example, or 'difficult to let' houses. In the latter case the GLC has operated a literal queue system, with the houses being advertised in the press and allocated on a 'first come, first served' basis. It is also used by building societies as an acceptable way of rationing mortgages.

It is, however, a most 'unprofessional' housing management practice. It denies one of the most important tenets of housing managers: that 'one must be scrupulously fair and endeavour to balance the needs of any particular family against those of others with equally strong claims for consideration'.[37] Indeed, its very advantages (of reducing the scope for administrative discretion) may be seen by housing managers as its essential shortcoming. Or, to use sociological terminology, it reduces the power (and prestige) of professionals (and also, in areas where political influence in the allocation of council houses lingers on, the power of elected members).

ACCESS

The effectiveness of a policy is dependent not only upon the resources which are allocated to its implementation, but also on matters such as the character of its administration, the capabilities and attitudes of the officials involved, the extent to which rights are accorded to the intended beneficiaries, the degree of publicity and public awareness, and the provision made for settling grievances and for hearing 'appeals'.

In this section a number of such issues are briefly discussed under the general heading of 'access'. This now popular term means more than geographical convenience: it signifies the particular difficulties facing the ordinary citizen in ascertaining (or even being aware of) the benefits and assistance to which he is entitled, and surmounting the barriers which he has to face in obtaining these. There is also the converse problem: that facing administrators in establishing predefined 'needs', in applying their book of rules to the infinite variety of human circumstances, in interpreting – and verifying – the claims of clients, and in using such discretion as is allowed.

All this is 'policy in practice'; and a sound policy will be one which is designed to overcome or avoid these problems. It is in this light that it can be seen that 'social administration' is not separable from 'social policy'. Policy is concerned, not with theoretical concepts, but with meeting needs. This necessarily involves 'administration'; and if the administration is deficient the likelihood is that the policy is inadequate. Access is thus not a fringe issue: it is a central one.

Given the right to a benefit, the first problem is that of providing the relevant information to the 'target group' of beneficiaries. The more 'universalist' the benefit and the larger the target group, the easier this is. Thus there is no general problem of providing the 'information' that there is a national health service or a comprehensive system of free education (though there are information problems on restricted benefits such as the remission of health service charges, education maintenance grants, nursery provision, and the like). Information problems increase when benefits are designed to meet a wide range of differing needs (as with supplementary benefits) or a particular section of the population (such as one-parent families).

With housing the problems are particularly difficult since benefits have to vary not only according to income and household needs but also according to tenure and housing costs. Of paramount difficulty is the extreme variation in housing costs, which makes it difficult to conceive of a practicable universal housing allowance (a matter which is discussed further in a later essay), or to make a standard allowance for it in other benefits. (It is for this reason that the standard supplementary benefit scales exclude an allowance for housing costs: this is calculated separately for each beneficiary.)

Here the problems may be compounded by barriers at 'the point of entry',[38] and by the attitudes of counter and interviewing staff. Such 'gatekeepers' can exert a considerable influence on the fate of an applicant.[39] Recognition of the importance of this has led to the 'managerialism thesis' – that the 'managers of the urban system' (the staff of local housing authorities, estate agencies, building societies, etc.) exert an independent influence on the allocation of benefits. They are the effective controllers of the access to housing.[40]

Much has been made of this by activist groups such as Shelter and the

Community Development Programme, and also by Marxist writers.[41] The same point, however, has been made in suitably restrained terms in the 1969 Central Housing Advisory Committee report (quoted on page 42 above).[42]

One answer lies in better training of management staff and more effective control over their work. These are neglected areas of housing policy.[43] Yet before too much blame is attached to the shortcomings of operational staff, regard must be taken of the extent to which they are simply carrying out the management policies of their political masters, which in turn may reflect public opinion. The CHAC report touched on this when it noted that 'some attitudes may reflect public opinion'. Elected bodies are by their nature subject to public attitudes and pressures, as is most clearly evidenced by the strong opposition to relaxing 'residential qualifications' and thereby allowing newcomers to compete with longer established residents. Another illustration of the problem is the anxiety felt in government circles that too much emphasis on the needs of coloured people might give rise to a white backlash.

There are, however, other difficulties; and some of these raise fundamental issues of policy. Elizabeth Burney's caustic verdict on access to council housing was that 'a clean person gets a clean house and a dirty person gets a dirty house'.[44] There is abundant evidence that this is so. Yet (ignoring the argument that this is as it should be) on what basis *should* local authorities allocate their 'dirty' houses? The stock of local authority housing is now very variable in quality, and there is evidence that the extent to which individual local authorities grade their applicants (and thus follow an explicit policy of 'differential access') is related to this variability in the quality of their stock.[45] This is an effective bureaucratic solution of the problem of ensuring that tenants are found for the poorer houses. What is the alternative? A market-type solution is rejected on the grounds that council tenancies are allocated according to need, not according to ability to pay. As a result the rent differentials between the best and the worst are small. Moreover, the rent rebate scheme (which, at the extreme, can reduce the rent to nil) operates to reduce the differentials facing any individual household. Increases in rents for the better houses would lead to larger rebates and thus defeat the objective. Issues of 'social polarisation' are also relevant: to charge much lower rents for the worst houses could exacerbate the problems of 'deprived estates'.

There is no easy solution to this problem, but to attempt to deal with it by the grading of tenants only diverts attention from the basic issue; and it creates additional problems as well. The crux of the matter is that council housing now performs a much wider function than that for which it was designed, that many non-housing issues impinge upon it, and that solutions to many of the problems which are now apparent in the council housing sector are not solvable by 'housing policies'.

3 Council Housing Finance

Exchequer subsidies should be examined to see whether
they are designed to produce the best possible results.

Milner Holland Report[1]

SUBSIDIES AND RENTS

A third of the housing stock of Great Britain is rented from public
authorities: a total of about 6½ million houses. Most of these are in the
ownership of local authorities (predominantly built as 'council houses'
but small numbers are acquired and 'municipalised' dwellings), a
quarter of a million have been built by new town development corporations (since 1948), and some 85,000 by the Scottish Special Housing
Association (since 1937). This discussion focuses on council housing.

Local authorities finance their housing over a sixty-year period, but
they do not borrow for such long periods, nor is borrowing for housing
separated from the borrowing for other purposes (though it forms a
major part of it). Typically, authorities operate a 'consolidated loans
fund' (otherwise known as a 'loans pool') which covers all their
borrowings. This means that all outstanding borrowings are amal-
gamated in one account and rates of interest are averaged. The pool in
turn lends, at this rate of interest, to a statutory housing revenue account
(which local authorities are required to maintain in association with
their subsidised council houses).[2] In times of rising interest rates the
effect is that a lower rate of interest is charged for housing than the
current rates; but as new loans are raised and old loans fall due for
repayment and have to be refinanced, the average rate will increase.

In such circumstances pooling of interest rates can result in a 'hidden
subsidy' to the authority's housing account (and therefore to council
tenants).[3] This, however, pales into insignificance against the impact
of changes in the cost of providing houses and the consequent outstanding loan debt per house. For example well over a million council houses
were built between the wars at total average costs of less than £500
(and in some years less than £400).[4] By 1967 the average had increased
to over £4,000,[5] and since then it has tripled. Moreover much of the
debt on the prewar houses has now been paid. Thus, whatever the

current rates of interest being charged on older houses of low historical cost, the actual repayment costs are comparatively very small.

This has the effect of considerably reducing the average current cost to local authorities of financing their housing. It thereby enables them to charge much lower rents than would be the case if they were paying on the basis of current market values.

Additionally, of course, local authorities receive Exchequer subsidies and they can themselves contribute from the rates. The statutory provisions have changed in form and amount since they were first introduced in 1919. Until 1956 they had to make 'rate fund contributions' in proportion to Exchequer subsidies; since then they have been required only to make such contributions as are necessary to keep the account in balance.

It is against this background that local authority rent policies are determined. Until the Housing Finance Acts of 1972 local authorities had a wide discretion in fixing rents. The only statutory requirements were that they had to charge 'reasonable' rents, to review rents 'from time to time', and to make such changes 'as circumstances may require'. They were also specifically empowered to give rent rebates on such terms 'as they may think fit'.

Local authorities varied widely in the ways in which they translated these very broad principles into policy. At one extreme were those who fixed their rents at a level sufficient to cover all outgoings (including management and maintenance) without any rate fund contribution. Tenants who were unable to pay the full rent determined in this manner could be given rebates (which themselves could be financed from the overall rent income or, alternatively, from the rates). At the other extreme were authorities who operated a low-rents policy under which heavy rate contributions were made to offset the increasing costs of building new houses and maintaining old ones. Whatever the 'policy', the scope for exercising it was significantly affected by the history of local authority building in each area. An authority with a high proportion of older houses could 'balance' its accounts at a much lower rent level than one with a low proportion. Continued building (at current costs) inevitably put a pressure on the 'balance' which could be met only by increases in rents or rate contributions or both.

The result was an extraordinarily wide range of rents for similar dwellings between different areas of the country. In 1964 the *average* weekly rent of a three-bedroom house ranged from less than £1 to nearly £4·50, while actual rents charged ranged from nil (owing to rent rebates) to £7·70. Scottish rents were much lower, averaging (for all houses) 60p, and ranging from about 40p to just over £1·00. (The Scottish Development Department, in an attempt to use psychological pressure, published an annual return of rents[6] which included a table showing the course of rents in the four Scottish cities from 1938 in current values. This demonstrated that, in real terms, rents had fallen significantly in three of them and hardly changed in the fourth.)

The position was widely condemned as chaotic and irrational,[7] and it gave rise to increasingly articulate criticism of the unnecessary and wasteful subsidisation of 'affluent council tenants'. Until the late sixties, however, central government action was largely confined to restraining the growth of Exchequer subsidies and encouraging local authorities to introduce rent rebate schemes (which it was hoped would facilitate increases in the general level of rents without creating hardship). More forceful steps were taken in Scotland where the device of public local inquiries was used to bring 'the worst offending' authorities to heel.[8]

In fact, the amount of unit subsidy fell in real terms. Though the English subsidy for a three-bedroom house doubled between 1930 and 1964 (from £11·25 to £24 a year) the cost of house building rose sixfold.[9] Though some of the increase in building costs was due to higher housing standards, the basic issue was not 'housing' but inflation; and this became abundantly clear in the late sixties when the Labour government felt compelled to increase subsidies significantly (in the context of increasing costs and an enlarged house-building programme), and later to cut back building and to restrain rent increases as part of counter-inflation policy.

The housing subsidy scheme introduced by the 1967 Housing Subsidies Act was designed to overcome two problems which were facing local authorities: the high (and fluctuating) rates of interest, and the variations in costs between different areas.[10] In addition to subsidies for the special costs involved in building on expensive sites or in mining subsidence areas, for high-rise buildings and such like, the new scheme replaced the main traditional fixed rate subsidy with subsidies which were related to the actual cost of building and financing. In brief, they met the difference between the loan charges on the whole capital cost at the going rate of interest and the loan charges which would have been payable had the rate of interest been 4 per cent.

The scheme was intended 'to provide a sound financial basis for public authority housing and to ensure that the new more generous subsidies are used to improve the quality as well as the quantity of housing'. Parker Morris standards[11] were now to become the norm. (They were made mandatory in January 1969.) Though it was stressed that 'the whole question of housing finance needs much deeper study than the government has yet had time to give to it', it was also maintained that 'the foundation for a comprehensive national housing plan has now been laid'.

The 'deeper study' was put in hand, and though it was completed before the Labour government fell in 1970, it was never made public. It is an open question how far the outcome would have met the increasing concern being expressed about the need for an equitable and rational system of finance for all housing sectors. Perhaps it was the sheer difficulty of politically achieving this which led to inaction (particularly at a time when an election was close). More generously it can be suggested that ministers were too preoccupied with more pressing economic problems to give time to such big issues. Be that as it may, the 'comprehensive national housing plan' was soon subject to setbacks in the economic difficulties of the following years. The expansion of the house-building programme was reversed and, as part of the prices and incomes policy, local authority rent increases were curtailed.

The Labour government had been somewhat coy about rents. The 1965 White Paper had stated:

Rent policies are for local decision. But if the extra subsidies now to be provided are to be used, as they should be, to relieve those with the greatest social need, these policies should reflect the fact that the financial circumstances of council tenants vary widely. This means that subsidies should not be used wholly or even mainly to keep general rent levels low. Help for those who most need it can be given only if the subsidies are in large part used to provide rebates for tenants whose means are small. A number of authorities have had the courage to adopt thoroughgoing rent rebate schemes and have found that it does not entail raising general rent levels beyond the means of the majority of their tenants. The more generous subsidies now to be provided create an opportunity for all authorities to review their rent policies along these lines. In doing so, they will be able to take into account the higher standards of accommodation which will increasingly be provided with the aid of the new subsidies.[12]

SUBSIDY POLICY AND COUNTER-INFLATION POLICY

This was the 'housing policy' line on rents. The 'prices and incomes policy line' was different. The 1966 White Paper, *The Period of Severe Restraint*,[13] asked local authorities to avoid or limit rent increases as far as they could, and paid tribute to the 'responsible attitude' which they had so far adopted. A 1967 White Paper[14] recognised that some rent increases were likely to prove unavoidable, and drew attention to the importance of rent rebates in protecting tenants on lower incomes. Most local authorities accordingly moderated the rent increases which were being forced on them by pressures of increasing costs. A minority, however, increased their rents by large amounts and, in November 1967, the Prime Minister (no less!) announced the government's intention to refer the matter to the National Board for Prices and Incomes.

The Prices and Incomes Act of 1968 made it unlawful for a local authority to increase rents unless the increases were in accordance with proposals approved by the minister. It was emphasised that the government had 'no intention of permanently restricting the long-established responsibility of local authorities for fixing the rents of their houses' and that this was a temporary measure which dealt only with rent increases, not rent levels.[15]

Such was the course of rent policy in the years when the basis for a 'comprehensive national housing plan' was supposedly being built. In fact no *rent policy* was possible: actions were dictated by wider considerations of incomes and prices policy. The actual rents charged rose, on average (in England and Wales) from £1·41 a week in April 1965 to £1·69 in April 1967 and £2·27 in April 1970.[16]

The increase in subsidies was very different. This was due, mainly, of course, to the new subsidy system. Exchequer subsidies rose from £129m. in 1967 to £210m. in 1970. Despite the 'generosity' of these subsidies, however, the rise in costs led to increased rate fund contributions: from £74m. in 1967 to £103m. in 1970.[17]

These rate fund subsidies would have increased even further had not a growing number of local authorities introduced rent rebate schemes (or improved existing ones). The ministry exhorted authorities to operate such schemes and even exerted a little pressure by making it clear that the introduction or extension of a scheme would be accepted as a justification for a rent increase under the prices and incomes policy.

Nevertheless, a considerable number of authorities – including some of the largest – refused to operate schemes (typically on grounds of objection to means testing), and the schemes in operation varied enormously in extent and character. There were, moreover, complications over the relationship between rent rebates and supplementary benefits. Local authorities were not slow to see that the exclusion from a rebate scheme of tenants on supplementary benefit would increase their rent income without any hardship being suffered by the tenant. It was even suspected that some local authorities allocated a disproportionate number of their newer (and hence high-cost) dwellings to tenants on supplementary benefit.

In short, the rent position had become even more confused and unjustifiable than before. Local authorities differed not only in their policies but also in their financial position (largely as a result of the history of council house building in each area), and there was an 'absence of any uniform principles governing the determination of rents'.[18]

Ironically, a major product of the government's decision to refer rent increases to the National Board for Prices and Incomes was the publication of a report which highlighted and elucidated this problem, and opened it up for more informed public debate. What the Milner Holland and Francis reports did for the privately rented sector, the NBPI Report did for council housing.

Following a detailed analysis of the position, the board concluded that the variations between authorities were so great as to make it 'impossible to make any general statement' of the reasons for the high rent increases which had been referred to them. They concluded not only that there was no uniform definition of the 'reasonable' rents which local authorities were statutorily required to charge, but also that there was no 'uniform set of principles for the determination of rents which can apply all over the country, while still making some allowance for conditions which will differ from place to place'. They then proceeded to discuss what these 'principles' might be.

Three concepts were considered: 'fair' rents, historic cost rents and replacement cost rents. Their examination of these, unfortunately, was cursory but they recommended that the long-term aim should be to set rents in relation to current costs of building.

THE FAIR RENT NEW DEAL, 1972

It is unlikely, had the Labour government been returned in 1970, that they would have continued with the cost-related subsidy scheme which they had introduced in 1967.[19] The costs to the Exchequer were assuming alarming proportions (by historical standards) and would continue to mount as authorities continued building. Despite their cost, the subsidies were proving inadequate for some authorities and overgenerous for others. They perpetuated (and increased) the anomalies between different areas. They were also administratively cumbersome. Unlike the former flat-rate subsidies (which were simple to administer) they necessarily involved the ministry in checking that the costs which were to be subsidised were reasonable. By the same token, they were likely to encourage 'extravagance' on the part of local authorities since the greater their costs, the larger the subsidy they received. It was for this reason that 'cost yardsticks' (in England and Wales) and 'indicative costs' (in Scotland) became such a bone of contention.[20]

More fundamentally, both cost-related and unit subsidy systems had become quite unrelated to the actuality of local housing finance, since they applied only to the margin (i.e. new building) of a total stock for which costs, interest rates and subsidies were pooled. They had no direct effect on the levels of rent which were charged, nor were they related to the needs of different authorities for financial assistance.

Public opposition to the 'indiscriminate' subsidisation of council houses was aroused – fed by anger at the (haphazard) rates levied on owner-occupiers 'struggling to stand on their own feet'. Much of this ill feeling was based on misconceptions, but there was abundant cause for concern. Not only was there a wasteful distribution of subsidies, but also there were some areas where needy council tenants were receiving inadequate assistance. And there were needy private tenants who received no assistance at all.

It was apparent that, if any rationality and equity was to be achieved in the world of local authority housing finance, an entirely new approach was needed. It was also now widely accepted that discriminating help to council tenants should be matched by a system of rent subsidies to private tenants. Whether a scheme should (or could) be devised to cover all tenures – including owner-occupiers – was less clear, but thinking was moving in this direction.

The issues had, of course, been subject to the 'deeper study' mounted by the Labour government. This provided a base on which a politically energetic new government could take some rapid decisions. Indeed, the Conservative government which was returned in June 1970 announced their 'broad conclusions' in Parliament in November of the same year. White Papers, *Fair Deal for Housing* and *The Reform of Housing Finance in Scotland*, followed in July 1971.[21]

The keynote of both was 'the principle of fairness'. The financial structure which had been assembled piecemeal over a half-century was to be swept away and replaced by a new system aimed to give help to 'areas of greatest need' and 'geared to meet the circumstances of the individual'. Parity of treatment was to be accorded to council tenants and private tenants. A 'fair balance' was to be established between owner-occupiers and tenants. Justice was to be done between landlord and tenant. And 'due regard' was to be paid to the 'reasonable claims' of the citizen as a taxpayer and as a ratepayer 'without placing on either the inflationary burden of unnecessary taxes'. The package of proposals would provide 'a fair deal in housing with increased help for areas and people in need'.

Legislative effect was given to the proposals in the Housing Finance Acts of 1972. Basically the new system provided for a common policy in relation to the public and private rented sectors. The principle of 'fair rents' (originally introduced by the previous Labour government for private lettings) was applied to council houses – with a new machinery of supervisory control – and a national system of rent rebates (for council tenants) and rent allowances (for private tenants) was introduced on a uniform basis.

There was an attractive simplicity and apparent fairness in this, but the political battles to which it gave rise virtually excluded the possibility of rational debate. Indeed, so violent was the political reaction that it could be suggested that the Act jeopardised the prospects for a long-term solution. The Labour opposition committed themselves to a repeal of the Act – and quickly did so when they returned to power a few years later. This 'repeal' was inevitably accompanied by a stop-gap measure which was itself to be replaced as soon as another comprehensive review of housing finance had been completed.

The unprecedented hostility to the new scheme arose mainly because of the removal from local authorities (in England and Wales) of their responsibility for determining the rents of their dwellings. (As is explained shortly, the Scottish legislation was fundamentally different on this point.) That some opposition to this was anticipated is suggested by the provision in the Act for the appointment of housing commissioners where a local authority was 'in default'. This removal of a highly prized political responsibility would have caused anger at any time, but as a prelude to legislation on local government reorganisation (the aim of which was to strengthen local government and reduce central control), it seemed particularly obnoxious.

Some of the objection may have masked unspoken relief that the central government was in future to bear the brunt of tenants' protests against rent increases. Less ritualistic and more open was the tactical opposition of authorities like Greenwich which 'appeared to want housing commissioners to be appointed in default so that the responsibility of the government would be made clear'.[22] Initially, some fifty local authorities announced their intention not to implement the Act, but by December 1972 the numbers had fallen to five. Faint-heartedness was less a reason than the prospect of losing subsidies (which the government had taken power to withhold). Housing commissioners were appointed for two Welsh authorities, but it was the north Derbyshire authority of Clay Cross which stuck out to the bitter end – and extremely bitter this was.[23] They finally achieved nothing but the addition of a new phrase to the vocabulary of local–central debate. 'Clay Cross' lives on in spite of the fact that the authority was abolished (for totally unconnected reasons) in the subsequent local government reorganisation.

It may be that the new system would have gradually been accepted had the 'fair rents' been regarded as such. This was far from the case. 'Fair rents' had been introduced in the 1965 Rent Act in relation to the private sector. Essentially they were conceived pragmatically as rents which would provide landlords with an income which was 'reasonable' in the theoretical context of an equilibrium between supply and demand. It was hoped that this income would be sufficient to enable landlords to maintain their property in reasonable condition. The vagueness of these concepts is all too apparent and, since opinions would vary, machinery was established to arbitrate between landlords and tenants.

It was difficult to see what relevance this had to council rents, though the adjective 'fair' (despite its political attractiveness) confused the issue. In the early days of local authority housing, when privately rented housing dominated the market, there was some justification for relating 'standard' local authority rents to those charged in the private sector,[24] but the situation was now totally different. Private rents did not, in any sense of the term, any longer represent an objective market criterion: they were artificial, arbitrated rents, designed to meet the political exigencies of the time. The justification for their application to local authority housing was illusory.

Such arguments, however, were somewhat academic and not easily conducted in the popular arenas of debate. Having chosen the term 'fair' for the artificial rents to be determined for the private sector, the Labour Party had some difficulty in denying its relevance to the public sector: their clothes had been stolen.

More telling were arguments on the prospective rent levels which would follow from the use of this 'fair' concept. The Conservatives made no secret of their hope – nay, intention – that council rents would steadily rise. This in itself was conducive to political argument, to which could be added a nice point about the consequent inflationary effects. More significant was the question of what was to happen to the 'profits' arising from the higher rent levels. Without entering into a discussion of the details of the new subsidy scheme, their overall effect was to channel 'profits' back to the Exchequer by way of reductions in housing subsidy. Some subsidies would rise (e.g. for slum clearance and, of course, for the new rent allowance scheme for private tenants). The net result was to be a containment of total subsidies to their current level, but with a different pattern of distribution.

The new system also raised in a sharp form the question of the function of council housing. Government policy was to encourage home ownership, and restrictions on the sale of council houses were lifted. Local authorities were also given power to pay the legal expenses incurred by purchasers. 'As a result authorities in areas of housing shortage will be helped to make additional accommodation available to help the badly housed and homeless.' Again this was apparently sensible and fair, but the implication seemed to be that council housing was primarily for those who could not afford to buy, and that the better-off council tenants should become owner-occupiers. They thereby became eligible for tax reliefs (or option mortgage) on any interest repayments, but they ceased to be a charge on 'public expenditure'. Some broad issues about the relationship of policies towards the different tenure sectors are thereby raised. This is discussed later, but meanwhile the operational success of the policy can be noted: nearly 100,000 public sector houses in England and Wales were sold in the four years 1970 to 1974.

The Scottish Act was different in a number of ways from the English one. Most importantly, it did not provide for 'fair rents' in the public sector: private sector rents were so low that, had they been used as a basis for comparison, the result would have been a *reduction* in public sector rents! Instead, local authorities were required to fix their rents in such a way that, with the new subsidies, they would be able to balance their housing revenue accounts. Another difference was that there was no explicit emphasis on the sale of council houses. (The Scottish White

Paper made no mention of this and, indeed, made only a passing reference to owner-occupation.) Despite the retention of rent fixing by local authorities, there was considerable opposition to the Act, and a number of public inquiries was held.[25]

THE 1972 SUBSIDY POLICY

Both of the 1972 Housing Finance Acts made a major break with preceding subsidy policy. All existing subsidies were to be phased out and in future were to be related, not to the housing activity of local authorities, but to the state of their housing revenue account. The intention, of course, was to reduce the cost of subsidies and to rationalise rents (at a higher level). Within the overall fall in subsidies, an increasing proportion was to go on direct rent assistance by way of rent rebates to council tenants and rent allowances to private tenants.

The subsidies were of three types. For present purposes, the 'transitional subsidies' can be ignored. The 'rent subsidies', however, are of particular interest. The finance of rent rebates (for council tenants) was different from that for rent allowances (for private tenants). Rent rebates, in effect, were met in the first instance from each local authority's rent income. Only if there was a deficit on the housing revenue account was an Exchequer subsidy payable. If the income on that account (after crediting various other subsidies) was sufficient to meet part or all of the cost of rebates, the Exchequer subsidy was either reduced or extinguished. The subsidy amounted initially to 90 per cent of the deficit, but it was to reduce gradually to 75 per cent. No subsidy was payable towards administrative costs.

Rent allowances, on the other hand, were initially to be met in full by Exchequer subsidies, though it was intended that these would later be reduced to 80 per cent in 1976–7. The other 20 per cent would then be met by local authorities. Again no subsidy was payable for administration. (In Scotland the provisions were somewhat different, and local authorities were to meet a proportion of the cost of rent rebates, rising from 10 per cent in the first year to 25 per cent in 1975–6.)

It could well be argued (as it indeed was) that an unfair share of the cost of the rent rebate scheme (and an increasing part of the rent allowance scheme) was to be borne by council tenants. Why should the relief of financial hardship (i.e. inability to pay fair rents) on the part of some council tenants be a burden on other council tenants? And what justification could there be for adding some of the burden of relieving private tenants? These welfare payments were arguably a national responsibility which ought to be borne by the taxpayer or ratepayer at large. These arguments were not accepted at the time, though they arose again in relation to later legislation and, indeed, are still relevant to contemporary debate.

The third class of subsidies (for slum clearance and 'rising costs') was designed to provide generous assistance to 'areas in need'. Slum clearance was now separated from the general run of housing finance on the grounds that this was a community benefit which should properly be financed by the community as a whole. This was less of a change from the existing situation than was commonly thought, but the position was somewhat confused.[26] The 1972 Act provided a slum clearance subsidy to meet 75 per cent of the loss to the general rate fund incurred through slum clearance. This subsidy was available irrespective of the future use of the land. In effect, the subsidy helped to meet the gap between the cost of acquiring and clearing land, and the value of the cleared site. It was hoped that, apart from achieving a greater fairness between council tenants and others, this would facilitate private redevelopment for owner-occupation – an issue which had been subject to an inquiry by the Building Economic Development Committee of the National Economic Development Council.[27]

The rising cost subsidy was intended as the main new subsidy and was payable to local authorities whose expenditure was rising faster than income and who, as a result, had a deficit on the housing revenue account. This was initially 90 per cent of the deficit but was to decrease to 75 per cent in 1975–6. The balance was met by a rate fund contribution.

Only the barest outline has been given here of the 1972 rent and subsidy system (and much of the Scottish system has been ignored). Whatever its merits, simplicity and comprehensibility were not among them. Indeed it gave rise to great administrative complexities. Thus one consequence of linking subsidy to the financial state of the housing revenue account was an increase in central controls. 'To prevent subsidy becoming open-ended local authorities became subject to more detailed control over their general expenditure levels, including spending on management, maintenance and improvement; these controls were in addition to the capital cost controls already existing through the cost yardstick system, which were retained.'[28] Whatever criteria might be adopted for future changes, it seemed clear that simplicity should be one of them.

In the outcome, and despite both the intentions of the government and the fears of the opposition, the 1972 system led to a large increase in subsidies. Whereas in 1970 the total housing subsidy had been £313m., in 1974 it was £740m.[29] Average English council rents increased from £2·27 a week in April 1970 to £3·31 in January 1974.[30] In April 1974, some 840,000 council tenants and 120,000 private tenants were receiving rent rebates and allowances (averaging about £2·40 a week).[31]

The 'take-up' of rebates and allowances was worrying. Even the relatively high take-up in the council sector (estimated at 70 per cent of those eligible) was disappointing; but the proportion in the privately rented sector (between a fifth and a quarter) was a matter of major concern.[32]

However, it was not the size of the subsidy bill, or administrative complexities, or 'take-up' which led to change: it was the return of a Labour government committed to repealing the 1972 Act which did this.

THE 1975 INTERIM POLICY

By 1975 the arena of debate on housing policy had widened. There was much talk of 'equity' between the different housing sectors, of easing mobility between them, and of aligning housing subsidy policy with the tax and social security systems. Such issues were not quickly to be settled by any government, let alone one which had just been returned to office. The commitment to 'repeal' the 1972 Act was essentially a promise to return to local authorities their 'freedom' to determine their rents. What was to underpin this was less clear. Indeed, the new Labour government was unable to do much more than replace 'fair rents' by locally determined 'reasonable' rents and to recast subsidies in such a way that they were related to current marginal expenditure rather than to the state of the housing revenue account. The new subsidies were now (1) an annual lump sum representing the consolidation of subsidies paid in 1974–5 under the 1972 Housing Finance Act, (2) 66 per cent of the loan charges on new expenditure on house building, acquisition of houses or land, and improvements, (3) 33 per cent of the extra costs incurred since 1974 on refinancing earlier borrowings, (4) 75 per cent of the cost of rent rebates. Additionally, there was a temporary 'special element subsidy' designed to cushion rent and rate fund increases.[33] This, of course, was not a 'housing policy subsidy', but an element in counter-inflation policy which (as is argued in the final essay) typically is also 'counter-rational housing policy'.

It was envisaged that this interim measure would be replaced by a major new Housing Act following the housing policy review. In the meantime subsidies have continued to mount, mainly because of high land costs and interest rates (which have fallen recently) and high construction costs (which have continued to rise). Indeed, the increase in subsidies assumed such alarming proportions that capital investment had to be reduced. By 1975–6 rents (in England and Wales) were meeting only 45 per cent of costs, compared with 75 per cent in 1967–8.[34]

THE HOUSING POLICY REVIEW

There is a wealth of analysis of public sector housing finance in the five volumes of the housing policy review. By contrast, proposals for redesigning the subsidy system (to contain – or reduce – the total subsidy bill and to provide the requisite assistance for needy areas) are decidedly thin. The 1975 subsidy scheme is shown to be too inflexible, and 'policy' is to be directed towards a more sensitive system which will provide subsidies related to the needs of different areas (in relation to their 'resources'), and which will be sufficiently flexible to take account of changing interest rates and costs both nationally and locally.

If, as is intended, financial assistance is to be focused on needy areas, clearly some measure of financial 'need' is required. Theoretically, the easiest way of doing this would seem to be to determine the gap between total expenditure and the income to be derived from reasonable rents. Basically this is what the Conservative 1972 Act did, and it is difficult to envisage any satisfactory alternative. Yet the 1972 solution (with external fixing of rents) is politically unacceptable. There would thus seem to be an impasse.

The impasse is to be broken, however, by an annual negotiation between central and local government on 'an appropriate level of increase' of rents (and rate fund contributions), together with a similar negotiation on the 'admissible' increase in expenditure. Not surprisingly, 'the details will need to be worked out in consultation with the local authority representatives'.[35]

Essentially the system envisaged is one of incremental change, the details of which will be settled by an annual hassle similar to that which occurs on the rate support grant, though presumably with separate negotiations with every local authority. A major element in all this will be the preparation of local 'housing investment programmes' which will encompass not only new building, but all forms of local authority spending on housing. These housing investment programmes will be based on local housing plans which will assess comprehensively the totality of local housing needs and the appropriate role of the local authority in meeting them.

The arena of debate has thus moved from the narrower one of council housing finance to one of the finance of housing in local areas. As later essays demonstrate, the issues involved both locally and nationally are extremely complex. They certainly cannot be solved – or even tackled – solely at the local level. Local housing plans will undoubtedly encourage a more co-ordinated and flexible approach to local problems, but they have to be worked out within the framework of national policies in relation, for example, to rent control, tax and tax reliefs, and income maintenance. Sadly, it is in these very areas that the housing policy review is at its weakest.

4 Rent Control

Many over 70 stay younger because of their property interests. A widow of 84 looks and acts twenty years younger discussing her apartments. They not only pay her a comfortable retirement income but help to preserve her youthful spirit. There is no question that property ownership has added years to the lives of many older members.[1]

The plain fact is that rented housing is not a proper field for private profit.

Harold Wilson[2]

PERMANENT/TEMPORARY CONTROLS

Policies in relation to the existing stock of housing are heavily influenced by perceptions of the character of the housing situation. If the overall situation is one of shortage, the emphasis is likely to be on new building to meet that shortage. The nature of policies in relation to existing houses will be determined by views on how long the shortage is likely to last. Typically, governments have been optimistic and have regarded shortages as being of a temporary nature. This was particularly so in the period immediately after the First World War when the foundations of housing policy (and of some of our current housing problems) were laid. Nowhere is this clearer than in relation to rent control.

Rent control was forced upon a reluctant government in 1915 by the political necessity of preventing landlords from benefiting from the effects of wartime shortages. At the time it was thought to be justified mainly on the ground that the 'normal peacetime remedy' for high rents – the building of more houses – was not possible. It was clear, however, that the government of the day felt that they were storing up problems for the future. Though the nature of the problem and the short-term remedy were obvious, it was difficult to feel confident that the remedy 'may not create some fresh difficulty which may be even more injurious to the people mainly concerned than the trouble under which they are suffering at the moment'.[3] As had so often been the case in the debates on housing during the previous half-century, the government felt out of their depth:

The whole question of the provision of housing accommodation
for the working classes is so difficult, so complicated, and so closely
bound up with many other commercial questions, notably the value
of money and the borrowing of money, that one approaches it with
very great anxiety, lest in removing one evil you may, by inadvert-
ence, set up another.

The normal reaction had been to do nothing (or as little as was possible
without interfering with economic forces) but now the political pressure
was too strong to resist. To allow rents to rise 'at a time when this
country is engaged in a life and death struggle, when the noblest and
best of her sons are giving their life's blood to defend hearth and home
from German horrors, to defend their wives and children, and also the
wives and children of landlords, is wrong'. So wrong in fact that 'logic
and economic grounds' had to give way to moral considerations.

The solution adopted was simple in the extreme: rents were frozen
at the level existing at the outbreak of war. The 1915 Rent Act, which
effected this, was due to remain in force until six months after the end
of the war 'and no longer'. But once having committed themselves to an
acknowledgement of the necessity to restrain the price mechanism in
'abnormal' circumstances, the government had assumed a responsibility
which they could not lightly shed. The housing shortage which was
reflected in the rising rents brought under control in 1915 was far more
acute in 1919. Furthermore the high costs of the immediate postwar
period meant that the building of working-class houses was 'so un-
remunerative an enterprise that there is very little reasonable prospect
of the deficiency being met for some time to come'.[4] In short, control
had to be extended, though (in order to assist landlords to meet the
greatly increased cost of repairs and maintenance) limited increases
in rents were allowed. The new Act (like the score which followed
it prior to 1965) was not meant to imply a permanent policy of control.
On the contrary, as the housing shortage became less severe the number
of houses subject to control was reduced. Nevertheless, over 4 million
houses remained controlled in 1939 when, with the onset of the Second
World War, control was again extended.

And so it remained until the mid-1950s, by which time controls were
as deficient in 'moral considerations' as they were on 'logical and
economic grounds'. Over 3 million dwellings were let at net weekly
rents of 50 pence or less, and of these nearly 1 million were only 25
pence or less.[5]

The political groundwork for change had been laid by the 'realistic
rents' policy applied to the public sector by the Housing Subsidies Act
of 1956. This aimed 'to restore sanity to housing finance' by a range of
measures including the abolition of the general needs subsidy, 'freeing

local authortiies' from the obligation to pay rate fund subsidies to their housing accounts, and restricting Exchequer subsidies to new building for specific needs such as slum clearance, overspill and the housing of the elderly and the single.

So far as the privately rented sector was concerned, the government's proposals were for the automatic decontrol of all dwellings with a rateable value over £40 in London and over £30 in the rest of England and Wales. It was estimated that there were 750,000 such dwellings (a figure which proved an overestimate by nearly 100 per cent).[6] Furthermore, any dwelling below these 'control limits' would become decontrolled when let to a new tenant. For the 4½ million dwellings remaining under control, a system of rent limits based on gross values was introduced. Existing rents which were below these limits could be increased, subject to the right of tenants to challenge them on the grounds of disrepair.

These proposals were incorporated in the 1957 Rent Act – one of the most controversial pieces of legislation of the fifties. In retrospect the debates on the Bill had a curious air of unreality.[7] In view of the fact that legislation was not preceded by any investigation of the problems it was designed to solve, nor even of the facts of the existing situation, this is not surprising: government spokesmen often seemed to be stating simple lessons in economic theory. Increased freedom (and rents) would restore the market situation. The condition of rented property would be improved. Under-occupation ('caused by artificially low rents') would be reduced by the simple process of small families in large houses moving and making way for large families previously living in small houses. For various reasons, the 'supply' of privately rented accommodation would increase: the basic reason being that it would now be profitable. But not too profitable: landlords were not the inhuman capitalists the opposition sometimes suggested; they were reasonable men (and women) merely interested in obtaining a fair price for the commodity they wished to sell. By permitting rent increases the government were simply restoring a measure of justice and sanity into the privately rented market – as they were attempting to do in the subsidised council house market by the revision of council house subsidies. Justice indeed figured largely in the debates: after all, since there were no adequate facts there was little apart from economic theory and justice to argue about! The opposition did stress the electoral implications of the Act (forgetting that a government can sometimes obtain support for its party by courageously tackling an unpopular subject), but concentrated on the injustices it would create, on the wage increases and inflation that would follow from it, and on the unreality of the government's predictions of its happy impact on the housing situation.

Several studies were made of privately rented housing after the Rent

Act came into operation.[8] These all showed that the Act made remarkably little impact. Large numbers of rents were increased (but a surprising number were not); more repairs were done but they were generally minor and superficial ones; the rate of movement did not seem to have been affected; and there was no observable increase in the supply of rented accommodation – indeed, the decline in the number of privately rented houses continued.

This was the national picture. A detailed local study in Lancaster came to similar conclusions.[9] The main assumption of the Rent Act was that owners and tenants would react in a textbook manner to economic incentives. This assumption was invalid: 'the majority of landlords are not (in relation to their ownership of rented housing) concerned with profit and loss accounts: their main concern is to rid themselves of the burden of owning old houses'. Decontrolled houses were generally sold, and rent increases in houses remaining under control encouraged tenants to buy rather than pay the higher rents. Landlords carried out few repairs, and most of these were minor.

Nevertheless the Act encouraged the improvement of old property in a roundabout way unexpected by its framers. Higher rents for privately rented accommodation narrowed the price gap between poor and good housing and thus destroyed the 'bargain element' of the former. Tenants were therefore stimulated to seek better housing, and many of them bought previously rented dwellings which they then improved themselves.

One other interesting point was the irrelevance of the legalistic approach to landlord–tenant relationships which the Act embodied (which was epitomised by the minister's statement that 'both tenants and landlords would be wise, when this Bill comes into operation, to take professional advice, if they are not themselves professionally qualified, as to their position under the Bill and as to the actions which they are taking under it').[10] Yet, in Lancaster, the relationships between landlords and tenants were usually personal and close. This was hardly surprising since three-quarters of the landlords owned only one or two houses. The 'typical' landlord was a pensioner owning a single house which had been acquired by inheritance. Most 'managed' their houses themselves: only a few employed professional agents. Responsibility for the upkeep of the houses was often shared between the landlord and tenant on the basis of an informal understanding. The legalism of the Rent Act was quite foreign to this loose social situation.

This, of course, was the situation in only one town, but there was no information available to the government (or anyone else) to demonstrate whether or not it was untypical.[11] Indeed there were no reliable figures on the number of privately rented houses, let alone on the character of their ownership.

RENT DECONTROL AND 'MULTIPLE OCCUPATION'
Nationally the 1957 Rent Act fulfilled neither the stated objectives of the government nor the fears expressed by the opposition. Nevertheless, it had serious repercussions on one of the housing stresses of London. Here housing problems were aggravated by racial discrimination and the operations of a few unscrupulous landlords. The Rachman[12] affair brought matters to a head, and new legislation had to be brought in to control 'houses in multiple occupation'. The term was new, but the problem was an old one – though it had for many years been submerged beneath the protective cloak of the Rent Acts.

'Multiple occupation' is the modern equivalent of 'houses let in lodgings'. These have for long met the needs of groups of people (from the otherwise homeless poor family to the grant aided student) for whom neither public authorities nor the private market has been able to make adequate provision. Commonly, the houses which today are in multiple occupation are the socially obsolete Victorian piles designed for an age when the distribution of wealth allowed rich families to live in large houses which could be serviced by a plentiful supply of cheap domestic labour. Properly converted and managed they can provide reasonable accommodation, particularly for smaller households, of which there are great numbers in the centre of large cities. This demand, particularly from newly formed households, migrant newcomers (British and foreign), single and childless people and the aged can – and does – result in abuses which have been forced on public attention in recent years. Unlike the nineteenth-century situation, the problem is not simply one of poverty: though the households in the worst conditions are those with the lowest incomes and those with average incomes but large families, the situation is made more difficult because of 'competition' from newcomers and from those with higher incomes. Indeed, the demand for better quality accommodation 'in multiple occupation' and the increasing trend in some areas (at least in London) for areas of working-class housing to be invaded by middle-class families has tended to reduce both the total supply of accommodation in general, and cheaper accommodation in particular.

The 1957 Rent Act added to the problems. Not only did 'block decontrol' reduce the availability of unfurnished rented accommodation (because of sales to owner-occupiers and conversions to 'freer' furnished lettings), but the 'creeping decontrol' gave unscrupulous landlords an incentive to evict tenants and then sell or relet at uncontrolled rents. Scandalous conditions developed in areas of acute housing pressure (particularly in London) where obsolete large houses were subdivided into multiple lettings. In these houses there was no proper conversion, and cooking and sanitary facilities were quite inadequate. Overcrowding further increased the squalor. (The Milner Holland Report – of which more anon – even quoted cases of a landlord dividing a room into separate lettings by chalking marks on the floor, and of a single room 'divided' for two households by blankets hung up across the room.)

Up to 1961 the powers of local authorities for dealing with conditions such as these was limited. Improvements generally could be made only if some of the families were rehoused, but almost by definition it was the shortage of alternative accommodation which gave rise to the bad conditions in the first place. Furthermore, the houses which were in the worst condition were frequently owned by landlords of a peculiar astuteness: their skill in managing property might be of a low order, but their skill in evading the provisions of the law could not be questioned. The position was made worse by the staff shortages of local authorities in the pressure areas.

The 1961 Act provided the first instalment of a new set of powers.[13] Multiple occupation was defined as 'a house which, or any part of which, is let in lodgings or which is occupied by members of more than one family'. Local authorities were enabled to apply a 'code of good management' to houses in multiple occupation, to require certain services to be provided and to fix the maximum number of inhabitants who should live in a house.

A study of the procedures which had to be followed under this Act suggests that the government were more infused with Victorian ideas on the sanctity of property rights than with a desire to give local authorities effective powers to control abuses. Certainly they proved largely ineffective and, after further press publicity in 1963 on the exploitation of tenants in this type of property, more drastic powers were provided in the 1964 Housing Act.[14] Where the situation is so bad that immediate action is required, a local authority can issue a 'control order' and summarily take over the control and management of the property. This constitutes a complete abrogation of the landlord's rights. He is entitled to compensation, but only at the rate of one-half of the gross value of the house. The procedure is peremptory and is designed to meet the special situation where tenants fear eviction (or worse) if they seek to invoke action by the local authority. No prior notice is given and any appeal to the courts comes after a *fait accompli*.

THE MILNER HOLLAND REPORT

The public concern which gave rise to this legislation also prompted the government to set up a committee of inquiry on the London housing situation as a whole. The decision was announced in 1963 (i.e. before the 1964 Act) within the context of a statement of broader policies for London[15] (which included the amendment of the 'third schedule' rights to add 10 per cent of cubic capacity in the course of office rebuilding). The committee was established in August 1963 under the chairmanship of Sir Milner Holland and reported (to a Labour government) in March 1965.[16]

Though they were not asked to make recommendations, the Milner Holland Committee drew some important 'conclusions' from their wide survey of London housing, some of which (particularly on rent control, the taxation of landlords and housing finance) were of significance to policy on a new scale. They stressed the parlous state of private landlordism. There had been half a century of fluctuating crude controls; there was an absence of any financial institution which catered for the requirements of private investment in rented property (as compared with the building societies for owner-occupiers and government sources for public sector housing); the current spread of decontrol was 'a haphazard and unpredictable process which depends on the behaviour of individual tenants, exposing their successors to rent increases without regard to their needs or resources, and tending in areas of great shortage to encourage abuses and bad relations between landlord and tenant'.[17]

The full list constituted an indictment of successive governments. An interesting account of the more sensible and sensitive policies followed in other countries pointed to the need for assisting those who build, own or live in privately rented housing, 'and regulating the price, management and distribution of this housing with the aid of effective local and judicial instruments'.

FAIR RENT REGULATION, 1965

Some of this thinking underlay Crossman's Rent Act of 1965. This was the first attempt to design a long-term – rather than an emergency – policy for the privately rented sector. The objects were twofold: 'to restore the security of tenure undermined by the Rent Act of 1957' and (unprecedentedly) 'to lay the foundation for a better relationship between the landlord and the tenant of rented property, by introducing a new and flexible system of rent regulation.'[18]

The detailed provisions of the act can be ignored here:[19] the important point is that, in addition to providing security of tenure for most privately rented housing, it introduced machinery for determining 'fair' rents. The concept of a fair rent is, in effect, a 'non-scarcity market rent': that is, the rent which the market would determine in a situation in which demand and supply were in balance. Such a concept is not one which commends itself to economists, since it 'specifically excludes from the reckoning the one economic factor likely to produce any easing of a situation of shortage',[20] namely, profit. But the intention was not to produce rent levels which would bring about a market response in terms of additional new supply: it was intended to maintain the existing supply, with rent levels which were 'fair' to the landlord and the tenant. Landlords would be able to keep their property in reasonable repair, and tenants would be protected from paying scarcity rents.

Accordingly, 'the age, character, locality and state of repair' of the house was to be taken into account, but not any personal circumstances of either the tenant or the landlord.

So much for the concept: but how was it to be operated? Clearly some machinery was required to ensure that fair rents were in fact being charged, but equally clearly it was inconceivable that machinery could be set up which would determine all rents. The solution adopted had a number of elements. First, the new system was to apply initially only to dwellings which were not controlled under the old system. Secondly, existing rents in the uncontrolled sector were to be frozen until a fair rent (at either a higher or lower level) was determined. Thirdly, since tenants now had security of tenure and the benefit of a rent freeze, it was felt that they were 'placed on something like equal terms' with their landlords and 'it is perhaps not too much to hope that agreement will become the normal practice'.[21] Fourthly, where the two parties could not reach agreement unaided, they would be able to call on the services of 'rent officers' who would 'bring the parties together and help them to settle the proper rent' in the light of the provisions of the legislation. Finally, if the rent officer's view was not acceptable to either party, the rent would be determined by a rent assessment committee.

The system was based on the assumption that the majority of rents would be fixed by agreement: otherwise the administrative apparatus would be unable to cope. This was Crossman's 'big gamble',[22] and it paid off (at least in political terms). By the end of 1969, the number of applications represented only 14 per cent of the 1·2 million regulated tenancies existing at that date (in England and Wales).[23] The Francis Committee, set up by the subsequent Conservative administration in 1971, commented that the evidence led them to the conclusion that 'most landlords charge reasonable rents, and that a correspondingly high proportion of tenants acknowledge this fact'.

This was not the whole story, of course: there were significant 'minority' problems, and there were factors such as ignorance and fear on the part of the tenants. Then there were other problems such as harassment (which the Act made an offence) and the intractable situation in the 'stress areas', but the Act was never envisaged as 'a complete solution': it was intended as the first step in laying 'a lasting foundation for a better relationship between landlord and tenant'.

The fair rents system applied at first only to dwellings which were not controlled under the pre-1957 Act system. Controlled rents were to be converted to fair rents only if a new tenancy was created (in cases, for example, where a dwelling became vacant and was relet). The Act did, however, provide for the extension of rent regulation to controlled tenancies by order (which could relate to particular classes of house or to area). This power was never exercised.

The Housing Act of 1969 also provided for conversion to a fair rent in cases where a dwelling was improved to a given standard. This was one part of the drive to encourage more improvement which is discussed in the following essay.

FAIR AND UNFAIR RENTS

The new system was not without its critics. Particular concern was expressed at the 'unduly high' level of rents being fixed by rent assessment committees in London, and at the weakness of the Act in dealing with harassment and unlawful eviction, and the need for greater protection for furnished tenants. Representatives of property owners, on the other hand, complained at such matters as the cumbersome nature of the system, the lack of consistency between rent officers in adjoining areas, and the need to free from control new buildings and winter lettings of holiday accommodation.

Many of the allegations and complaints were difficult to assess and, expectedly, another committee of inquiry was set up in 1969. Their report (the Francis Report) was published in 1971 by which time a Conservative government was in power.

The Francis Committee concluded that the rent fixing machinery was working well and that, though rent levels in London were relatively high, this was only to be expected owing to the special 'amenity value' and employment opportunities in the metropolis. They did, however, propose that new provisions should be made for 'stress areas' (where there was clear evidence of harassment, particularly in multiple occupied property) giving local authorities stronger powers of enforcement and the right to take over the management of houses where landlords were acting oppressively towards their tenants.

A majority of the committee recommended that newly erected dwellings should be excluded from rent regulation and that the security provisions should be relaxed in relation to certain classes of single unfurnished lettings of part of a landlord's home.

Of particular importance (in the light of subsequent legislation) were their recommendations on controlled tenancies and on furnished accommodation. Since no order had been made to convert controlled tenancies into regulated tenancies, two systems of restriction applied to the privately rented housing market. Whether a dwelling was controlled or regulated was simply – and arbitrarily – a matter of history. Identical adjacent dwellings could have widely different rents (the committee instanced a Glasgow tenement block where two similar flats were let at £28 and £115). Quite apart from the obvious unfairness of this, 'it creates the impression among regulated tenants that the rents fixed by the rent officers are unduly high, and generally undermines confidence in the fair rent system'.[24]

The political justification for maintaining two separate systems was that many of the tenants of controlled dwellings were elderly and could not afford to pay fair rents – a point constantly made within the Labour Party. The only alternative solution, of course, was to introduce some system of subsidies to the tenants, but this fell outside the terms of reference of the Francis Committee. Nevertheless, 'the perpetuation of the controlled system has undoubtedly created an acute sense of injustice among landlords of controlled premises', many of whom 'are no better off, and are not infrequently less well off, than their tenants'. The situation 'has on the one hand produced an attitude of indifference to the state of repair of those premises, and on the other hand has engendered a determination to have nothing more to do with letting them but rather to sell them as soon as they become vacant'.[25] The case for converting controlled tenancies into regulated tenancies was therefore 'overwhelming'.

Furnished dwellings were subject to different controls, with a separate appellate machinery (rent tribunals) charged with fixed 'reasonable rents' but empowered to give security of tenure for a limited period only. The 'most difficult' question facing the Francis Committee was whether the system of control over furnished accommodation should be assimilated with the system relating to unfurnished lettings. A unanimous recommendation proved impossible, though the members agreed to the assimilation of the rent fixing systems. Where fundamental differences arose was on the issue of security of tenure. The majority concluded that furnished tenants should not have 'the right of indefinite occupation' enjoyed by unfurnished tenants, since this 'would lead, sooner or later, to a considerable reduction in the supply of privately rented accommodation'. They continued:

> Greater security for those in occupation when the extended security code came into force could well be bought at the cost of greater hardship and difficulty for the much larger number of households seeking such accommodation in the following weeks, months and years. Such, in our considered view, is the dilemma which faces Parliament in deciding whether or not to extend full security to the furnished tenant. For the reasons we have indicated, we cannot recommend such extension. On the contrary, we venture to sound a solemn warning against it.[26]

A minority report[27] argued that the distinction between unfurnished and furnished tenancies was 'wholly illogical', since it depended solely on the amount of furniture provided by the landlord at the commencement of the tenancy. The distinction had 'given rise to a marked switch of accommodation from unfurnished to furnished in stress areas', and had 'deprived of security those tenants most in need of it, the young couples starting a family who would move into permanent houses if they could, the immigrants to the cities, and those families least able to manage their affairs'. The real distinction was not between furnished and unfurnished accommodation, but between commercial lettings by a company or a landlord who lived elsewhere, and accommodation that was part of a landlord's own home. Among the latter:

> The householder may be a widow whose family house is far too big for her needs, or a young couple who buy a house which they will occupy fully when their family gets older, but while the children are young some spare rooms can be let, and the rent helps to meet their expenses. Many of these landlords would prefer to let their accommodation unfurnished if they were satisfied that they could recover possession of it within a reasonable time.

The minority report therefore recommended that all unfurnished and furnished lettings should be subject to full security other than lettings of 'small premises' where the landlord lived in the building.

It fell to the Conservative government of 1970–4 to act upon the Francis Committee report. They accepted the recommendation to convert controlled tenancies into rent regulation. This was to be done under a staged programme and was to apply to all controlled dwellings except those which were unfit. Of fundamental significance was the introduction of rent allowances for private tenants. These were introduced initially for unfurnished tenants but, by the Furnished Lettings (Rent Allowances) Act of 1973 they were extended to certain classes of furnished tenants (though it did not alter their insecurity of tenure). This rent allowance scheme transformed the position of the private tenant and, in effect, began a process of transferring the financial benefits received by the private sector from the dwellings to the tenants (the 'cost' now being met by the state, not the landlord). The scheme, and the wider context in which it was conceived, is discussed in a later essay.

FURNISHED LETTINGS

The extension of rent allowances in 1973 to (some) furnished tenants was the result of intense political pressure, and the scheme was initially a cautious one. A more comprehensive measure came in 1974 with the Labour government's Rent Act. Not only was the rent allowance scheme extended to all furnished tenants but, following the minority report of the Francis Committee, the anomalous distinction between furnished and unfurnished tenancies was abolished as the basis for determining the extent to which the tenant was provided with security of tenure. The anomalous nature of the distinction was that it depended on the amount of furniture provided: a dwelling was to be regarded as furnished only if 'the amount of rent which is fairly attributable to the use of furniture . . . forms a substantial part of the whole rent'. (These provisions were derived from the Rent Act of 1923 which were apparently intended to safeguard 'lino tenancies' – where a trifling amount of linoleum was likely to be sufficient to take the tenancy out of protection.)[28] This gave rise to some legal niceties and offered considerable scope for argument and litigation.[29] Moreover, once the 1965 Act introduced machinery for determining 'fair rents' for unfurnished lettings, there were two quite separate rent fixing systems. This was difficult to justify, and it became even more so when the membership of the rent assessment panels (for unfurnished tenancies) and the rent tribunals (for furnished tenancies) were integrated in the late sixties. But it was the illogical, and often spurious, test of furniture which created the biggest anomaly, particularly since (following the extension of controls in 1965) the provision of a few bits of furniture enabled landlords conveniently to avoid the restrictions to which unfurnished tenancies were subject.[30] Not surprisingly, after 1965 there was a big switch of unfurnished lettings into 'furnished' ones. (A similar situation arose with 'board' and 'holiday' lettings which provided other ways of escaping controls.)

The 1974 Act – like its many predecessors – is complex. It did not provide a comprehensive new code replacing previous enactments: it amended and added to them. The distinction between furnished and unfurnished tenancies was abolished and replaced by a distinction between resident and non-resident landlords. In other words, a 'resident landlord test' was substituted for the 'furniture test'.

Furnished lettings with no resident landlord came into the fair rent system, while unfurnished lettings with a resident landlord moved over to the reasonable rent system operated by rent tribunals (though special provisions were made for existing tenants).

Finally, student lettings and holiday lettings were made exempt from both systems: hence the rash of signs for 'holiday lets' that can now be seen on vacant properties which were previously controlled or regulated.

THE RENT ACTS UNDER REVIEW, 1977

Despite the centrality of the issue of rent control to the housing policy review, the difficulties to which it gives rise proved too great for the government to tackle within the compass of that review. A separate review was therefore mounted and a consultative paper was issued in January 1977.[31] This pointed to the significant changes which have taken place in housing markets and conditions since the Francis Committee reported in 1971 and disarmingly stated the government's willingness' to consider new ideas or reconsider previously rejected proposals'. One major proviso, however, was made: 'the general principle of security of tenure for the tenant in his home is to be maintained'. Since security of tenure is meaningless without rent control it follows that control is to remain. The issue thus is what form of control will meet policy objectives.

Despite a seemingly imposing list of 'objectives'[32] it is clear that the government's over-riding concern is with the physical condition of the stock of housing in the privately rented sector. There is certainly no intention of resuscitating private investment in this field, though reference is made (in the housing policy review) to the difficulties, particularly for new and mobile households, which may be created by the continued shrinkage of the sector (currently declining at the rate of about 100,000 a year). It is suggested that 'to guard against' such difficulties, 'we need to consider what action can be taken to stimulate the supply of lettings within the private sector', but the thought is not developed beyond a tentative proposal for a new 'publicly accountable letting agency' which might provide sufficient confidence for the attraction of private capital.[33]

For the most part both the stated objectives of the Rent Acts review and the thirty-six questions posed in the consultation paper are concerned with tidying up and rationalising the complex of controls which have grown by accretion over a long period of time. Given the over-riding concern for safeguarding 'the interests of private tenants', the only major policy issue is that of preserving and improving the physical stock. It is to this subject that the following essay is devoted. Here one can conclude with the observation that, had it been the long-term objective to kill off the private landlord, British housing policy has achieved a remarkable degree of success.

5 Improvement and Slum Clearance

> Houses are not like wine or cheese – they do not improve
> with keeping
>
> *The Sanitary Aspects of Philanthropy*, 1866[1]

IMPROVEMENT POLICIES

Rent control and decontrol, together with measures to deal with problems such as that of multiple occupancy, were all 'reactive' policies: they were intended to deal with immediate problems of hardship or injustice. None was designed to make a positive contribution to the furtherance of housing policy objectives. At best they were conceived as means of removing impediments to the smooth working of the housing market. Yet the housing sector to which they applied – privately rented housing – was becoming more obsolescent and inadequate by the standards of the time as each year passed. Only slowly did the point emerge that something more than 'justice' was needed if the decaying legacy of private landlordism was to be salvaged. One school of thought holds the view that private landlordism has no place in a just society and, thus, the sooner it passes into history the better. At the other extreme is the view that a free society needs a privately rented sector – a view which was translated into policy with the Conservative government's (unsuccessful) pump-priming measures of 1961. This debate now has a contemporary twist with the wider concern being expressed about the inadequacies of twentieth-century housing suppliers to cater for all needs.

There has been, however, one element of policy which, beginning in 1949, was gradually brought to bear on the problems of the privately rented sector – house improvement.[2] Its slow move into the mainstream of policy is accounted for by the fact that it had to be conceived in the framework of rent controls. It was not easy to marry a system of controls over private rents with one of a subsidy to encourage improvement. The early attempts foundered because the over-riding concern was to prevent landlords securing unseemly profits – or, indeed, any real profit at all. Success on one front meant failure on another.

The Housing Act of 1949 made improvement grants available for houses which, after improvement, would have an expected life of thirty years or more. The intention was, in the revealing words of Mr Bevan, not to 'rescue slums' or 'to permit landlords to make good the arrears of repairs that they should themselves have carried out long ago'. The grants were not for repairs, but for 'improvements' such as the installation of a bath, a water closet and a piped water supply.

Critics argued with some irony that this 'public assistance for landlords' was necessitated by the government's refusal to touch rent control: 'So long as the Rent Restriction Acts prevent a landlord from so increasing his rents as to make the holding of property profitable, there is no way in which it can reasonably be expected that these improvements will be carried out unless a grant of this kind is made.'[3] Nevertheless, though there was considerable discussion on the morality of giving government grants to landlords who had no 'need' of them, it was generally accepted that the object was a laudable one. And in the case of the reluctant landlord who was 'not sufficiently attracted' by the grants, there were the already existing powers of compulsory acquisition. The local authority could purchase the house, undertake the necessary improvements and claim the grant.

Little use was made of these grants, partly because of lack of publicity and the fact that local authorities did not wish to promote any activity which might draw resources of men and materials away from their building programmes, and partly because the conditions were restrictive. Between 1949 and 1953 only 7,000 grants were given in the whole of Britain.

THE 'BETTER HOUSING CAMPAIGN'

The essence of the matter was that no effective policy in relation to older houses was considered practicable until some tangible inroad had been made into the huge quantitative housing shortage of the immediate postwar years. Priority was accorded to new building: and that meant ignoring the mounting problem which was arising in the ageing stock. The stance, of course, was a political one, and it would be interesting (though not very fruitful) to speculate whether policy would have been different with a government of a different political persuasion. Be that as it may, increasing concern was being expressed at the beginning of the fifties about the ravages of time and inflation on the housing stock.[4]

At last, in November 1953, a major reorientation of official housing policy was announced. Now that the house-building programme had been expanded by over 50 per cent since 1951 and was running at 300,000 houses a year, attention could be turned to the less spectacular problem of maintenance and improvement, and to the resumption of slum clearance. Two White Papers gave a broad analysis of 'the many aspects of the national housing problem', and outlined the government's

'comprehensive plan of repair, maintenance, improvement and demolition which covers all types and conditions of house. It is a better
housing campaign.'[5] This is of particular interest in that it was the first
attempt to devise a set of complementary policies for the range of
problems arising in the existing stock.

At this date there were some $13\frac{1}{2}$ million dwellings in Great Britain.
Of these, $6\frac{1}{4}$ million were owned either by their occupiers or by public
authorities. The remaining $7\frac{1}{4}$ million were privately rented. Most of
the latter were very old: $2\frac{1}{4}$ million were a hundred years old or more
and a further $2\frac{1}{4}$ million were over sixty-five years old. As the government pointed out, these figures of age were 'striking'. Though there were
no national data on condition, it was obvious that a policy which
concentrated almost solely on building additional houses should not
continue any longer than was absolutely necessary.

The great bulk of privately rented houses were thought to be either in
good condition or capable of being put in good condition if rents were
raised to a sufficient level. This was not taken to imply that a general
decontrol of rents was justified: the housing shortage was still too severe
to allow this. Some method was needed which would enable and
encourage landlords to undertake repairs, but at the same time would
ensure that rents were raised only if the necessary repairs were in fact
carried out. For this purpose a system was devised to enable landlords
to claim a 'repairs increase' for fit dwellings on which they could demonstrate that a given sum had in fact been spent on repairs.

At the other extreme from these 'essentially sound houses' were
'hundreds of thousands' which were 'unfit for human habitation and
cannot be made fit at reasonable expense, or which, by reason of their
bad arrangement or the narrowness or bad arrangement of the streets,
are dangerous or injurious to the health of the inhabitants' – in short,
slums. The slum clearance campaign which had been interrupted by the
war was to be resumed immediately.

Between the slums and the improvable houses was an intermediate
category of 'dilapidated' houses which could be brought into the
'essentially sound' category if sufficient repairs were undertaken.
Technically, such houses were 'unfit for human habitation – but at the
same time capable of being made fit at a reasonable cost. Expenditure
on such repairs would not of itself be sufficient to warrant a repairs
increase since the 'conditions justifying an increase of rent' stipulated a
higher standard than that which was used in determining mere 'fitness'.
Nevertheless, landlords were statutorily bound to keep their houses in
a fit condition and local authorities had powers to ensure that this was
done. They could even carry out the works in default and recover the
cost from the landlord. These powers had been little used during the
war and postwar periods, but local authorities were now to be exhorted
to bring them into operation. It was hoped that the use of these powers

would not only ensure that dilapidated houses were made fit but would also encourage unwilling landlords to make the 'extra effort' and bring these houses up to the higher standard of 'good repair'. There was thus both a 'stick' and a 'carrot'.

The final category was of houses which 'could give years of good service if they were improved' or (in the case of large, socially obsolete houses) properly converted into flats. Grants were already available, under the 1949 Act, to local authorities and private owners who wished to undertake improvements or conversions, but the 1954 Housing Repairs and Rents Act made them more generous, and eased the conditions under which they were given.

The main thrusts of this 'better housing campaign' were effectively with slum clearance (discussed separately in a later section) and improvements. The new improvement grant system with its easier conditions (and increased publicity) resulted in a sharp rise in approvals. The number of grant aided conversions and improvements in England and Wales in 1954 (13,710) was more than double the number for the whole period 1949-53. In 1955 there was a further very large increase: to a total of 36,423; the numbers stabilised at around 35,000 until 1959. Most of the grants were given for the installation of baths and hot water systems.

In spite of this progress, few improvements were undertaken in privately owned *rented* property: most of the grants went to owner-occupiers. Either the conditions were still too restrictive or (as was now increasingly being suggested) rented houses had ceased to be an economic asset to their owners. Certainly a major problem facing landlords was the cost of repairs which were necessary before improvements could be carried out. These did not rank for grant and naturally (even with the repairs increase) reduced the landlord's return.

DEVELOPMENT OF IMPROVEMENT POLICIES

A rate of improvement of 35,000 a year was very modest in relation to the scale of the problem to which the improvement policy was directed, and it was clear that significant changes would be needed in the scheme if it were to be more effective. One of the barriers was the reluctance of some authorities to give grants to owners whose financial position was such that they had no 'need' of them. A few (particularly in Scotland) categorically refused to operate the scheme on the grounds that it was wrong to give public money to private owners. Other authorities were overzealous in requiring the carrying out of an excessive number of repairs (which were not grant aided) as a condition of grant aid. Moreover, the general standard of improvement which had to be achieved was a high one. Though there was provision for a 'waiver' where normal standards could not be met, it was generally held that a high standard should be insisted upon in order to ensure that public funds were well invested. It was certainly contrary to the prevailing concept that an owner might be subsidised to 'half-improve' his house by, say, installing a bath or a hot water supply. Yet there were some $4\frac{1}{4}$ million non-slum houses in England and Wales which lacked such amenities. Clearly, the policy was a nice case of the best being the enemy of the good.

A major change came in 1959 when a new system of 'standard' grants (in addition to the existing 'discretionary' ones) was introduced. These were for the installation of basic amenities: a fixed bath, a wash hand basin, a hot and cold water supply, a water closet and a food store. At the same time the conditions applying to grants were further eased. The effect was dramatic: in 1960 alone over 130,000 grants were made, and a similarly high rate continued. Two-thirds of the grants in the years 1960 to 1964 were 'standard'.

The success of the new scheme was marred, however, by the low take up in the privately rented sector (where housing conditions were the worst). It had been hoped that an increase in the return allowed to landlords (from 8 to $12\frac{1}{2}$ per cent of his share of the cost) would encourage improvement, but the real problems were much deeper. First, the increase of $12\frac{1}{2}$ per cent related only to the expenditure incurred by the landlord and, if the controlled 'pre-improvement' rent was low, the resulting new rent was still low. Secondly, it was highly misleading to think of the $12\frac{1}{2}$ per cent increase in net terms. The Milner Holland Committee convincingly demonstrated that the actual return was very much lower because of the tax position of the private landlord.[6] (On a property having a life of twenty-five years the net return was 6·2 per cent; on one having a life of fifteen years, it was a mere 0·43 per cent.)

IMPROVEMENT BY ORDER

The reaction (strange in itself; remarkable as one of a Conservative government) was to introduce powers to *compel* landlords to improve. The 1963 White Paper blandly stated that, with loans from local authorities and the right to charge a higher rent, 'it does not seem that any hardship would be entailed in requiring owners to carry out improvements'.[7] The new powers, however, were to apply only in designated 'improvement areas' (where half the houses lacking standard amenities could be improved to the five-point standard). The compulsory powers would be applicable only to tenanted property and then only when there was a change of tenant or when requested by the tenant.

The emphasis was on improving *areas*, and the justification for compulsion was that without it the benefits of an area approach would be unrealisable. The 1964 Act gave local authorities the duty to inspect their areas with a view to identifying areas suitable for comprehensive improvement. The intention, however, was not only to secure the provision of amenities in individual houses and to ensure that the good effect was not offset by deterioration of adjacent properties; it was also intended to be part of a process of urban renewal – involving such measures as providing trees, parking facilities, better open spaces, new street furniture – indeed, any action (including smoke control) which would improve the quality of the environment.

Though the principle of compulsion was accepted in relation to such areas, the remarkably cumbersome procedures imposed upon local authorities almost guaranteed that the principle would only rarely be applied. After advertising the declaration of an improvement area, the next step was for the local authority to select those tenanted dwellings which could be improved at reasonable expense to this standard. A 'preliminary notice' was then served on both the owner and the tenant specifying the works required and their estimated costs, together with the time and place at which the future of the dwelling would be discussed. If the dwelling could only be brought up to a reduced standard at reasonable expense, the notice would specify accordingly. There was no statutory time limit for the service of a preliminary notice, but after it had been served, follow-up action had to be taken within two years of the declaration of the area. This was intended to allow sufficient time before taking any formal action for the council to make a final effort to persuade the owner to carry out the needed improvements voluntarily. At the 'discussion' the local authority could accept a formal undertaking by the owner (with the consent of the tenant) to carry out the necessary work. If such an undertaking was not given – with the consent of the tenant – or was not fulfilled, the local authority could serve an 'improvement notice'. If the tenant agreed to the improvements being made, an 'immediate improvement notice' was served, requiring completion of the works within twelve months. If the consent of the tenant had not been received, the authority could serve a 'suspended improvement notice'; this could be converted into a 'final improvement notice' (which had the same effect as an immediate improvement notice) if the tenant's consent was obtained or if there was a change of occupier. The local authority could serve a final improvement notice without having obtained the tenant's consent subject to certain conditions, including offering the tenant a council house, but only after five years had elapsed since the declaration of the improvement area. There were certain rights of appeal to the county court.

Outside improvement areas the compulsory improvement procedure could be used on the application of a tenant. In other words, if the tenant wanted the improvements, compulsion could be used against the landlord.

The new Act was accompanied by unprecedented publicity, with press advertising, pamphlets, mobile exhibition vans, a colour film and a colour filmstrip entitled *Yours for the Taking*.[8] It also attracted a great deal of criticism. The public health inspectors (who had pressed strongly for compulsory powers)[9] attacked the cumbersome nature of the procedure, the exemption of owner-occupiers from the compulsory provisions, and the right of tenants to object to improvements. Others, however, were strongly averse to the compulsory powers, including the present author who argued that, while compulsion would be justified to ensure adequate maintenance, there was no such case in relation to improvement.[10]

HOUSE IMPROVEMENTS AND THE ENVIRONMENT

The improvement area and compulsory improvement powers were not successful. In four years only 136 of the 1,400 local authorities in England and Wales had declared improvement areas. There were 379 of these areas containing about 35,000 improvable dwellings of which about 18,000 were tenanted, and therefore 'susceptible to compulsory improvement'. About 3,500 of these had been improved. Outside improvement areas, a further 1,400 dwellings were compulsorily improved.[11]

With hindsight, it was a pity that the idea of area improvement had been so associated with compulsory improvement. The compulsory powers were hedged with so many restrictions that the whole process became cumbersome in the extreme. Moreover, the provisions related essentially to 'houses in areas' rather than areas within which both houses and the environment were to be improved. The ministry did advise local authorities to take a broader view, and stressed that 'area improvement is something more than a means of providing amenities in individual houses: it is part of the process of urban renewal'.[12] But no grants were provided for anything other than 'providing amenities in individual houses' and, by 1968, it had to be admitted that the powers 'do not really enable an authority to improve an area as a whole'.[13]

The 1969 Housing Act embraced a new approach. The emphasis was now on voluntary improvement with more informal and flexible procedures, higher grants for house improvements (with the maximum for discretionary grants raised from £400 to £1,000), and a new grant for environmental improvement. Local authorities were given powers to declare 'general improvement areas' in which the aim would be 'to help and persuade owners to improve their houses, and to help them also by improving the environment'.

As an incentive to the improvement of privately rented houses, rent increases following improvement were to be dealt with under the fair rent system. This included controlled dwellings which, of course, had lower rents than those which had already passed into the fair rent scheme.

A striking illustration of the importance attached by the government to the expansion of the improvement programme was the abolition of virtually all the conditions which previously applied to the making of a grant. In particular, if an improved house was sold, there was no obligation to repay the grant. The possibility of someone making a profit out of the improvement grant scheme was thus thought to be of less significance than the fact that a house had thereby been improved. This was a quite remarkable change in that it effectively provided a real profit motive for improvement – a most unusual feature of any British housing policy. As we shall see, these profits attracted considerable criticism and eventually (in 1974) amending legislation.

The 1969 Act brought about an immediate increase in the rate of improvements – from 124,000 in 1969 to 180,000 in 1970, and 233,000 in 1971. That year saw an amending Act which pushed the figures even higher: this was the further increase in the maximum home improvement grant (from £1,000 to £1,500), a doubling of the environmental improvement grant (from £100 per dwelling to £200), and the payment of grants at the rate of 75 per cent (instead of 50 per cent) in the 'development areas' and 'intermediate areas' – which covered the whole of Scotland and the older industrial areas of England and Wales. These 'assisted areas' were, of course, areas of high unemployment and thus the higher rates of grant could be considered as much a matter of 'employment policy' as of 'housing policy'; but they were also areas where the take-up of the new grants was well below the national average.[14]

As a result, improvements rose greatly (particularly in the assisted areas). In 1972 the number increased to 368,000, and in 1973 reached the incredibly high figure of 454,000. Two-fifths of these were council houses and an equal proportion were owner-occupied; but 74,000 (16 per cent) were privately rented. It thus seemed at last that the improvement grant policy was having an impact on the poorest housing sector. Yet the statistics were too crude to support such a simple conclusion: they did not show what types of privately rented houses were being improved or, indeed, whether they remained privately rented after improvement. The policy was a 'non-discriminating' one which involved more than a sixfold real increase in subsidies over the period 1969–70 to 1973 4 (from £87·7m. to £568·7m. in 1974 prices).[15] At the same time slum clearance was beginning to fall dramatically

Before this discussion is carried further, however, it is necessary to examine the course of slum clearance policy up to this time.

SLUM CLEARANCE

Slum clearance has a very long history in Britain: a consequence of the fact that the industrial revolution started at a time when incomes and housing standards were low. (The contrast with, say, Sweden is striking.) The industrial towns of the nineteenth century were unknown in history: they gave rise to housing conditions which became intolerable even by the standards of the day. The development of medical knowledge, the realisation that overcrowded insanitary urban areas resulted in an economic loss which had to be borne at least in part by local ratepayers, the experience of the classless visitation by cholera, the fear of social unrest, and a gradual appreciation of the necessity for some interference with market forces and private property rights in the interests of social well-being – all these factors combined to force action in the field of public health and housing. An Act of 1868 (the Artisans and Labourers Dwellings Act, more commonly known as the Torrens Act) made it the duty of owners to keep their houses in good repair, and empowered local authorities to act in default and to close insanitary houses. Ineffective though this proved to be, it established the principle that the state could interfere with property rights in the interests of the public health. Later legislation reinforced this principle and attempted to make its administration more effective.

The biggest obstacle was the compensation which had to be paid to owners of slum property. Until the end of the First World War, compensation in effect had to be paid for the market value of slums, and more generally compulsory acquisition of land involved a 10 per cent *solatium* in recognition of the fact that the sale was a forced one. As a result 'housing policy' was inordinately expensive, and no significant progress could have been made without changes in 'land policy'.

Both problems were tackled in 1919. The Housing, Town Planning, etc., Act provided that the compensation for an unfit house should be the value of its cleared site alone, and the Acquisition of Land (Assessment of Compensation) Act settled the principle that no allowance was to be made in assessing compensation for the fact that the acquisition was compulsory.[16]

Despite these new provisions (and other relevant changes such as simplified procedures), little slum clearance took place during the twenties. As in the period after the Second World War, the backlog of shortage was too great to permit any large-scale programme of demolition. Thus policy was focused on adding to the stock rather than on improvement and slum clearance. By the end of the twenties, however, there was mounting concern about 'the appalling slums',[17] and slum clearance became an issue in the general election of 1929. A change in policy – and the first effective slum clearance drive – was heralded by the Greenwood Act of 1930, though it was not until 1933 that local authorities in general began earnestly to devote their attention to it.

Over a third of a million houses were demolished in the decade before the Second World War. By 1938 demolitions were running at the rate of 90,000 a year. Had it not been for the war, over a million of Britain's older housing stock might have been cleared by 1951. Instead, the programme came to an abrupt end, not to be resumed until the mid-fifties.

The resumption was part of the Conservative government's 'better housing campaign' which has already been outlined. The first major step in this was to obtain an assessment of the scale of the problem – on the basis of a new definition of 'unfitness' (the statutory term for slum conditions) which was introduced by the 1954 Housing Repairs and Rents Act.[18] Local authorities were required to make a 'return' of the number of unfit houses in their area, and the number they proposed to demolish or to 'retain for temporary accommodation' during the next few years (five in England and Wales and three in Scotland). The results gave a total of nearly a million unfit houses: 6·5 per cent of the stock in England and Wales and 7·7 per cent in Scotland.[19]

Despite the large number, it was clear that it was a considerable underestimate. Some of the authorities with the worst problems (Salford and Glasgow, for example) simply 'returned' their clearance programme rather than the total problem to which this would be only a contribution.

However, for authorities giving a total assessment it was clear that only a fraction of the problem would be dealt with in five years. Thus Manchester (with 68,000 – 32 per cent – of its houses returned as unfit) was proposing to demolish only 7,500 within this time, and Liverpool (with the even higher figures of 88,000 unfit houses – 43 per cent of the stock) was to demolish only 7,000. It was against this background that a boost to slum clearance was given by the withdrawal of the subsidy for 'general needs' building (under the Housing Subsidies Act, 1956).

Slum clearance rapidly gathered momentum, and over the twenty years from 1954 to 1973 was estimated at a high level (with a peak in 1970 and 1971 ov over 90,000 houses in Great Britain as a whole: over 71,000 in England and Wales, and around 19,000 in Scotland). The total number of houses demolished or closed during this period was of the order of 1½ million: this was 50 per cent more than the estimated total number of unfit houses in 1954.

The campaign opened with almost religious fervour, and though criticisms of lack of sensitivity to human and social issues were heard intermittently during the fifties and early sixties, it was not until the seventies that a significant groundswell grew against clearance. Improvement – of environments as well as of houses – then became viewed as an alternative to wholesale clearance. But initially improvement was seen as a distinctively separate policy for dealing with a different category of house.

In the main, the criticism of the slum clearance campaign was not that it was 'a brutal destroyer of communities', or that it was proceeding too rapidly, but that the programme was inadequate to deal with the enormity of the problem – which, it soon became clear, was much larger than had been officially estimated.[20] Estimates varied, but ranged from a need for an annual programme (in England and Wales) of over 100,000 to 200,000 Despite ministerial assurances that the programme was to be accelerated,[21] the number of slums dealt with in England and Wales remained obstinately at around the 60,000 mark until the mid-sixties.

The Labour government which was returned in 1964 was committed to giving housing a higher priority, and both new building and slum clearance were stepped up. Local authorities were asked in 1965 to reassess the total number of unfit houses in their areas 'regardless of the time needed to clear them'. The revised estimate was of 771,400 unfit houses containing 823,858 'separate dwellings'. Manchester and Liverpool accounted for a fifth of these, and a further twenty-two authorities (mainly in Lancashire, the West Riding and the west midlands) accounted for an additional 30 per cent.[22]

The government's broad estimate (made before these figures were forthcoming) was of a need for 'about 1 million new houses to replace unfit houses already identified as slums' and 'up to 2 million more to replace old houses not yet slums but not worth improving'. Of these 500,000 were required in Scotland.[23] The problem was to be met by a greatly enlarged building programme (including further new and expanding towns), but emphasis was laid on the need for better information on conditions, needs and aspirations. A committee was set up to review standards relating to old houses (the Denington Committee) and a series of house condition surveys was mounted (at first in the main conurbations, and later nationally).

STANDARDS UNDER REVIEW

The Denington Committee[24] concluded that there was 'a need for a comprehensive approach to the problems presented by older houses and a coherent pattern of standards', aided by research on a range of relevant issues including the economic criteria for deciding between replacement and improvement. The size of the problem of old houses was so great and the rate of improvement so inadequate that 'effective compulsion' was needed to improve and maintain the better old houses. Standards could be made more objective, 'but a substantial element of judgement must remain'. Standards were recommended for a 'satisfactory' dwelling but, since there were so many unfit houses still remaining, it was considered unrealistic to raise the minimum fitness standard (though minor alterations were suggested). As the problem was concentrated in particular areas of the country, 'the necessary resources must be channelled by the government to those local authorities with the most serious problems'. Unfortunately it was 'by no means easy to suggest ways of doing this'. More generally, better and more detailed information was needed on the condition of the housing stock.

Work was already under way on this last recommendation, and a national house condition survey (in England and Wales) was carried out in 1967.[25] This showed that the problem was different in scale and character than had been assumed. The total of unfit dwellings numbered 1·8 million (more than double the estimate based on local authority returns) and they were less concentrated in particular areas than the earlier figures had suggested. There was also a massive backlog of repair to be made up.

The result was an even greater emphasis on (to use the title of the 1968 English White Paper) *Old Houses into New Homes*, and on further acceleration of the slum clearance programme. In England and Wales, the number of slums dealt with rose from around 60,000 in the years 1961 to 1965, to 67,000 in 1966 and 72,000 in 1967.

THE SCOTTISH SLUMS

Events followed a parallel course in Scotland where the slum problem (above all in Glasgow) was even greater than in England and Wales. There were, however, some significant differences. Of particular interest was the abolition of the concept of 'unfitness' and its replacement by one of 'tolerability'. This was proposed by a subcommittee of the Scottish Housing Advisory Committee[26] as a more objective standard. It was not a 'satisfactory' standard (for which – as with the Denington Committee – a separate formulation was proposed); instead it was a condemnatory standard 'below which houses should not be allowed to exist'. The subcommittee argued:

We have no doubt in our minds that the present 'standard' is interpreted in widely different ways in different parts of the country. To a large extent this is a reflection of the variation in housing conditions, but this is not the only factor. Local authorities differ in the urgency with which they are tackling their problems and this is partly due to the lack of clarity in the present 'standard'. A clearer and more objective standard will enable local authorities to assess their problems more accurately and will enable the secretary of state to assess the resources which are needed both nationally and locally to deal with the problem. Last, but not least, it will enable property owners – landlords and owner-occupiers – to establish more easily whether their property falls below the statutory standard.

As we have already stated we think that the public health basis of the minimum standard should be superseded by a concept more in line with modern thinking. As an indication of this, we propose that the terms 'unfitness' and 'fitness' should be discarded. In their place we suggest the term 'tolerable', and we define the tolerable standard by reference to our proposed satisfactory standard. This has, incidentally, allowed us to express the standard in positive terms, as many of our witnesses proposed. This will make for greater clarity and objectivity.[27]

The proposed standard was largely adopted in the Housing (Scotland) Act, 1969.

Also of interest in the SHAC report was the emphasis which was placed on environmental issues (which in the Scottish context needed little justification). The committee even went so far as to suggest that there should be new provisions for 'areas of unsatisfactory environment'. An illustrative definition was given:

An area of unsatisfactory environment is an area in which the majority of the houses fall below the standard for a satisfactory house, or where the arrangement of the streets is unsatisfactory, or where there are unsatisfactory environmental conditions such as those of noise, smell, dust, dirt, smoke, inadequate open space (including plays pace for children) or inadequate provision for the garaging and parking of cars.[28]

Such areas were not necessarily to be *clearance* areas: on the contrary, the intention was to devise a concept which would allow a flexible approach with action being taken which was appropriate to the particular circumstances of an area. Thus, while clearance might be appropriate in some cases, elsewhere improvement (or a combination of improvement and clearance) might be preferable.

The 1969 Scottish Act went some way in this direction by introducing 'housing treatment areas' in which clearance and/or improvement could be undertaken.[29]

IMPROVEMENT VERSUS SLUM CLEARANCE

Slum clearance continued at a high rate in the early seventies, averaging about 67,000 a year in England and Wales and 18,000 in Scotland: a total of around 85,000. The year 1974, however, saw a marked downturn (to 53,000), and clearance appears to be stabilising at this lower rate. There are several reasons for this. First, much of the worst housing has now gone: but with 700,000 unfit dwellings remaining in England and Wales and 160,000 in Scotland[30] – which is roughly the number thought to be unfit at the start of the clearance drive in the fifties – this is clearly not the only factor. More important is the increased emphasis which has been placed on improvement and (the underlying reason for this) disillusionment about large-scale clearance.

There had always been critics of slum clearance – from M'Gonigle's pioneer study of the effect of rehousing on poverty and health in 1933,[31] through the famous 'Bethnal Green' studies of Young and Willmott,[32] to a veritable spate of researches in the later sixties and early seventies.[33] Some of these focused on the inadequacies of the process of clearance,[34] while a few debated the comparative economics of clearance and improvement.[35] The Milner Holland Report of 1965 contained three short case studies of the impact of redevelopment and rehabilitation on the housing market[36] – a theme which was taken up and expanded by Della Nevitt in 1972:

> Few people have any understanding of the chaos which has been caused in the London housing market by the 1957–72 slum clearance programmes . . . The operation has been carried out in a thoroughly haphazard and unco-ordinated manner, and the social pressures created culminated in angry campaigns of squatting. In the next decade it is essential that slum clearance should be fully co-ordinated with transport, employment and private housebuilding plans. Every delay in co-ordinated development is automatically reflected in further pressures upon the very limited stock of conveniently sited existing houses, and appears automatically in rising house prices.[37]

By the turn of the seventies, there was an increasing clamour for 'stop slum clearance now' (to quote the title of a representative article).[38] Disillusion was spreading, problems were being redefined, public participation had become the vogue, more sensitive and socially oriented policies were being thought through, and 'the slum clearance problem' became ousted by the 'inner city problem'.

The government, however, were preoccupied with more politically pressing issues such as housing subsidies, land prices, the declining privately rented sector (and related issues such as rent allowances for private tenants and the promotion of housing associations as the private landlord's legatee).

The year 1973 saw the publication of *four* White Papers on housing.[39] The first English White Paper reiterated current policies for 'the elimination of unfit or substandard housing', and looked forward to the time when local authorities would have 'substantially the primary tasks of building for rent, clearing slums and promoting improvement'. Its Scottish counterpart heralded 'a renewed drive to deal with Scotland's remaining substandard houses': this was 'in the forefront of the government's plans' and was to be achieved 'either by clearing away old houses which are below the tolerable standard, and building new houses to replace them; or by renovating old houses, wherever this is possible, so that people can continue to live in the same neighbourhoods and communities'.

HOUSING ACTION AREAS

Indicative of the new approach was the introduction of the concept of 'housing action areas'. Confusingly, the term has quite different meanings north and south of the border. While the Scots use the term to apply to all areas where action is to be taken, whether improvement or clearance (or a combination of the two), the English use is in relation to areas of particular housing stress where special action is required *in the interests of the residents.* In marked contrast to the long-standing emphasis on physical structure and plumbing, there is now a strong social element actually embodied in the legislation.

Housing action areas in England and Wales are areas where 'the living conditions are unsatisfactory and can most effectively be dealt with within a period of five years so as to secure – (a) the improvement of the housing accommodation in the area as a whole, and (b) the well-being of the persons for the time being resident in the area, and (c) the proper and effective management and use of that accommodation'. Physical conditions are to be measured by traditional indices, but particular importance is attached to social conditions, including not only the proportion of households lacking amenities or living in overcrowded conditions, but also the proportion living in privately rented accommodation, and 'the concentration in the area of households likely to have special housing problems – for instance old age pensioners, large families, single-parent families, or families whose head is unemployed or in a low-income group'.[40]

It should be noted that, in a housing action area, *action* is of the essence – 'within a period of five years'. To achieve this, there is a range of powers: for acquisition, rehabilitation, protection from eviction, environmental improvement – indeed, for any action which is required to remove the underlying causes of housing stress in the area, to arrest and reverse deterioration, and to effect real improvements in the living conditions of those living in the area. But 'a basic – and novel – feature of housing action areas is the statutory provision which makes the well-being of the people living in them one of the requirements for, and objects of, declarations. This means involving people and groups, in the scale, nature, and timing of proposed action programmes'. There is thus an explicit role for neighbourhood groups and such organisations as tenants' co-operatives and housing associations.

This striking break with the sanitary tradition did not come suddenly, though the 1974 Housing Act is its legislative landmark. There were many contributory causes, particularly the wider perspectives on 'deprived areas' and 'positive discrimination'.[41] In narrower 'housing' terms, the 1969 Housing Act created a great push towards socially oriented thinking: indeed that Act was much criticised for failing to do what it did not aim to do. As the Expenditure Committee noted:

In retrospect, it is clear that objectives other than purely housing ones have subsequently been attributed to the 1969 Acts. It has come to be realised by local communities, and now by planners, that improvement is a housing technique which attempts to meet the needs of existing residents of an area, and prevents the blight of a neighbourhood while a redevelopment is being planned, as well as the social disruption of communities caused by the eventual clearance. Social objectives were not made clear during the passing of the Acts, but they have figured prominently in discussion of the effects of the legislation. The new White Papers finally recognise their role, especially in relation to the criteria for deciding on a housing action area.[42]

In 1969 the objective was to stimulate improvements and to obtain the maximum possible within the available resources. In these terms, the policy was a huge success: $1\frac{2}{3}$ million houses were improved during the years 1969 to 1974. The extraordinary flexibility of the grants scheme and the virtual absence of conditions contributed to this. So also did the emphasis on areas where improvement was relatively easy – and the avoidance of the difficult, needy areas. Indeed, the greater part of the improvements carried out were outside general improvement areas. What had been intended as the backbone of the policy – area treatment – proved the weakest part. Between 1969 and 1974, some 900 general improvement areas were declared, but only 75,000 grants approved. Moreover, many of the general improvement areas were interwar local authority estates: they were certainly in need of some improvement, but they could hardly have been regarded as a priority against the background of large numbers of much more inadequate houses.

Yet, given the policies of 1969, the results were not surprising, and the criticisms made of the lack of emphasis on the most needy areas emanated from later thinking – not that of 1969. The 1969 Acts were rooted in the discretionary grant 'tradition', and they were 'too broad in scale and conception to tackle areas of greatest housing stress'.[43] It was the objective of the housing action area policy to do precisely this.

ABUSES, GENTRIFICATION AND SPECULATION

The essentially physical character of the 1969–74 policy is underlined by the lack of concern about the opportunities which the freer grants gave for profit making or, more surprisingly, the social impact on a neighbourhood which came to be called 'gentrification'. Speculation in the purchase (sometimes with 100 per cent local authority house loans) and improvement of old property might well be justifiable if the aim is purely a physical one: profit will oil the wheels; but the change in the social character of an area as a result of speculation could create increased housing difficulties for lower income households (other than those who themselves contributed to the change by selling on a rising market). There was much evidence of this in London (Barnsbury being one of the best-known cases).[44]

The profits to be made increased markedly in the house price explosion of these years (to which it may even have made some contribution, not only in London but elsewhere).[45] Not surprisingly, there were thus opportunities for the unscrupulous to evict or harass tenants of potentially valuable improvable houses, or to offer financial inducements to obtain vacant possession.

As the Royal Town Planning Institute noted in their evidence to the Expenditure Committee, all this posed important

... questions about what and who the present legislation is for? Is it intended to upgrade existing areas of substandard housing or is it to improve the conditions of the existing residents of the area? This becomes an urgent problem when those tenants displaced as a result of improvement, by the need for vacant possession by landlords or higher rents, suffer a decline in their housing standards.[46]

A similar issue arose in relation to 'second homes' which gave particular concern to some rural and coastal authorities. There was, however, a dilemma here, as the Rural District Councils Association pointed out:

The number of second homes is increasing in attractive areas within reach of the large cities as well as in coastal areas. A few councils have for long made it their policy not to give grants on such properties, but the department have always taken the view that the aim is to save housing and that who should occupy it is immaterial because, even if a house is owned as a second home, it may be sold for a primary home at a later date. The willingness of outsiders to spend money on second homes has helped to preserve many properties which would otherwise have been lost, frequently to the detriment of the appearance of the locality.[47]

But feelings ran high in some areas about the 'morality' of grants to second home owners, and the Expenditure Committee unequivocally supported the decision already announced in the White Papers to prohibit them.

It was against a background of this character that the 1974 Act reintroduced conditions on grants, designed 'to stamp out abuses' which had been encouraged by the *laissez-faire* philosophy of the 1969 Acts. In addition to the prohibition of grants on second homes, controls were placed over the occupancy of grant aided improved dwellings. These were designed to prevent sales of improved owner-occupied houses at a profit, or letting for 'holiday' purposes, or the selling of improved rented property. There was also an introduction of a rough and ready means test for owner-occupiers of houses which already had the basic amenities: grants for improvements to such houses were restricted to those within certain rateable value limits.

FOCUS ON THE NEEDY AREAS

These new conditions were a corollary of the policy to concentrate more resources on the needy areas. The main instrument of this was the housing action area which, as already explained, is an area of 'housing stress'. In these areas the normal grants (which had been raised to higher levels) are payable at the rate of 75 per cent – or even up to 90 per cent where this is justified by the financial circumstances of the owner. A (discretionary) repairs grant is also available for repairs and replacements in housing action areas, but only where the local authority considers that the applicant could not finance these himself without undue hardship. Yet a further grant (known as a 'special grant') is payable for the provision of standard amenities in multiple occupied houses. Finally environmental grants for local authority work on such matters as new street works, stone cleaning and planting (up to £200 per dwelling) are supplemented by grants to individual owners for environmental improvements. The four housing grants were now known collectively as 'house renovation grants'.

General improvement areas are now envisaged as being areas 'of fundamentally sound houses capable of providing good living conditions for many years to come and unlikely to be affected by known re-development or major planning proposals'. Here grants are payable at a 60 per cent rate, and environmental grants are also available. Outside general improvement areas and housing action areas, grants are paid at the normal 50 per cent rate (and no environmental grants are available).

As is apparent, the system is a complicated one, with different types of area and different amounts and rates of grant (not all of which have been listed here). This is partly a consequence of the policy of providing the greatest assistance to the worst areas, but also as a means to meet the great variety of circumstances in different parts of the country.

CENTRALLY CONTROLLED POLICY

Under the 1969 schemes, informality had been the keynote. Local authorities were free to declare general improvement areas and follow whatever housing and environmental policies seemed to them to be most appropriate. There was no provision for central government approval, or for formal inquiries or appeals (unless, of course, compulsory purchase was involved – which was unusual, and certainly contrary to the general philosophy of maximum voluntary action and co-operation between local authorities and owners). Such an informal system was quite remarkable. It stemmed from a belief that central government involvement would delay progress and reduce flexibility. Conditions varied widely, and it was the local authorities who understood the local problems and the policies which would be most effective locally. Central government therefore (very untypically) took a back seat, and merely issued 'advice' – which had no legal status.

The 1974 Act did the opposite. Since local authorities are required to devote their main energies to the priorities determined by central government, proposals for housing action areas and general improvement areas have to be referred to the secretary of state. One example will suffice to illustrate the new procedures: the secretary of state can 'prevent an area which appears to him to be inappropriate' from being declared a general improvement area. In short, there is now central control over area policies.

SCOTTISH HOUSING ACTION AREAS

In Scotland the 'housing action area' was largely the same as the former 'housing treatment area'. This was an area in which at least half of the houses were below the tolerable standard and in which 'treatment' was by clearance, by improvement or by a combination of the two. There was, however, one important difference; before detailing this it is helpful to go back to the SHAC report and its proposals for 'areas of unsatisfactory environment'. Such areas were proposed where the majority of the houses fell below the standard for a satisfactory house. The 1969 Act, however, provided that treatment areas should have a majority of houses below the *tolerable* standard. There was much discussion on what the standard should be for a housing action area. The White Paper suggested that it might be 'on the lines of the twelve-point standard' where improvement was to be the main action, and 'probably a lower standard' where clearance was contemplated.[48] The former, of course, was in accordance with the SHAC recommendation but it was felt to be too high a standard (as well as being insufficiently objective) and, in the event, the lower five-point standard was taken.[49]

The Scottish 1974 Act provided for three types of housing action area. For an area to be declared a 'housing action area for demolition', more than half the houses must be below the tolerable standard. A 'housing action area for improvement' or 'for demolition and improvement' can be declared where more than half the houses are either below the tolerable standard or lack one or more of the five standard amenities. (The English reader should note that the Scots use the term 'house' to mean the same as the English 'dwelling': it thus embraces a flat and a 'house' in a tenement.)

All area policies in Scotland are dealt with under their housing action area procedures. Differential grants and rates of grant for improvement follow the English pattern.

It is not possible here to detail all the provisions relating to Scottish procedures, but one new requirement is of interest. This provides that a local authority must allow two months 'for representations from the people affected and must take account of these before making a final resolution declaring a housing action area'. This is a legalistic formulation of an obligation on local authorities to act sensitively in accordance with the wishes of the people living in housing action areas. As an SDD circular explains:

> The secretary of state attaches particular importance to this requirement, and he would urge local authorities to make the fullest use of this period to consult those affected, explaining and discussing the proposals with them. He considers that full consultation with the residents and a sensitive and sympathetic response to their wishes for the future of the area will go far to obviate opposition or resistance to what is proposed, and to ensure that once a final resolution is made the work which it entails will proceed as quickly as possible.[50]

By contrast with the elaborate statutory provisions for improvement in England and Wales, the Scottish system appears remarkably simple. This is not the place to speculate on the reasons for this difference (which can equally be seen in the planning field): suffice it to say that while the English try to attain flexibility by a complex range of powers to be *adopted* by local authorities according to their various circumstances, the Scots prefer broad powers within which flexibility can be attained by local *adaptation*.

Reference can also be usefully made to the extensive powers in Scotland for the compulsory improvement of houses in areas where the majority of the houses lack one or more of the standard amenities. The need for this (certainly in tenemental property – where the biggest problem lies) stems from the fact that the improvement of *some* of the houses in a tenement cannot normally be carried out without affecting the other houses: it frequently is a case of 'all or nothing'. The declaration of an 'improvement housing action area' is, however, in essence a declaration of intent: it is a clear and definite proclamation by the local authority that the future of the area is to be safeguarded and that marked improvements are to be made – to the environment as well as to the houses.

Given the peculiar characteristics of tenemental property, it is typically necessary to ensure that improvements are planned *as one operation* to all the houses (at least in a close or stair, if not the block as a whole). Concerted action of this kind can sometimes be done by the landlords or, more frequently, their factors (agents), but in any case some 'external organisation' is necessary. One method of doing this is by the establishment of *ad hoc* housing associations. Experiments in this direction are under way (particularly in Glasgow) with the assistance of the Housing Corporation.[51]

RENEWAL STRATEGIES

The 1974 policies have been in operation for only a short period and it is too soon to evaluate them, though one major point on the adequacy of the area approach will be dealt with shortly. Successive departmental circulars have continued to stress the need 'to concentrate resources more positively than hitherto within housing areas most in need of improvement, and upon dwellings which are manifestly substandard'.[52] Of particular importance is the 1975 DoE circular on 'renewal strategies'.[53] This notes that, with few exceptions, 'the programme of large-scale slum clearance should now be drawing to a close'. Emphasis is laid on implementing a policy of 'gradual renewal':

Gradual renewal is a continuous process of minor rebuilding and renovation which sustains and reinforces the vitality of a neighbourhood in ways responsive to social and physical needs as they develop and change. Rehabilitation should take place to varying standards to match the effective demand of individual occupiers. Successful management of rehabilitation, in particular, will call for a more flexible attitude by local authorities towards the rate at which desirable standards of renovation are adopted. It must be accepted – and willingly – that some houses of low quality meet a real need for cheap accommodation, a need which might not otherwise be satisfied. It would not always be sensible to press for the immediate rehabilitation of all dwellings in an area to the full standard or more, or to clear them, until they cease to fulfil their present social function. For example, substandard dwellings occupied by elderly persons could, *if this were the residents' wish*, remain largely undisturbed for the time being, except for the carrying out of basic repairs and elementary improvements (e.g. hot water supply, better heating) with the help of the new grants where appropriate. Authorities should also consider the possibility of selective acquisition of dwellings, or rehousing of certain residents, to prevent the undue deterioration of a neighbourhood or enable better use to be made of the housing stock.

Renewal similar to that described above has traditionally taken place in areas able to attract private investment, but has rarely been an explicit aim of local authority housing policy. Authorities have tended to see the normal life-cycle for housing areas as one of development, decay, clearance and redevelopment, with rehabilitation postponing the necessity for clearance, notwithstanding the fact that individual houses were in different stages of obsolescence. Policies of comprehensive redevelopment have, however, blighted all the dwellings in the area uniformly and experience has shown that social conflicts and tensions can arise as the point of demolition is reached. Gradual renewal, on the other hand, can serve to minimise the disruption of established communities in a variety of housing areas.

This is a marked change in the policy of only a decade earlier. As in other fields, the objective is one of 'putting people first'. (This was the subtitle of the White Paper which preceded legislation on compensation: among the provisions were new home loan payments and disturbance payments for people displaced from their homes.)[54]

Measured in crude numerical terms, the result has been a big drop in both slum clearance and improvement. But the objective of the new policies cannot be fully measured in such a way. Unfortunately there is little easy alternative, and discussion on why 'faster progress' is not being made is developing.

Some of the reasons follow from the policy itself, for example, the imposition of rateable value limits, the conditions of resale and the limits on rent increases. Yet, if the objective is to be the maximum feasible rate of improvement, it may be that the biggest weakness of the present policy is its emphasis on the area approach. Despite the obvious advantages of this, it is time-consuming and may distract efforts from the large number of inadequate houses which are not spatially concentrated. The area approach is of limited value 'when progress depends so heavily on the propensity of individual owners to invest (or on the capacity of the public authorities to compensate for the lack of such propensity)'.[55] It would appear that new thought needs to be given to the houses and households in greatest need as distinct from areas.[56] The short experience of the 75 per cent grant in the areas of high unemployment suggests that this 'created an impetus in lower income areas which did not exist with 50 per cent grants'. The grant structure could also be changed to provide for a higher rate of grant for basic improvements and a lower rate for less essential ones.[57]

As with so many issues of policy, much depends on the objectives of policy which, in turn, depends on the way in which problems are perceived. All too frequently policies follow simply from the definition of 'problems'. The slum clearance policy was conceived as precisely that: to clear the slums. The improvement policy developed separately – for 'non-slum' houses. Later it became recognised that these were alternative ways of dealing with 'the same problem'. Initially this was defined in physical terms, but increasingly a more socially sensitive approach was adopted. And so the focus shifted to social areas, communities and individual needs. This is uncertain territory within which time-honoured signposts (such as plumbing deficiencies) are inadequate and perhaps even misleading. To introduce concepts of the 'social function' of substandard housing and the role of low-quality housing in meeting 'a real need for cheap accommodation' undermines the traditional base of housing policy. If such housing has a social and economic function, programmes based on 'house condition surveys' and the like are misconceived. The basic sanitary approach to housing problems becomes irrelevant. To suggest that substandard dwellings might be retained 'until they cease to fulfil their present social function' is to put social function on a more important level than substandard conditions. It also implies that replacement housing is not able to serve the same social function.

The message is revolutionary: it is tantamount to an abandonment of a century of housing philosophy. What is to take its place? Can a social function be as easily recognised as the absence of a hot water supply or the presence of structural instability? How is the function of an area to be established? What if it is in the process of change: should the process be facilitated or hindered? Will not *any* improvement be likely to change an area's function (by making it more attractive physically and probably more costly)? What if an area has two or more social functions which clash with each other? Mason's study in Manchester points to 'the potential heterogeneity of housing function within even quite small stress areas'.[58] How is the favoured function to be determined?

In truth it is extremely unlikely that improvement can be carried out without some effect on the function of an area; and the result may be stress in other areas. Since a 'comprehensive functional area policy' over the whole of a housing market area is inconceivable, the conclusion is that 'a parallel policy to improve conditions on a non area basis, particularly in the privately rented sector as a whole, will be necessary'.[59]

The problems which arise with an area approach are exacerbated by the tendency of local authorities to require 'high standards' of improvement. The higher these are, the more the function of an area is likely to be affected. It is with good reason that the housing policy review proposed 'a change of emphasis', with the aim of improving a large number of the worst houses to a decent basic standard rather than a smaller number to a higher standard.[60] The evidence of the 1976 house condition survey shows a fall in the numbers of houses which are unfit or lacking standard amenities, but a significant increase in the number requiring major repairs. As a result 'repairs grants' are to be extended.

Housing stock policies are thus changing as the character of the stock changes. However, experience with area improvement policy and with a range of 'deprived area' policies[61] reinforces the conclusion from American experience that 'the deterioration which the programs strive to halt involves housing dynamics of a broader nature than a neighborhood focus would seem to imply. Both favourable and unfavourable neighborhood trends often result from a variety of circumstances in the larger world which localized programs are powerless to affect'.[62] Added testimony to this is given by the rapid deterioration which is affecting some public authority estates. The perceived 'housing' problem is here clearly symptomatic of deeper problems in relation to which 'housing policy' is neither effective nor appropriate.

6 Owner-Occupation

Give a man the secure possession of a bleak rock and he
will turn it into a garden. Give him a nine years' lease of a
garden and he will turn it into a desert.

Arthur Young[1]

The popular image of the owner-occupied sector is that of a young
couple buying a newly built house on a mortgage. In fact, a third of
owner-occupied dwellings were built before 1919, a third are occupied
by retired people, and 45 per cent are owned outright. Very large numbers of houses which are now owner-occupied were previously privately
rented. Additionally, possibly as many as 200,000 were previously
owned by local authorities, or new town development corporations.
(In total 3·7 million rented dwellings in England and Wales were sold to
owner-occupiers between 1914 and 1975.)[2] In England, over a quarter
of a million owner-occupied houses are unfit and 470,000 lack basic
amenities.[3]

As these figures illustrate there is a great variety both of houses and
households in the owner-occupied stock. The market is a complex one.
The current supply is made up of new building, sales of existing owner-
occupied houses, and sales of previously rented dwellings – less houses
withdrawn by demolition or changes of use. New building is affected by
general economic conditions, the supply of mortgage funds and land
availability. Supply from the existing stock is affected by the rate of
household 'dissolution' (by death, movement into institutional accommodation, emigration, or amalgamation of households), by the
rate at which rented dwellings are sold, and by the amount of 'residential
mobility' and 'geographical mobility' of households. Demand is
affected by prices, incomes and mortgage availability, by the relative
prices and ease of access into other tenure sectors. It also varies according to local traditions (with high levels in areas such as north-east
Lancashire or south Wales and low levels in Scotland), and the differing
aspirations of different age groups (as witness the increase in demand on
the part of younger households even in areas of 'low tradition').

It is within this complex framework that 'housing policy' in relation
to owner-occupation operates. Its ramifications are wide. Planning

policies restricting the supply of land or insisting on provision for car parking may counteract housing policies designed to encourage owner-occupation. Rent policies for the public sector may stimulate (or restrain) demand for home ownership. Policies aimed at preserving the privately rented sector (or at promoting large-scale slum clearance programmes) may reduce the supply of cheaper houses for sale. Subsidisation of commuter transport or the building of motorways can open up lower cost areas for development and thus have the opposite effect. Taxation and tax relief provisions are of great significance, even though their origins may have had nothing whatsoever to do with 'housing policy'. And inflation may be the most important of all incentives to house purchase.

Governments face a difficult issue in determining how far owner-occupation should be encouraged. Social surveys clearly demonstrate that there are large unsatisfied aspirations,[4] despite the huge growth in home ownership (which has doubled in the last twenty-five years). How far is the apparently high level of demand due to the difficulty in obtaining decent alternatives? How far does it represent a fundamental change in attitude? How far is it prompted by a desire for protection against inflation? Is there an 'optimum' level of owner-occupation in the context of national economic considerations?

There are no easy answers to these questions – which of course is why the issue is such a political one. In any case, the questions have to be considered alongside others relating, for example, to the future of the rented sectors. They therefore fall to be considered in the final essay. Here we examine the financial policies which have developed in relation to owner occupation and the range of benefits and costs which it involves.

FINANCIAL INCENTIVES TO OWNER-OCCUPATION

The 'housing emergency' of the post-1918 period led not only to subsidised council housing but also to subsidised private enterprise housing. Of the 3 million private houses built in Britain in the interwar years, some 460,000 were subsidised (14 per cent of the total in England and Wales, and 32 per cent in Scotland).[5] Most of these houses were sold to owner-occupiers, as was the intention. Similar subsidies were envisaged after the Second World War[6] and were proposed by the Conservative caretaker government of 1945,[7] but they were rejected by the Labour government and have never been reintroduced (except, of course, in respect of improvement). The Labour government's policy (within a heavily restricted total building programme) was to give priority to 'the need for houses for letting at reasonable rents to the families in greatest need'. Private house building was subject to licensing control, the aim of which initially was to maintain a balance of at least four houses for letting to one for sale.[8] Of the 1 million houses built in Britain between 1945 and 1951, only 180,000 were for owner-occupation.

The return of the Conservative government in 1951 led to a much larger role for private enterprise (within an enlarged building programme), particularly after the abolition of licensing. It now became official policy to promote 'by all possible means' the building of new houses for owner-occupation. It was held that 'of all forms of saving, this is one of the best; of all forms of ownership this is one of the most satisfying to the individual and the most beneficial to the nation'.[9] Nevertheless, with the exception of the abolition of licensing (and development charges) no positive measures were taken, and the statement that the government 'will take every opportunity that offers to promote the private building of houses'[10] had a hollow ring.

Apart from the extension of the powers of local authorities to make home loans and the provision of £100m. of Exchequer loans to enable building societies to lend on older properties,[11] policy in the fifties remained benignly passive rather than forcefully active. Indeed, there was no apparent need for anything else. Private building was steadily increasing, and owner-occupation was spreading rapidly within the existing housing stock. (In the forties and fifties more houses were sold by private landlords than were built for owner-occupation.) By 1960, 42 per cent of the entire housing stock was owner-occupied, and it was growing at a rate of some 250,000 to 280,000 a year.[12]

However, one change which was made in 1963 (under a 'tax policy' rather than a 'housing policy' umbrella) was the abolition of the highly unpopular Schedule A tax on owner-occupied houses. It is most unlikely that this made any impact on the demand for owner-occupation, but it highlighted the relevance of taxation to housing policy. This was to become a matter of increasing debate, though little was made of it at the time.

Schedule A was one of the five 'schedules' into which tax was divided in 1803.[13] It was levied on income from land and buildings. For owner-occupiers the 'imputed' income was taxed. This provided equitable treatment between those who received rent in cash and those who received it in kind, though in fact most houses were rented at the time. The tax was based on the actual rent of houses which were let and the estimated rental values of houses which were owner-occupied. Deductions were allowed for repairs in both cases. Owing to the postponement of revaluation (and special provisions relating to the valuation of housing in the fifties), Schedule A tax on owner-occupiers fell in real terms, particularly since deductions were made on the current cost of repairs. This at one and the same time meant that it would be politically difficult to reassess the tax in current terms (particularly for a government committed 'to take every further opportunity that offers' to promote owner-occupation), and that the tax loss involved in abolition was relatively small.

The abolition of Schedule A tax for owner-occupiers seemed a minor change at the time, and few could have foreseen how significant it would become in later debate.

By one of those curiosities which abound in political history, it was a Labour (not a Conservative) government which introduced positive measures to encourage owner-occupation. In addition to exempting owner-occupied houses from the capital gains tax of 1965, they announced the 'stimulation of the planned growth of owner occupation by financial measures designed to widen its economic basis'.[14] The proposals were at first somewhat vague: plans would be published 'as soon as the country's economic situation allows'. The first instalment promised was the provision of powers to the Land Commission to dispose of land for owner-occupied housing on favourable terms.[15] Another (stimulated by the particular difficulty in certain parts of the country of the fall in of long residential leases) was leasehold reform. This was to enable certain classes of leaseholder to purchase their freeholds or to have their leases extended by fifty years.[16] The main thrust, however, came with the introduction of the option mortgage scheme.[17]

The option mortgage scheme was an explicit recognition of the importance of tax reliefs for mortgagors. Those who paid income tax at the standard or higher rates obtained substantial relief by the long-standing provision which allowed interest payments to be deducted from income in their tax assessment. Those who paid at lower than standard rates received less relief and, of course, those who paid no tax did not qualify for any relief. This 'regressive' and 'socially unjust' system was now complemented by the option mortgage scheme which was intended to provide similar benefits for the low-tax and non tax payer.

The option mortgage subsidy will reduce the annual payment a man of modest means has to make for a given sum borrowed and, as a result, lenders will often be willing to advance a larger sum, or to make advances which would otherwise not have been possible. In this way, home ownership will be open for many more people.[18]

The option mortgage benefit, it should be noted, was termed a 'subsidy', thus distinguishing it from 'tax relief'. Being a subsidy it counts as 'public expenditure' and is included in the total cost of housing subsidies. Though this distinction is now outdated and confusing, it had some justification in 1967 in that whereas the option mortgage subsidy was unequivocally a 'housing' benefit, the tax relief on mortgage interest flowed from the general provision that interest payments on any personal debt was not to be reckoned as taxable income. This provision was repealed in the 1969 budget when relief was limited (except for businesses) to interest on housing loans. A further change came in 1974 when relief was restricted to loans with an upper limit of £25,000.

Little information is available on the operation of the option mortgage scheme. It had a slow start mainly because of its inflexibility in relation to rising interest rates and because the decision to opt was, at first, irrevocable. By the end of 1969 some 200,000 mortgagors had opted for the scheme, but the numbers increased when revised provisions enabled the subsidy to be varied with the ordinary mortgage interest rate, thus ensuring that the subsidy and the tax relief were always roughly equivalent.[19] In 1975 about a seventh of building society loans were option mortgages; and the proportion for local authority loans was slightly over a quarter.[20] In 1977 almost a fifth of all new mortgages were option mortgages, giving rise to a subsidy of £140m.[21]

The total cost of tax relief on option mortgage subsidy rose from £125m. in 1965–6 to £1,240m. in 1976–7.[22]

THE DEMAND FOR OWNER-OCCUPATION

At the outbreak of the First World War, owner-occupied housing formed a small proportion of the total market. In England and Wales, less than 1 million of the 8 million dwellings were then owner-occupied: the great majority were privately rented. Today there are 10 million owner-occupied houses, and they form some 55 per cent of the total stock. Whatever allowance might be made for 'involuntary' house purchase (on the part of those whose preference for an alternative was thwarted by lack of supply), there can be no question that the demand for home ownership has been a large one. (The position in Scotland is somewhat different, and is discussed separately in a following section.)

How much *additional* demand there may be is a different matter. Social surveys have uniformly shown a large latent demand among existing renters,[23] and a half of new mortgages from building societies go to buyers who were not previously owner-occupiers.[24] Moreover, a high proportion of newly married couples opt for owner-occupation (sometimes after a short stay with relatives, or in privately rented accommodation or even in council housing – in those areas where there is easy access).[25]

If policy is to be based on people's aspirations, there is clear justification for the expressed intention of successive governments to support, and perhaps even stimulate, increased owner-occupation. What this leaves out of account, however, is the extent to which both demand and aspirations have been stimulated by taxes, subsidies and inflation. The position in the owner-occupied housing boom of the thirties was very different: costs were falling, tax reliefs were less significant (because tax levels were lower and the tax threshold was so much higher than it is today), mortgage funds were in good supply (sometimes embarrassingly so), and council house rents were much less subsidised; indeed, at times it was as cheap to buy as to rent.[26]

The current position makes a striking contrast: once entry has been gained to the owner-occupied market, real costs fall, and the greater the rate of inflation, the greater is the extent of the fall. It might seem academic to argue that an 11 per cent mortgage rate (reduced to 7 per cent by tax reliefs) is turned into a negative rate by inflation. Such arguments can be carried much further by including freedom from capital gains tax and such like. The debates may be heated or semi-philosophical, but certainly complicated.[27] The would-be house buyer would find it all very perplexing, but he is well aware of the essential point and, if he can possibly get on to the owner-occupation ladder, he will do so.

Whether governments should continue to encourage this with a vast amount of tax relief and option mortgage subsidy seems debatable, to put it no higher. The issue is not one which should be decided within the context of owner-occupation alone though, in fact, it may well be. The basic questions relate to the housing market as a whole and the extent of government intervention in the various sectors. This, however, is likely to be too academic an approach. The 'bargain' of owner-occupation is now so impressed upon the public mind that governments will tend to respond by making it available to marginal groups who 'find that they fall just short of current requirements for a mortgage'.[28] This is the approach of the housing policy review in its proposals for 'low-start' mortgages, higher percentage mortgages, easier loans on older properties and 'special assistance' for first-time buyers.[29] The stated objective is to 'support' the demand for home ownership on the grounds that 'for most people owning one's own home is a basic and natural desire, which for more and more people is becoming attainable'; and the reason for this preference is not simply 'financial advantage' but 'the sense of greater personal independence' which home ownership brings.[30]

Before discussing the validity of this, it is useful to ask whether the promotion of owner-occupation serves other goals such as regional development, and whether it is equally applicable to all areas of the country and to inner city as well as to suburban locations. A discussion of such issues leads to the conclusion that, even if governments refuse to tackle major questions of housing finance (the case for which is argued in the final essay), *general* policies in relation to owner-occupation are not sufficient.

OWNER-OCCUPATION AND REGIONAL DEVELOPMENT

At the local authority level there is no organisation, other than the local authority itself, which is responsible for assessing the needs for non-council housing. This is one of the reasons why local authorities are now being exhorted to concern themselves with the totality of housing needs in their areas, and the adequacy or otherwise of the supply. This is a new and difficult role for local authorities. They have a massive stock of their own housing and a long tradition of concern for their waiting lists: it is not easy for a legatee of this stock and tradition to change its character.

It is, however, interesting to note the strong comments and recommendations of a wide range of economic advisory bodies on the role of owner-occupied housing in regional development – particularly in areas where there is a relatively high proportion of council housing. The various reports of the regional economic planning councils are replete with references to this issue. One of the most recent is that of the Northern Region Strategy Team which, after a detailed analysis, concluded that 'there is an expressed demand for an increase in the number of houses for owner-occupation, for more better quality houses, particularly "executive type" houses in the Tyneside and Wearside markets, and for the elderly and single, and for second homes in rural areas . . . New building may thus be provided to satisfy demand, rather than need.'[31]

The last sentence is probably the most striking in highlighting, not simply a type of thinking which is typically alien to local authorities, but also a very different conception of the role of housing policy. It is not, of course, a totally new conception: thirteen years earlier a government White Paper on the north-east complained:

There is in the region a pressing need for houses of the standard sought by the higher salaried worker. The introduction of many new firms and the recent economic revival have brought a demand for higher quality houses from managerial, scientific and technical staff to which there has so far been a slow response.[32]

There is no need to labour the point: whatever the successes of local authorities in meeting local housing needs (and these are undoubtedly of great significance), they have given insufficient attention to the wider context within which they are operating, and this (coupled with the easier prospects of mobility for owner-occupiers, able to 'trade up' in a rising market and in inflationary conditions) has made the provision of owner-occupied housing an important feature of regional development.

There are (at least partial) alternatives, as the experience of the 'undemocratic' Scottish Special Housing Association has demonstrated. More generally, owner-occupation provides a means by which a kind of new law of settlement is circumvented. An owner-occupier does not need to pass the eligiblity tests of a local authority: if he can sell his existing house and buy another, he is free to move as he pleases. Moreover, since in development areas (except in Scotland) owner-occupied houses tend to be cheaper than those in the more prosperous areas, a move can result in a considerable amount of trading 'up market' – if the up market houses are there.[33]

This short summary is intended to be an explanation, not a justification. It does seem, however, that given the present framework within which the various housing markets operate (and particularly the huge importance attached to *local* people by *local* authorities responsible for *local* authority housing), owner-occupation has a significant role to play in furthering wider policy objectives such as regional development. It is sad that this should be so, but it is perhaps an inevitable price that has to be paid for a system which works with a high degree of effective public accountability on a local scale.

The perhaps somewhat surprising conclusion of this is not that owner-occupation has inherent advantages in the promotion of regional development (via easy residential mobility), but that it does not exhibit the shortcomings of local authority controlled housing. The implication is that if good quality council housing were easily available to new-comers, there might be less concern for advancing owner-occupation.

There is, however, a danger of overgeneralisation. Conditions and attitudes vary greatly between different areas, and a policy of 'promoting owner-occupation' may be appropriate to deal with the symptoms of a problem of one area it may be quite inappropriate to another. (Those who know Glasgow, Tower Hamlets and Nottingham – to select almost at random – will appreciate the great importance of differing local situations.)

The particular case of Scotland generally (and Glasgow in particular) illustrates the difficulty of determining what the optimum level of owner occupation might be.

OWNER-OCCUPATION IN SCOTLAND

The extent of owner-occupation varies between the different regions of England (from 45 per cent in the northern region to 61 per cent in the south-west) and between England and Wales (55 per cent and 58 per cent respectively), but the most striking contrast is with Scotland where the proportion is only 33 per cent.[34]

This difference is of long standing. In 1947, for example, while there was 27 per cent owner-occupation in England and Wales, the Scottish figure was 17 per cent.[35] In the interwar years, while nearly three-quarters of house building south of the border was in the private sector, in Scotland it was less than a third.

The reasons are largely historical. As a result of general economic conditions and relatively low incomes in the past there has been little provision of medium-priced housing. The private building boom of the thirties which was so significant in England had little counterpart in Scotland. Moreover, whereas there is in many English areas a good supply of pre-1914 terraced housing available for house purchase, the equivalent in Scotland is typically a tenemental flat which all too frequently is a poor equivalent (and which presents very difficult physical problems for improvement). In short, there is a crucially important 'gap' in 'the Scottish owner-occupation ladder'. There is a reasonable supply of good, modern but relatively high-cost housing for sale, and similarly with poor quality, old tenemental housing: but there is little in between. For reasons of economic history this 'gap' was filled by public sector housing; and since 1945 the emphasis of policy has been on increasing the supply of rented housing for which there has been a priority need.

There is also the so-called 'tradition of low council rents' in Scotland which is alleged to be a major factor in depressing the effective demand for owner occupation. (To the extent that it is a 'tradition' it is not a very long one as is evidenced by the long battle in the interwar years between central and local government when the central department was exerting strong pressure on local authorities to *reduce* rents.)[36] Nevertheless, Scottish rents have been low in the postwar years and this has widened the gap between the costs of buying and renting.

Additionally, Scottish house prices are high relative to most of the other parts of Britain. This cannot be explained away by the higher costs of standards of building in Scotland, nor by land prices (which in fact are substantially lower). More to the point is the small number of builders in Scotland who are responsible for a large proportion of the building. In short, there is a greater profit element – though not great enough to attract competitors into the market. Searching inquiry has put the matter more diplomatically: 'demand influences did not appear to account for the relatively higher house prices in Scotland';[37] and the 'massive contribution from a small group of large firms raises serious economic implications'.[38]

Despite all this, owner-occupation is growing in Scotland, and it is clear from an analysis of incomes and tenure that there could be a large potential. Though recent buyers in Scotland have similar incomes to all recent buyers in Great Britain, the proportion of Scottish households who are owner-occupiers is lower in all income groups.[39] In England and Wales (as a whole – not necessarily in individual regions) any significant extension of owner-occupation could be achieved only by making special provision for lower income purchasers. In Scotland, however, there is a high proportion of households who could afford to buy if suitably priced houses were available.

The policy implications of this are of great importance: in Scotland, the problem is essentially one of increasing the supply of houses for owner-occupation and of gearing financial arrangements to enable more households who have both the aspirations and sufficient incomes to buy their own houses. No special subsidies are needed for this purpose: the problem is simply one of organising *housing supply*. To quote from the *Quarterly Bulletin of the Building Societies Association:*

> The likely consequence of a strong demand for owner-occupied housing together with a shortage of houses available for home buyers is an increase in house prices. In the fourth quarter of 1975, house prices in Scotland at the mortgage completion stage were 22 per cent higher than a year earlier, compared with a national average of 8 per cent . . . If the shift of demand in Scotland from council housing to owner-occupied housing is to be met, rather than merely lead to an increase in house prices, then there will need to be a significant increase in the number of houses that are available for purchase.[40]

Without this, the subsidies for first-time buyers proposed in the housing policy review[41] will simply inflate prices. However, as already indicated, there is a gap in the Scottish owner-occupation ladder. A household aspiring to owner occupation has restricted choice between cheap and often nasty old housing and good (but expensive) new housing. Important 'rungs on the ladder' are missing and, as a result, households who would prefer to become owner-occupiers have no choice (if they are to improve their housing conditions) except to become public authority tenants.

In short, housing choices are distorted by supply. If households are to be given the real opportunity to choose the tenure they prefer, then considerable adjustments are needed in the pattern of real alternatives available to them. This cannot be achieved simply by new building: this is inevitably relatively expensive and, in any case, can only make a small marginal contribution. There is thus a strong case for infusing the supply with good quality, older and cheaper housing: in short, the sale of public sector houses. There is no other way in which the 'missing rung' of the ladder can be provided.

This is an issue which, though of particular relevance to Scotland, is of far wider import. It is therefore more usefully discussed in a British, rather than distinctive Scottish, context.

THE SALE OF COUNCIL HOUSES

It would not be difficult to write at length on the sale of council houses: there are good precedents.[42] The subject is also one which raises strong passions. These were politically polarised until very recently with the Conservatives being strongly in favour, and Labour being strongly opposed. Attitudes, however, are changing. A few years ago there would have been no doubt about the part of the political spectrum from which the following came: 'There is a certain sourness, not to say bitterness in

the land . . . as tenants become more and more aware of the extent of the
serfdom imposed upon them by their council tenancies.' In fact, it comes
from a pamphlet by Frank Field, director of the Child Poverty Action
Group.[43] He claims three 'immensely important advantages' from
taking a more open approach to the question of the sale of council
houses. In his own words:

In the first place it would be a massive redistribution of wealth in our
community. Secondly, it would extend the new dimensions of individual freedom to a large number of people: freedom from the
petty rules and restrictions imposed by bureaucracy, and also freedom
in the ability to move around the country. Thirdly, and I think this is
one of the most important reasons for at least keeping an open mind
on this option until we have thought it through much more carefully,
is that this approach would be a direct attack on the cycle of poverty
in that we would for the first time be giving many poor people that
crucial thing they lack – and that is access to wealth.

Perhaps even more eloquent of the change in attitudes is the debate
within the Glasgow Labour Party of selling council houses in their city.[44]
This would have been unthinkable only a few years ago.
    The issue is, of course, a highly political one but, like many such
issues, it is intertwined with highly technical matters, such as the implications for local authorities' borrowing requirements, for the total
subsidy bill (with a decrease in Exchequer subsidies and an increase in
tax reliefs and option mortgage subsidy), for short-term and long-term
'management' problems in the public housing stock, for social polarisation, for filtering, and so forth.
    It is also confused, as all such issues are, by many cross-currents. For
example, if the root cause is what Field calls 'the sourness of serfdom',
is not at least part of the answer to give tenants greater responsibility
and control over their estates? On the other hand, if aspirations for
ownership are depressed by the restriction of financial assistance to lower
income households in rented property, could not a system be devised to
give equivalent help on change of tenure? ('Equivalence' may be much
easier to define politically than technically.) If the objection to sales is
that councils are thereby restricted in the help they can give to families
in need of housing, is this not a further argument for changing their
function from managers of council houses to local agencies for ensuring
that all needs are met within a range of tenures? If there is concern that
only the better council housing will prove saleable (leaving local
authorities with a rump of unpopular housing) is not the answer to
follow policies of restricting sales on certain estates and encouraging
them on others, perhaps with positive policies designed to improve the
unpopular estates?

A related issue is the extent to which the growth of owner-occupation has been possible only because of the sales of previously privately rented houses. Now that this supply is drying up (at least outside the major urban areas), it is arguable that the sale of council houses should take its place. On this line of argument, the policy ought to place emphasis on sales of the poorest and cheapest council houses (with a transfer of the present tenants to better accommodation). Already there are mounting vacancy rates in 'difficult to let' areas: are these not the ones which should be sold at the bargain prices currently being proposed by opposition spokesmen (for example Hugh Rossi's promise of 'discounts' up to 50 per cent)?[45]

There is a host of such questions to which the answers are neither clear nor applicable in the same way in all areas. A simple-minded view would be that both the questions and the answers would be different in an area which had a housing stock containing 5 per cent of council housing from one which contained 50 per cent.

There is scope for boundless speculation, and so far little research has been carried out. What there is tends (rightly) to be confined to particular local areas. Birmingham and the west midlands is the area which has had the most attention.[46] There it was found that the typical buyer of a council house is a long-established, middle-aged tenant with a fairly large growing family, above-average wages and often with more than one earner. An identical picture emerged in Manchester.[47] The typical council house buyers in these areas are thus different from the typical council tenants. More interestingly, they are generally better off than those who obtain local authority mortgage loans for the purchase of private property. The conclusion is that the sale of council houses does not do much to extend owner-occupation to groups who could not have gained access through the private market.[48]

The comment can be made that this is irrelevant, though it is more questionable whether heavily discounted prices are justified. But this cannot be considered in isolation from the benefits received by other groups in the housing market; and, in any case, is the discount greater than the capitalised value of the subsidy they would have continued to receive had they remained council tenants?

Such questions are unanswerable, and so attention should focus on the demerits of council sales. Given that the purchaser benefits, who loses? Again the issues are complex, and Forrest and Murie make much of the fact that (not unsurprisingly) sales are concentrated in those parts of the council house market which is in greatest demand from tenants.[49] Thus the higher income tenants are buying better houses and, though the numbers are, as yet, small, the long-term effect is to reduce the range of choice open to the remaining tenants and, at some point 'the erosion of the council stock would fundamentally affect the social role of public stock: the recipe is one for social segregation and stigmatisation'.[50]

The conclusion seems a hefty one to base on a limited survey, but Murie is clearly worried about the 'wholesale' policy advocated by the political Right. He calls in aid the horrifying effects of social segregation in American public housing (eloquently set out by David Harvey),[51] and argues that the sale of council houses 'reflects a greater value attached to individual ownership than to allocation according to need.[52] And so the research worker finds himself clearly on the political stage and embroiled in Marxist debate.[53]

Nevertheless, Murie's essential practical message is that the question of the sale of council housing raises much broader issues of equity and of the management of resources. It is but one more addition to 'an incoherent collection of (often conflicting) *ad hoc* adjustments to a variety of immediate crises and basic beliefs'.[54] Some of the benefits which accrue from council house sales (and, indeed, from owner-occupation) can be obtained in other ways. If this is translated into legal terms, different tenures provide different 'bundles of rights'. Some consideration is now being given to the issues involved here, for example, by study of alternative forms of tenure and tenant participation. Even some of the financial benefits to be obtained from owner-occupation can be made available to tenants.

In the longer term, an adequate answer to the question of the sale of council houses can be provided only when the housing system as a whole exhibits a far greater degree of rationality and equity than it does currently. There is little evidence that that day is nigh. We are therefore likely to be left with a continuing debate on a narrower issue: how many of which council houses should be sold to whom at what price?

The answer will hopefully be a pragmatic one determined at the local level by local authorities whose responsibilities are effectively (and sensitively) deployed across the whole spectrum of housing in their areas. Whether alternative forms of tenure may provide 'a means of defeating doctrinaire and sterile argument between the major political parties over the sale of council housing' (as Gilmour has suggested)[55] is, however, even more debatable.

INNER CITY OWNER-OCCUPATION[56]

Nationally – and in every region of Britain – owner-occupied housing is on the increase. With few exceptions, this is not the case in inner cities. Indeed, the effect of slum clearance, redevelopment and urban motorways has been to decrease it. Virtually all the new housing which has been built has been provided by local authorities, and thus both the number and the proportion of owner-occupied houses have fallen.

There can be much scope for argument as to how far this is because of demand or supply factors. Certainly new housing in suburban locations can be provided more cheaply than in inner cities, since land prices are cheaper and no redevelopment is required. Private redevelopment takes place only when the price which can be obtained for new dwellings is sufficient to cover not only the cost of building these dwellings but also the cost of purchasing and clearing the structures existing on the site. In economic terms this is not a typical situation. Other factors, however, add considerable complications. Land has to be assembled, existing tenants have to be rehoused, planning restrictions tend to be more onerous than in suburban locations, and site preparation costs are frequently higher.

On the demand side there are great uncertainties. The demand for inner city housing is affected by the supply of outer city or suburban housing, the relative quality of environments and services, the transport network and the cost of the journey to work, the location of employment and a host of similar factors. Perhaps the most important of these factors is the quality of the environment: it is not easy to provide an inner city environment which is accepted as being as good, in physical and social terms, as a suburban environment. It is difficult enough for a public authority: for a private developer it presents exceptional problems. And finally, why should the private sector enter this problem-laden field while suburban developments are booming? It is perhaps significant that private sector interest in residential rehabilitation has been stimulated by forecasts of the decline in demand for additional housing [based largely on demographic changes] and the prediction that future housing requirements will be much more dependent upon slum clearance.

Before examining these issues further it needs to be stressed that London, as always, has to be considered separately. Its sheer size, its attractions and the functions which it serves put it in a class entirely of its own. Here the high market prices paid for new and rehabilitated housing evidence the demand which exists for inner city residential location. Nevertheless, the market for *new* private housing in London would seem to be restricted to a small luxury sector: the major demand appears to be for rehabilitated dwellings – or, probably even more significant, old dwellings which can (with the aid of improvement grants) be rehabilitated by individual owner-occupiers. It must, however, be admitted that, except to a limited extent in London, there is little hard evidence on the potential demand for new private inner urban housing.

A survey commissioned by the National Economic Development Office throws some light on the attitudes of suburban owner-occupiers to the purchase of new housing in redevelopment areas.[57] The survey covered two groups of owner-occupiers in the fifteen largest towns (outside London) in England and Wales:[58] owner-occupiers of 'new' houses (built between 1967 and 1969) and owner-occupiers of 'older' houses (built between 1930 and 1959).

Only about 4 to 5 per cent of those who were likely to move within five years were attracted by the idea of buying a new house in a re-developed urban area. The report concluded that 'given the inherent inaccuracies of predictive data, the evidence discourages much reliance on these sectors of house owners as a market for the proposed new housing' – though, if the sample was representative, the number of owner-occupiers of post-1930 houses who might be interested could be between 16,000 and 20,000 annually.

Of greater interest, however, are the reported attitudes to environment. Great importance is clearly attached to a 'semi-rural' environment: the fresh air and cleanliness which was provided by the estates on which these owner-occupiers lived. In striking contrast is the dirty, noisy and unpleasant image of the inner urban areas. Descriptions of the environmental improvements which would form part of a redevelopment scheme did not dispel this image. This general attitude was not over-ridden by the perceived advantages of an inner area: better transport, shopping, indoor entertainment, job opportunities for women, and facilities for teenagers. Shopping and transport were the most important of these: both were also a source of dissatisfaction with suburban estates.

Younger house owners (under the age of 35) and those with children show the greatest interest in the idea of moving to a redeveloped area. Attitudes hardened with age, though the length of time spent in the suburbs did not appear to be important: 'Once the move to the suburbs has been made, the pressures to stay there are clearly very great.'

The survey did not include households living in inner urban areas but there is a presumption (and scattered evidence) that they would be more attracted by the idea of buying in a redeveloped area. However, there is little evidence to show what prices they would be prepared to pay for new houses: this is the crux of the issue.

Two other aspects are also clearly of importance: the general environment and the type of houses that are provided.

The inner urban environment is surely more than a question of 'image': it is a very big issue of urban quality which 'skilful landscaping' will not fundamentally change. More easily changeable is density. Private suburban development is typically at a density of ten to twelve dwellings to the acre. Public authority development in new and expanding towns is generally around sixteen dwellings to the acre, while redevelopment is rarely less than twenty, and can rise to a hundred in schemes with tower blocks. The evidence from the private sector (outside London) suggests that lower densities are necessary if private sales are to be achieved.

This, however, raises several major issues. Given present land prices, lower densities would lead to higher dwelling costs (probably above the level at which they could be sold). Yet, if this is a reflection of demand, why are land prices so high? And why is it that there is an apparently large demand for public authority housing in inner cities? Indeed, why can public authorities do what the private sector cannot?

There are no certain answers to these questions, but a number of points can be made. First, it seems clear that public authority redevelopment is 'uneconomic' in the sense that a private developer could not undertake it at a commercially acceptable return on the capital employed. In other words the dwellings would not sell (or let) at a profit on the open market. The NEDO report produced figures which illustrate this. They obtained the actual costs of a number of local authority redevelopment schemes which were considered to be 'not too dissimilar from the kind of development a private builder might carry out'. (Unfortunately, no details are given.) These costs were compared with valuations which were made of the dwellings for vacant freehold possession and for letting at fair market rents. The conclusion was that none of the schemes would have been commercially viable.

The difference between costs and value was ascribed to the high density of the redevelopment. Yet, for a local authority, high density is desirable both to meet (its assessment of) the local demand and to minimise the land cost per dwelling unit. To some extent the latter is a function of the subsidy system while the former is not unrelated to the rents at which local authority dwellings are provided. It is an exaggeration to say that the land prices are 'artificially' raised by local authority action and that the demand exists only because of the heavily subsidised rent. Nevertheless, there is a sufficient element of truth in this to make further discussion appropriate.

Local authority redevelopment is not, of course, undertaken because it is 'economic'. Indeed, it is precisely because it is not that public action is necessary. The cost of land acquisition may be higher than it would be if local authorities were not 'in the market', but this is not a relevant point since they are and must be if slums are to be cleared and new roads, schools and other public services provided. Neither is it valid to argue that local authorities should hold back until values fall to a level at which redevelopment becomes economic. This is appropriate for commercial redevelopment, but if slum clearances were held back until the value of the properties fell to a level which made redevelopment profitable, very little clearance would ever take place. In fact, the properties in clearance areas typically do have very low values (except where there is multiple occupation), and houses which are statutorily 'unfit for human habitation' are acquired at site value – though this harsh rule has been considerably modified, particularly for owner-occupiers.

However, clearance areas typically are densely developed and, as a result, the site values are consequently higher than is the case with undeveloped land. Furthermore, areas of slum housing are frequently peppered with commercial and industrial premises which have considerably higher values but whose clearance is necessary if a satisfactory redevelopment scheme is to be achieved. This can very significantly increase the cost of acquisition. Figures quoted for inner London showed that areas containing mixed uses are twice as 'valuable' as areas consisting solely of housing.[59] In the provinces, costs of acquiring central slum clearance sites are working out at ten times those of peripheral sites.

There is also the cost of the clearance itself which can amount, in areas of terraced housing at forty to the acre, to £4,000 an acre (in 1970 prices). Demolition costs do not, of course, bear any relation to the value of the property and they are, therefore, more important when values are low. Further additional costs are involved on account of the length of time taken by clearance and redevelopment (democratic processes are necessarily time-consuming), of site preparation and of construction itself: all these tend to be higher in redevelopment schemes than on virgin sites.

Redevelopment is thus inevitably costly. A commercial 'return' could be anticipated only if the new use were highly profitable. But those who are displaced by clearance require to be rehoused, and local authorities (rightly) have a statutory responsibility in this connection. Occupiers of dwellings in redevelopment areas are not numbered among the most affluent. The gap between their rent-paying ability and current 'cost rents' is a large one which has to be met by subsidies.

Until 1972, these subsidies were available only in connection with local authority redevelopment. The cost of land acquisition and clearance was grant aided through housing subsidies to local authorities. Under the Housing Finance Acts of 1972, subsidies for slum clearance were provided separately from those for new building. The slum clearance subsidy (payable for at least fifteen years) meets 75 per cent of the difference between the cost and the value of cleared land. This 'value' is determined by the use to which the land is put.

The point immediately relevant to the current discussion is that this subsidy was intended, *inter alia*, to enable local authorities to dispose of cleared land to private developers for building owner-occupied housing. By selling the land at a price reflecting its value (not the cost of acquisition and clearance) private development in clearance areas would no longer be thwarted by the burden of the costs of the non-market operation of slum clearance.

Unfortunately, it does not appear to have had the desired effect, but it is not at all clear whether this is due to the reluctance of local authorities to dispose of the land or the reluctance of private developers to buy it. Nor does much appear to have resulted from a parallel attempt to promote 'local authority/private enterprise partnership schemes'.[60]

It is extraordinary that, despite the almost frenetic intensity of studies on housing and inner city problems during recent years, little is known about the basic land problems and little inquiry has been made of measures which might make private redevelopment possible. Why is it, for instance, that there is so much neglected, vacant and apparently abandoned land in inner cities? Is it true that much of this is in public ownership and is being held on to in the hope of 'a price the land market is disinclined to give'?[61] And, if public ownership of the land is regarded as desirable, could not there be a return to the traditional leasehold system or some variant of it such as was envisaged in the Land Commission legislation?

TENURE CHOICE

Though the discussion in this essay has been selective, it is apparent that it is highly misleading to think in terms of a single issue of owner-occupation. There are in fact many different issues within which owner-occupation needs to be considered. The difficulty lies in framing policies which reflect this variety. To promote owner-occupation generally would be to deny the differences between different areas and between the inner city and the suburbs. Indeed, the housing policy review's proposal to give assistance to first-time buyers could exacerbate the problems of the inner cities. Moreover, it may be that some of the 'demand' for owner-occupation reflects a dissatisfaction with the management of council houses and the limited rights accorded to tenants. More clearly it must be affected by the financial advantages of owner-occupation over other forms of tenure, and the sheer difficulty of obtaining decent accommodation in the privately rented sector. The crux of the matter, however, is likely to be the financial one. This is discussed in the final essay where some reference is made also to broader questions which need addressing. First, however, it is useful to look briefly at the campaign for 'alternative forms' of tenure which has been stimulated largely by the decline of private landlordism.

7 Alternative Tenures

No aspect of public policy causes more frustration than housing.[1]

The nineteenth-century financial system for the provision of private rented housing has already been outlined, while the long history of rent control has been discussed in some detail. Rent control has certainly not eased the lot of the private landlord, but his decline was inevitable as the circumstances of the nineteenth century in which his operations flourished changed: particularly the development of new and easier investment opportunities. The building societies figure largely here, not only because they were a good avenue of investment, but also because they funded housing which could be provided at a price with which the private landlord could not compete. Though new investment in private rented housing was free of control throughout the interwar years, the prospects of falling prices over much of the period made it an unprofitable venture. The price stability of the Victorian era had ended, and with it went security and confidence in this investment market.

There were, as already indicated, other factors, such as taxation and competition from subsidised council housing. Against this background, little could be expected by way of new investment in the privately rented market, though there was some activity in the late thirties. There is little evidence on this but it seems that, apart from some 'luxury' building, part of it was simply forced upon builders because they had saturated the owner-occupied market and had no alternative but to let. As war approached, some even put their houses on the rental market in the hope of large capital profits which might be made after the expectedly short war was over.[2]

Had there been no war, it is possible that the saturation of the owner-occupied market would have led to new thinking on the finance of private rented housing investment. A 1933 guarantee scheme did bring a modest response from the building societies, and produced some 75,000 rented houses;[3] and before the advent of the Labour government in 1945 some discussion was proceeding about the role which might be played by the building societies. In February 1944, the chairman of the Building Societies Association declared that, in the immediate postwar period, the societies would indeed do this:

We must be ready to play our part in the provision of houses for letting. That means a development of a side of our business which we have always regarded as secondary. It will, I am convinced, have to take place during the early postwar years. We must see to it that it is used by us wisely in the national interest, so that tenants may become home owners.[4]

But the real interest was revealed by the final comment.

There has been intermittent interest in the resuscitation of private investment, but it has never been taken seriously. (If it had, means could have been found of promoting it, or at least removing the major tax disincentives.) Instead, attention has been focused on rescuing the property from deterioration (or replacing it), improving the living conditions of private tenants, and providing an alternative to the privately rented sector, and directly assisting tenants by way of rent allowances (thereby hopefully reducing the disincentives to landlords).

The first of these (improvement and clearance) has already been discussed, while the rent allowance scheme is analysed in the following essay. Here we proceed to a discussion of the alternatives to the private landlord of which housing associations constitute the current favourite.

HOUSING ASSOCIATIONS

Housing associations have a long history, though in terms of numbers of houses provided they were of minor importance until very recently. Their nineteenth-century significance was as a forerunner and catalyst of public provision. The attention they then attracted 'was out of proportion to the scale of their activities',[5] and they clearly demonstrated that neither 'philanthropy and 5 per cent' nor private subsidies such as charitable donations could bridge the gap between the rent-paying capacity of the poor and the cost of providing decent housing (even by the much lower standards of the time).

When it was at last conceded, in 1919, that the deficiency had to be met by subsidies, these were made available to housing associations (or public utility societies and housing trusts as they were then termed) and, indeed, to private enterprise. Moreover, local authorities were empowered to assist in the promotion of voluntary housing bodies, and in the thirties provision was made for many of the housing functions of local authorities to be carried out through housing associations, for example, in rehousing from unfit houses and providing accommodation for 'the abatement of overcrowding'.[6] Generally, subsidies have been available on the same basis as for local authorities.

Originally housing associations, like local authorities, provided housing for the working classes at below-market rents. Until the end of the fifties, these 'traditional' associations made a modest but useful contribution. Most of the associations were small, though there were notable exceptions such as the Coal Industry Housing Association (set up by the National Coal Board) and the long-established Peabody, Guinness, Bournville and Sutton organisations.

Government concern at the continued decline of the privately rented sector (and the failure of the 1957 Rent Act to stop this) led to a central initiative for priority 'new-style' housing associations. A pump-priming operation (involving £25m. of Exchequer loans to approved housing associations) was mounted in 1961 with the hope that 'it will serve to show the way to the investment of private capital once again in building houses to let'.[7] No subsidies were payable to these 'cost-rent societies' and 'housing co-operatives' (except in the case of purpose-built accommodation for old people – where the objective was simply to increase the supply for this group, rather than to demonstrate the viability of the concept of 'cost rent').

The success of this modest scheme led to the expansion of the programme in 1964, with the establishment of a national Housing Corporation as a promotional body and channel of finance. The 1964 Act provided for Exchequer loans of up to £100m. which, it was intended, would supplement finance from building societies. The arrangements were complex, but the basic idea was that building societies would lend about two-thirds of the cost to each society, while the Housing Corporation would lend the remainder on second mortgage. Loans were made over a period of forty years. The intention remained to provide for the needs 'of those who cannot afford or do not want owner-occupation but who yet do not feel that they should look to the local authorities for housing'.[8] Reference to trail blazing for the resumption of private building for renting, however, was now muted, and the emphasis shifted to 'the development of a housing society movement which will build and manage houses for people at large who are able to meet the cost'. Indeed, it was envisaged that 'once societies have been established, they might well extend their activities to taking over and managing existing rented houses where management by a trust would be appropriate'.[9]

The 1964 scheme did not work smoothly. Building societies (with a few significant exceptions) were not really interested in financing these curious new bodies (even after the Housing Corporation's share was raised from a third to a half). The administrative arrangements were complex and, for the cost-rent societies, rising interest rates led to letting difficulties. (Unlike owner-occupiers who received tax relief on their mortgage interest payments, and council tenants who had the benefit of subsidies, cost-rent tenants had to bear the full brunt of the higher interest rates.)

Co-ownership schemes, on the other hand, began to prosper, particularly when the option mortgage scheme was made available to them. This subsidy was more important than the tax relief which co-owners had individually been able to obtain (if their incomes were sufficiently high) since it operated most effectively 'at just the income level of the tenants whom cost-rent and co-ownership societies set out to attract – those just not able to afford normal house ownership'. Radical changes in the rules imposed by the Housing Corporation also had a major impact. Deposits (which had originally been equal to 5 per cent of the cost of the dwelling) were reduced to a mere six months' rent; and the minimum length of lease (originally kept long in order to ensure a security of tenure as similar as possible to that of an owner-occupier) was reduced to a simple monthly tenancy.[10] With the additional attraction of a share in the equity, co-ownership was clearly a much better buy than cost renting. By 1969 cost rent was dead: indeed, many schemes which had started in this way changed over to co-operatives. At the end of 1970, only 1,575 dwellings remained in cost-rent projects (compared with a total of some 12,000 approvals).[11]

But even co-operative schemes suffered from the shortage of building society funds. Nevertheless, 11,000 dwellings were built in the two years 1969 and 1970.[12]

THE COHEN COMMITTEE DEBACLE

Some of the difficulties facing the housing association movement – traditional and new style – would probably have been resolved had there been greater government interest; but the Labour government (like many local authorities) had no heart in this funny little sector. There were political antagonisms to competition for land and building resources; there were doubts about the integrity of some of the promoters of the new-style societies; there was concern about possible exploitation of the assets; and there was only a small band of 'real believers', regarded by some as being of a slightly cranky character.

Inevitably a committee of inquiry was set up (in 1968) but, untypically, the civil service machine did not succeed in finding an appropriately neutral chairman. The person appointed (Sir Karl Cohen) was not only a leading local housing authority protagonist: he was firmly of the belief that there was nothing a housing association could do that a local authority could not do better. After over two years internal wrangling the committee (to its own great relief) was disbanded in July 1970, one month after the return of the Conservative government. In place of a 'report', the material gathered by the committee was put together by the department and published as 'a working paper'.[13]

Clearly there could be no recommendations in such a document, but the department were asked to submit 'such tentative indications as officials might feel able to give of the conclusions which seemed likely to emerge from it'.[14] These were straightforward. The decline in the number of properties let by private landlords offered a great opportunity for voluntary housing. 'Yet because it is voluntary, its effectiveness depends in the last resort on the energy and capacity of those engaged in it, for their efforts cannot be commanded, in the way in which those of authorities are by virtue of statutory obligation. Hence all that can be done is to make it possible for voluntary housing to prosper by removing impediments.'

Some of the impediments were serious. There was a vast number of associations (over 3,000) and a bewildering range of types. Most were small and had few assets. Arrangements for finance were complicated and confused. There was a real risk of the exploitation of housing association assets (created with the aid of public funds) because of an archaic and inappropriate system of registration which applied to those associations which were not technically charities.

The answers suggested themselves: simplification of both the types of housing association and the financial arrangements; and a new system for registration.

FAIR DEAL FOR VOLUNTARY HOUSING, 1971

The working paper was published in April 1971 – nicely in time for its findings to be incorporated in the Conservative government's 'fair deal' White Paper.[15] Unlike the previous government's rather negative (if not hostilely alloyed) attitude to the voluntary housing movement (as it was now coming to be termed), the new government envisaged 'a special place' for it in housing policy, and promised 'encouragement and support'. In particular, those associations and societies providing rented accommodation would be brought into the fair rent system and their tenants made eligible for rent allowances. This would neatly secure a greatly increased rent income for housing associations without hardship to tenants. Existing subsidies would be phased out in line with phased increases in rents. New building would attract a deficit subsidy to meet the gap between costs and income from fair rents.

Housing Corporation funding would be made available to traditional associations in the same way as for the new-style societies, though loans from local authorities would continue in cases where the authority had nomination rights over not less than 50 per cent of the dwellings concerned. (The nomination issue is an important one, to be discussed later.)

Further consideration was to be given to simplifying the dual system of loans from the Corporation and the building societies; and to measures which might be necessary 'to consolidate and streamline the movement if it is to realise its full potential in a reformed system of housing finance'.

Though the point was not made explicit, this reorganisation effectively abolished the old distinction between the traditional subsidised associations and the new-style rental societies.

Legislative effect was given to these proposals in the 1972 Housing
Finance Acts. They had a short life because of the change in government in 1974 – committed to the repeal of these Acts. But so far as
housing associations were concerned, the Conservatives were already
preparing major new legislation. They were alarmed at the current
house price crisis and its effects on the demand for public sector
building; at the continued decline of the privately rented sector (and the
Labour threats of municipalisation); and at the trend towards 'polarisation' between the public sector for renting and the private sector for
buying. It now seemed clear that any hope of resuscitating private
investment in rented housing was doomed to failure. Even with fair
rents, the gap between rental value and sale value was too great to be
bridged; and the gap was rapidly increasing with the house price boom.

The answer therefore was seen to be a major expansion of the
voluntary housing movement – to be promoted by a strengthened
Housing Corporation under a new chairman (who would also chair the
National Building Agency with whom the corporation would work
closely).[16]

ALL-PARTY SUPPORT, 1973–4

The Conservative government's proposals for housing associations
were incorporated in the 1973 Housing and Planning Bill and, on the
change of government, formed the basis of the 1974 Housing Act.[17]
Both dealt with other issues, some of which (particularly improvement
grants) are discussed elsewhere in this book.

There was now all-party support for housing associations, though
for different reasons. The Conservatives saw them as a safeguard
against municipal monopolisation of rented housing. The Labour view
was more complicated, and certainly less homogeneous. (There still
lingered the view that housing associations were not really necessary.)
Crosland (Secretary of State for the Environment) expressed his firm
support for the housing association movement, initially in terms harmonious with those of the Conservatives:

> It would be intolerable if we ever reached a situation in which only
> two forms of housing were available in this country – in which
> everyone either had to become a tenant of a local authority or had to
> buy his own home. Monopoly is as undesirable in housing as else-
> where. But this does not mean . . . that we endorse the policy of our
> predecessors towards housing associations. Expansion, yes: but it is
> utterly misconceived to regard the voluntary housing movement as
> in any sense an alternative to municipal renting. Local authorities
> alone have the capacity and responsibility to tackle the major housing
> needs in their areas, and they will become the principal suppliers of

rented accommodation. Housing associations can and will have a growing role in supporting local authorities, particularly in meeting special needs and in the worst areas of housing stress. They also have a role in the extension of social ownership of rented accommodation. But in all this they must complement and supplement local authorities, not supplant or compete with them. I also see a role for housing associations in developing and experimenting with new forms of tenant participation in the management of their dwellings. This is an area in which they could provide a much-needed stimulus.'[18]

This in fact touched on the issues which worried some Labour supporters: the relationship between the roles of housing associations and local authorities (a point to which we return).

The Act transformed the Housing Corporation from a relatively modest organisation channelling Exchequer aid to the voluntary housing movement (and badgering the building societies to do likewise), to the dominant promotional, supervisory and financial institution in the field. Its role was underpinned, first by its financial strength, and secondly by the new statutory requirement that before any association could borrow from public funds and obtain the very generous new grants, it had to secure registration with the corporation. (Registration is approved only if an association can demonstrate that its control and supervision, financial stability, performance and capability are sound, and that its operating methods are above suspicion.) The corporation was also greatly strengthened in staff (which doubled between 1973–4 and 1975–6 to 363), and developed a close link with the technical side of the National Building Agency, both of whom were chaired by the powerful Lord Goodman.

The new subsidy system was so generous as to be beyond the wildest dreams of the most ardent supporters of voluntary housing: it was designed to meet the total deficit on each scheme, with rents fixed by the 'fair rent' system. (The tenants thus qualify, as in the earlier scheme, for rent allowances.) The subsidy – which at the time of writing is still operative – is known as the housing association grant (inevitably but ungenerously shortened to HAG). It is payable as a capital sum for all projects, whether new building or rehabilitation, and encompasses acquisition or building costs, improvements and repairs, and management and maintenance. Most unusually, it is paid as a capital sum (and is therefore based on assumptions about future income and expenditure).

The level of grant paid works out at an extremely high level, averaging 75 to 80 per cent of a fair rent scheme. Not surprisingly, with subsidies at this level, the voluntary housing movement expanded rapidly, and the corporation had to operate for a time under severe pressure – not simply to administer the grant system, but also to check the eligibility of applicant associations for registration. This 'policeman' function as it is known in the trade is, of course, essential as a means of protecting the public interest. It proved 'more exacting' than expected, and good use was made of the statutory Housing Associations Registration Advisory Committee. The backlog of registration (which, of course, applied to all existing associations as well as new ones) was not overtaken until well into 1977 (when 2,400 associations had been registered).[19]

This, coupled with the teething troubles of its new and greatly expanded role, the detailed work involved in approving projects, and the complexities of calculating HAG, soon gave the corporation a reputation for bureaucratic bumbledom which it has yet to live down. But there is no gainsaying the results of the new system. Some 30,000 dwellings a year are being built or improved, and in 1976 completions of new dwellings reached the unprecedented figure of 15,760 – 5 per cent of total house building.

FINANCIAL PROBLEMS REMAIN

With the high level of subsidies for housing associations, the fixing of rents under the fair rent system and the application of the rent allowance scheme to tenants unable to meet fair rents, one would expect that the financial problems of this sector would be solved. Unfortunately this is not so: for two reasons. First, there is a problem caused by the fact that the fair rents set for new housing association dwellings 'are often significantly higher than the reasonable rents set by local authorities for similar properties and intended to house similar people.'[20] This follows from the different rent-fixing systems in the two sectors and the fact that, despite the very high subsidy on new housing association building, the true subsidy on an identical council house will be even higher (mainly because of rent pooling). There is, however, an added difficulty which flows from the structure of the rent allowance scheme: this operates only up to a certain level. Beyond this, even if the rent is 'fair', no allowance is given.

The other problem facing housing associations has been the public expenditure cuts. There was, of course, no justification for shielding housing associations completely from the cold climate of 1976–7 and, though they were treated relatively kindly at first, eventually the cuts applied to the corporation became so severe as to threaten the 'decimation' of their programme. To avoid this, the corporation set about searching for private funding (with government guarantees). This involved establishing a separate organisation – the Housing Corporation Finance Company Ltd – with 40 per cent of the shares being held by the Housing Corporation and the remainder by some of the larger housing associations (such as the Guinness Trust, the Sutton Trust and the London and Quadrant Trust). With this respectable backing, and working through a City merchant bank, £35m. of private funds were raised. The scheme was gilt edged for the private market since, as already explained, 75 per cent or more of the cost of schemes so funded would be met immediately by Exchequer grants and the remainder over time by income from fair rents.

This is a blatant dodge to avoid operations being technically counted as public expenditure, and it was possible only because housing associations (despite their huge dependence on public money) are regarded as being part of the private sector. The Expenditure Committee had some sharp comments to make on this – not because of the acumen of the Housing Corporation or the undesirability of the outcome in housing terms, but because of the nonsense of public expenditure conventions.[21]

CO-OWNERSHIP REVIVED

Just as the changes in the financial context killed off cost-rent housing associations and pushed co-ownership schemes to the forefront, so the new subsidy arrangements did the opposite. In 1976, however, new initiatives on the part of the Housing Corporation (with the backing of the DoE) were intended to revive such schemes. A limited pilot project was launched with the housing association grant providing about a third of the cost.

The details are somewhat complex (and increasing complexity is a marked characteristic of all contemporary attempts to provide 'alternative forms of tenure'). There are two main versions of the new co-ownership schemes: co-ownership equity sharing and community leasehold.[22]

Co-ownership (equity sharing) is based on the form of co-ownership housing first sponsored by the corporation. Under that form, half the cost of a housing development is borrowed from a building society, and half from the corporation, and the total joint mortgage net of option mortgage is repaid out of the rent paid by the co-owner tenants. When the co-owner leaves, he receives a premium payment linked to the increase in the value of his flat or house while he lived there, minus administrative and other costs. The estate remains in the ownership of the co-ownership society.

Under this scheme around half the capital cost is financed by a block building society option mortgage, around a third is funded by HAG, and the remainder is financed by the corporation on second mortgage. The corporation retains the freehold of the land or property, and that part of the equity funded by HAG will thus remain in social ownership. But any outgoing co-owner will be able to take out 50 per cent of any appreciation in the value of the property, provided he has lived there for at least a year (as opposed to five years for the old co-ownership premium payment), and there is a guarantee of no financial loss.

The other part of the pilot programme consists of homes where the occupier buys an individual lease for a proportion (initially set at 50 per cent) of the total value of the home and will benefit from its increasing value. Thus if he paid half the initial value, he will get half the new value when he decides to leave. There are two ways in which these leasehold schemes will operate. In one, 'community leasehold', designed primarily for young couples in housing need, it is expected that the occupiers will take out individual building society mortgages to cover the purchase of a lease. In the other, 'leasehold schemes for the elderly', sheltered housing is provided for those of retirement age and the occupiers' contribution comes in the form of a lump sum; generally, it is expected that this will result from the sale of their previous home, now too large for their needs. In both these leasehold schemes that part of the costs not raised by the individual's contribution is covered by public funds – and the occupier pays a 'rent' for this portion.

HOUSING CO-OPERATIVES

Terminology has always been problematic in the voluntary housing movement – trusts, associations, societies, co-ownerships, co-operatives, and a host of variations on each. The same terms have had different meanings at different times and in different contexts. Moreover, there are some terms on which there is no general agreement on definition. This is particularly the case with 'co-operatives'. In the last section, we discussed 'co-ownerships' (where the distinctive feature is that the occupiers not only collectively own and manage their property, but also have a share in the equity which they can realise). In this section, we discuss 'co-operatives', where the crucial characteristic is taken to be that the 'co-operators' have either no individual stake in the equity or a stake limited to a share repayable on leaving at its original par value. (The latter are known as 'par value co-operatives'.)

Confusingly, the DoE use the term co-operative in a generic way to include both of these, as well as 'management co-operatives' in which the tenants have collective responsibility for some or all management functions, but do not own or lease the property.[23] This is by no means all there is to the matter, but there is no reason here for delving further into the deeper mysteries of this area.

In the narrower sense given above, co-operative housing is envisaged by its protagonists, not as a halfway stage between renting and buying, but as a distinctive form of tenure emanating from the objectives of the early co-operative pioneers: 'the building of a number of houses in which those members desiring to assist each other in improving their domestic and social condition may reside'.[24]

The case has been put forward eloquently by John Hands and in the Campbell *Report of the Working Party on Housing Co-operatives*[25] (of which he was a member). The stress is on 'fundamental human needs', not on the final nexus, though there can be material benefit from the distribution of annual surpluses (or their investment in additional amenities) arising from self help maintenance and management. To quote the working party report:

> Co-operative housing represents a highly desirable departure from traditionally remote and depersonalised forms of housing management. It can on the one hand provide a greater sense of community than individual owner-occupation, underpinned by shared responsibility and involvement, and on the other hand provide people who would otherwise feel the insecurity (and perhaps indignity) of being subject to the arbitrary decisions of even an efficient and well-meaning landlord with the right to self-determination where their own houses are concerned.[26]

Despite the fact that Britain is the birthplace of the co-operative movement, it has few housing co-operatives,[27] mainly because of the development of public authority housing and owner-occupation, and the lack of support and interest. As a result, there has been no adequate financial system (or even legal framework) within which it could flourish. Indeed, there have been strong objections raised against co-operative housing, partly from the vested interests of existing institutions (who are pained at the implied – and sometimes explicit – slurs which the promoters of the idea cast upon them). More generally, there is a scepticism that 'it won't work here', reinforced by fears that 'an apathetic majority could end up being dominated by an interested minority'. The biggest source of scepticism is on the argument that 'any attempt to give *individuals* a financial stake in housing destroys the co-operative principle': this is seen as being remote from reality.[28]

Nevertheless, a combination of circumstances, including dissatisfaction with the present housing system, the increasing interest in alternative forms of tenure, wider support for grass-roots initiatives, and some effective lobbying, have combined to arouse official interest. Though this can hardly be described as enthusiastic, it is now sufficiently encouraging to have led to some action. The first significant step was a new statutory provision enabling co-operatives to be set up in local authority and housing association schemes with full entitlement to subsidy. The second came with a new remit for the Housing Corporation to act as midwife to a new Co-operative Housing Agency (headed by the movement's leading pioneer – John Hands).

There was considerable agreement that the Housing Corporation was not a suitable body to take this on itself. Indeed, spokesmen for the co-operative movement argued that it was 'dominated by a staff absorbed in administrative procedures and with little or no understanding of the creative and social processes essential to the task of securing tenant involvement'. Moreover, its traditional concern for co-ownership housing would confuse a new role for co-operative housing.[29] Whatever justification there might have been for such criticisms, it was decided that the Housing Corporation was the appropriate body to 'foster' a new agency.

In the outcome, the Co-operative Housing Agency has been established under the Housing Corporation's wing, located in separate premises near to the corporation's headquarters. Its role is to work with and through co-operatives

. . . to create a legislative and administrative framework which will enable co-operatives to develop in response to local needs; to help make available financial resources for co-operative development and help members exercise proper financial control; to promote the principles and techniques of co-operative housing nationally, and to provide a national resources centre for co-operative education in housing; and to provide some direct assistance in legal, financial, educational, project development and housing management matters to co-operatives and co-op development groups.

The Housing Corporation have commented that 'no one expects co-operative housing to be an easy concept to promote but there is great interest in it and enormous enthusiasm for what is for many almost a new life-style'.[30]

THE ROLE OF HOUSING ASSOCIATIONS

The role which housing associations are intended to play in the British housing scene has always been far from clear. This is partly because local conditions have differed widely, but also because both local housing authorities and local housing associations have varied greatly in their outlooks, and, indeed, competence. Until the Housing Corporation was established, there was no effective alternative source of finance for housing associations, and most associations operated on a local basis. A great deal therefore depended on local initiative and local response. Some local authorities were keen to see associations making a contribution to local needs (whether supplementary or complementary to public provision). Others saw them as unnecessary competitors for scarce resources or as an out-of-date and redundant form of housing provision. Then again there were a few authorities who envisaged a large role for associations which would reduce the need for further public authority housing and, indeed, might even take over a significant part of the local authority's stock.

Attitudes were – and still are – highlighted by the issue of 'nomination rights'. Some local authorities have been prepared to assist housing associations only on condition that a certain proportion (or, on occasion, all) tenants shall be nominated by them. Others impose no conditions. Nominations may involve the submission of local authority applicants for approval by the housing association, or vice versa.

Though the Housing Corporation is now the predominant organisation in promoting and financing housing associations, there is still considerable funding by local authorities; and the issue of nomination arrangements is still very much a live one, irrespective of the source of finance. A DoE circular of 1974[31] set out 'the government's general policy': a significant proportion of local authority nominations should be accepted in order to ensure that housing association schemes, which are heavily subsidised by the taxpayer, help local authorities to meet the whole range of housing needs, especially in stress areas. Where schemes were financed by the Housing Corporation, the corporation would expect to be satisfied that reasonable nomination arrangements had been made with the local authority (in practice, normally on a fifty-fifty basis).

Nevertheless, it was also pointed out that housing associations could bring 'greater flexibility to the selection of tenants in public sector housing by providing for people who, although in pressing need, have little expectation of being offered a local authority tenancy, because they lack residential qualifications or for other reasons'.

The circular did not lay down detailed figures for the proportion of nominations because it was thought right to allow these to be negotiated in the light of local circumstances. By the end of 1975, however, it had become apparent that some local authorities were still seeking to insist on the right to nominate *all* of the tenants in certain housing association developments. 'This, of course, removes the degree of flexibility that it was considered essential for housing associations to provide.' The DoE therefore issued 'clear' guidance: 'Both housing association schemes in which virtually all the places are reserved to the local authority and, on the other hand, schemes in which little or no provision is made for local authority nomination will not normally be regarded as acceptable for grant.'[32]

This begs the essential question of whether housing associations are to *supplement* the work of local authorities (simply doing what a local authority might do), or to *complement* them (meeting needs which a local authority considers to be outside its own field of responsibility). How far should housing associations be made an instrument of government policy and how far should they operate independently – seeking out needs and experimenting in areas where public authorities fear to tread?

There are, for instance, relatively well-off single people, young married couples, and retired people who fail, for one reason or another, to pass the eligibility tests of the managers of council houses and the managers of building societies. Moreover, there are needs which neither sector can easily meet, such as those of students, elderly people who wish to move to a retirement area (or to the area in which their married children live), mobile young professionals and executives, ex-prisoners, migrant workers, and the family wanting temporary accommodation in a new area before deciding on a house to buy.

In the lengthy recent debates on institutional arrangements, finance and subsidies, there has been surprisingly little serious discussion of this matter of role. The fact that housing associations are heavily subsidised is not the main point: so are most other providers of housing. As with so many current housing issues, the problems of provision, allocation, subsidy and level of payments for occupiers are horribly confused.

The policy operated by the Housing Corporation since 1977 gives priority to three groups of need:

(1) inner city rehabilitation in housing action areas and priority neighbourhoods;
(2) general family housing only in areas of acute housing stress, or to relieve such stress, and with the emphasis on small units (of which there is a particular shortage);
(3) housing to meet the special needs of the elderly, the handicapped, and others such as ex-offenders, ex-psychiatric patients and one-parent families whose needs are rarely met by the local authority or the private sector.

Such a statement of policy in relation to housing associations fits in well with the conception of a national movement, overseen and heavily financed by a national organisation which operates 'very strictly in line with government policy and priorities'.[33] And the policy may well be judged right, but there is a real danger that having now provided massive funds for the housing association movement, governments will end up with a supplementary public (or semi public) sector, rather than an effective substitute for the privately rented sector.

In any case policy may well be forced in this direction by pressure of other considerations. For instance, if the housing associations continue to prosper, for how long will it seem 'sensible' to operate two systems of housing finance in each area - particularly if the local authority housing accounts develop surpluses as a result of the impact of inflation on their historically determined loan charges? Much, of course, will depend on the way in which future subsidy policy develops, but the indications in the housing policy review are clearly towards a situation in which it will appear natural to bring the two systems of finance to-gether. Not only is it proposed to treat housing associations 'on very similar lines to local authorities', it is also suggested that the system for determining housing association rents should be changed to achieve 'a more logical relationship with local authority rents'.[34]

The writing is on the wall: what started off as an 'alternative' may finish up as more of the same thing.

ALTERNATIVE TO WHAT?

The truth of the matter is that there has been inadequate clarity about the questions at issue. 'Alternative forms of tenure' has been a banner under which many different campaigns are being waged.[35] Some earnestly search for more sensitive 'housing processes' within which the consumer plays a positively active role. Some are academically critical of the increasing 'power duopoly' of building societies and public authorities, and the 'managerialism' which thereby confronts those seeking 'entry' to the 'housing system'. More pragmatically (though essentially bothered about the same thing) are those who see the division of housing provision into two main sectors effectively controlled by bureaucracies as being unhealthy if not politically dangerous, since the rules by which bureaucracies operate (however well intentioned and enlightened) will exclude some needy groups. Alternatively, there is apprehension at the amount of discretion which is exercised in such a scheme of things – a discretion which is effectively (and inevitably) in the hands of relatively junior staff. (The head of the housing department or the building society may sit on a high-level committee advocating more sensitivity and fairness, but the active decisions are taken in his name at a much lower level where discrimination, prejudice and arbitrary decisions might be taken without anyone being aware that this is happening.)

Others see the problem in terms of making the two main sectors 'more responsive', or of building easier 'bridges' between them, or of 'breaking down barriers', or obtaining more 'equity' between the sectors, or giving tenants some 'equity' in their accommodation, or simply providing tenants with more opportunities for 'participation' in management.

Then again there are those who see all these issues as being diversionary to 'the basic problems which need tackling', such as 'the fragmentation of the working class introduced by tenure differences'.[36]

In fact, of course, since most people are well housed the orators in these debating chambers are small in number; and even those who have opted for an alternative form of tenure seem often to have done so for the simple reason that it was the only alternative available to them at the time they needed a house.[37] Even with the self-build groups it seems from one investigation that members 'do not show any characteristics of user control beyond those demonstrated by all owner-occupiers: the problem for us as investigators has been that we have been looking for alternatives in housing but they have not'.[38]

The evidence suggests that there is little demand for alternative forms of tenure *as such*, but rather a series of perceived problems relating either to the management of or the access to the traditional tenures. As was seen in the previous essay on owner-occupation, the multiplicity of the relevant issues is denied by the use of generic slogans. Politicians may find it electorally profitable to espouse the general cause of owner-occupation or of 'alternative forms of tenure', but these are seductive oversimplifications which fail to recognise the true nature of the complex of problems to which they are supposedly the answer.

8 Housing Allowances

The aim of discriminating finely has reached the point of being self-defeating.

P. H. Levin[1]

THE FAIR DEAL

The cornerstone of the Conservative government's 1972 'fair deal for housing'[2] was that 'of subsidising people, not bricks and mortar'. All rents were to be brought on to a common 'fair' basis and (effectively) the subsidies to dwellings were to be reduced (i.e. the direct subsidies received by public authority tenants, and the indirect subsidies – through rent controls – received by private unfurnished tenants). At the same time, a national housing allowance scheme would enable tenants to claim reductions in rent to bring their payments down to a level which was 'fair in relation to their means and family circumstances'. (Technically there are two schemes: rent rebates for council tenants, and rent allowances for private tenants. They are essentially the same, and it is convenient to use the term 'housing allowances' when the discussion applies to both of them.)

Though the scheme was intended as a housing policy measure (or, to be more precise a rents policy measure), it was also seen as 'an important new weapon against family poverty'. The family income supplement – a means tested benefit payable to low-income families with children – was another such device. That scheme was aimed at helping those whose incomes were low in relation to their family responsibilities; 'but people with low incomes and high rents need more help than those with low incomes and low rents'. This was precisely the problem to be met by housing allowances.

This immediately raises an issue which has been recurrent in discussions of the housing allowance scheme (and possible successors): are they to be considered a form of income support which should therefore properly be dealt with primarily in combination with other forms of social benefit? Or are they essentially (or primarily, or additionally) better regarded as an instrument of housing policy?

The Advisory Committee on Rent Rebates and Rent Allowances

have stated that 'actually or potentially, they are both' and the question as to which function is more important appeared to them as an academic one.[3] This may seem a sensible enough view but, as we shall see, decisions on the future of the scheme will be greatly affected by the priority which is accorded to one or the other. Historically, despite the references to 'weapons against family poverty', the housing allowance scheme was unequivocally designed to facilitate the injection of some rationality in the haphazard and arbitrary pattern of rents. Its aim was to ensure that this could be done without causing hardship to those who could not afford fair rents.

The housing allowance scheme for private tenants was quite new (apart from the scheme introduced by Birmingham City Council under local act powers in 1968). Rent rebate schemes, however, had been operated by local authorities for many years, though these varied greatly in character and scope – and some local authorities had none at all. (In 1972, about two-thirds of the authorities in England and Wales had schemes.) The national scheme was made mandatory on all local authorities with only a small scope for local discretionary additional benefits.

It is not intended here to discuss the schemes in detail: they are complex (and increasingly so) and are constantly changing in detail. In summary, however, they operate on the basis of determining the basic expenditure needs of a household (termed the needs allowance) and charging a rent related to the amount by which income exceeds this. There is a 'minimum rent' payable (which has remained since the introduction of the schemes) of 40 per cent of the actual rent – with a floor of £1 a week. However, this minimum is reduced (if necessary to nil) where a tenant's income is less than his needs allowance.

For tenants whose incomes are in excess of the needs allowance, a percentage of this excess is added to the minimum rent. This percentage is fixed at the apparently curious figure of 17 per cent. The reason for this is that it was felt that not more than a half of income above the needs allowance should be taken by tax and other such payments: tax takes a third, thus leaving one-sixth (17 per cent) for increased rent.

For the purpose of the scheme, 'income' is taken as the gross income of the tenant and his spouse. (Gross income is easier to deal with administratively and avoids the necessity of assessing relevant deductions, and deciding which are obligatory and which are voluntary.) Income of other non-dependants in a household is ignored, but a flat rate decuction from the allowance is made according to their age and circumstances.[4]

TAKE-UP OF BENEFITS

A major problem facing any new scheme which depends upon positive knowledge and action by the intended beneficiaries is that of 'take-up'.

The difficulties are more than that of providing information: people have to understand the scheme, its purpose and scope; they have to know how to obtain the benefit and perhaps overcome anxiety at making an approach to a local authority; and they have to have attitudes (particularly concerning stigma) which do not prevent them from obtaining their rights.

These difficulties are especially acute in the housing allowance scheme where eligibility extends much higher up the income scale than is the case with other means tested benefits. Take-up (i.e. the proportion of eligible tenants who receive benefits) has been officially estimated at 75 to 80 per cent for council tenants and around 40 per cent for tenants of private unfurnished accommodation. (Tenants on supplementary benefit are excluded from these figures, since their housing costs are met automatically.)

The higher figure for council tenants is related to the fact that rent rebates have been much longer established in that sector, and that the authority responsible for rent collection is the same as the authority responsible for administering rent rebates. Even so, a 20 per cent 'failure rate' seems disturbingly high, even if some allowance is made for the possibility that for some high-income households their eligible benefit may be considered too low to be bothered with.

Much more serious is the low take-up in the private sector. Increased publicity and familiarity has gradually raised take-up from between 10 and 15 per cent in May 1973 to between 35 and 40 per cent in January 1976, but this only serves to underline the problem of reaching an acceptable take-up rate.

Research in this field has demonstrated the difficulties. A project in the London Borough of Haringey showed that, even after intensive publicity in selected areas,

> . . . surprisingly few people understood the schemes. Only a very small proportion of eligible non-claimants were aware that they were eligible, and people continued to think that all means tested benefits were for those handicapped by old age, physical disability, low income, etc. Few grasped that eligibility for allowance extends further up the income scale than for other means tested benefits, or that it is determined by the relation of income to rent, and not by the absolute levels of either.[5]

More research and more publicity might raise the take-up figures further, as might compulsory registration of rents. Nevertheless, it does appear that inadequate take-up is an inherent shortcoming of the housing allowance scheme.

Added weight is given to this conclusion by the extremely high costs involved in reaching eligible non-claimants. In Haringey, the take-up rate was increased during the course of the experiment from 8 per cent to 22 per cent at an average cost of £32·60 per successful applicant. (The costs ranged from £6·90 with the direct mailing of a DoE leaflet to £431 with the cost of a promotional caravan.)[6] The total cost of publicity by local authorities is not known, but the DoE spent £1,103,000 on national publicity between September 1972 and April 1975.[7]

The cost of administering the scheme is also high. In 1974–5 it was estimated that the annual average was about £8 per rent rebate and £15 to £20 per allowance.[8] These costs appear to be increasing dramatically in this labour intensive scheme. Thus in Hammersmith the annual cost per rebate rose from £6 in 1974–5 to £15 in 1975–6, and per allowance from £11 to £36.[9]

THE PROBLEM OF 'HIGH' RENTS

Some limit clearly has to be set to the level of individual rents which can be allowed for benefit. (It would be generally regarded as unacceptable that a low-income family should be subsidised to the full extent to enable them to live in a luxury flat in Mayfair.) This poses a problem of administrative discretion about which little is known.[10] It applies equally in the case of supplementary benefit where less than 1 per cent of claimants in 1975 had 'unreasonably high' rents which were not met in full.[11]

Of much wider significance is the maximum rebate allowable under the scheme. (This was increased in November 1977 from £8 to £13 in London and from £6·50 to £10 elsewhere.) The secretary of state has power to 'authorise' higher benefits (on application by a local authority) where the general level of rents in an area, or the rents of a particular class of dwellings in an area, can be regarded as 'exceptionally high. This is one of those dark corners of administration where it is not easy to establish how things work, but at the end of 1976, fourteen local authorities (all in Greater London) had 'authorisations'.[12]

There are technical aspects of this issue into which the general reader would not wish to be led. It may be asked, however, why it is necessary to have a maximum rebate at all as long as the rent is registered as a fair one. In their first report, the Advisory Committee on Rent Rebates and Rent Allowances did recommend that the limit should be abolished, 'since it is not evident that a tenant's resources are necessarily commensurate with higher rent levels when they occur sporadically rather than generally in an authority's area'.[13] The recommendation was rejected, presumably because it would have involved an unlimited additional Exchequer liability (though this could not be very great),[14] or because it might have brought into the scheme an unacceptable number of higher income tenants paying rents which, though high, are not incommensurate with their affordable aspirations. Alternatively, it might have been feared that it would remove a constraint on tenants' aspirations (and thus bring into greater prominence the issue of administrative discretion).

Another point which arises in connection with the high-rents issue stems from the fact that many rents in the private sector are not registered. The law requires that 'fair rents' shall be charged – but, if the landlord and tenant agree what this should be, there is no requirement that it be registered. This can give rise to problems in determining allowances. The local authority has to assess whether the rent actually agreed and paid accords with its estimate of what the fair rent if registered would be. (Without this there could be collusion between landlord and tenant to maximise the allowance.) This system of 'estimated fair rents' inevitably leaves room for differences of judgement, and cases arise where tenants find that their allowance is based on a rent which is lower than that which they are paying.

There is no satisfactory solution to this other than the compulsory registration of all rents. The Advisory Committee for Rent Rebates and Rent Allowances have so recommended, partly to avoid this problem (and the administrative complexities and costs to which it gives rise), and also because they felt that it would enable more effective measures to be taken by local authorities to improve take-up.[15]

HOUSING ALLOWANCES FOR FURNISHED TENANCIES

The housing allowance scheme initially applied only to unfurnished tenancies, and the government strongly resisted attempts to extend it to the furnished sector,[16] mainly because of administrative problems of the type just discussed. (The full technicalities of this have been ignored in this summary discussion, but one important point to note is that furnished tenancies operate under a different code, with a separate system of rent tribunals which can determine 'reasonable' rents.) However, in response to sustained pressure, a limited scheme was introduced by the Furnished Lettings (Rent Allowances) Act, 1973. The scheme was intended to meet the needs of poorer families who had been forced into furnished accommodation because of the impossibility of obtaining anything else. It was not intended to cover young people without family responsibilities 'who were more mobile and could generally share rooms with others in their age group'.[17]

The groups to be covered by the scheme were not specified in the Act: instead they were to be defined by regulation.[18] They included families with dependent children, single-parent families, pensioners (and households containing a pensioner dependant) – all of whom had to have a local residential qualification of three months; the 'non-young' (those aged over 30) who had lived in their present area for six months; and households containing someone who was chronically sick, handicapped or disabled (for whom no residential qualification was required).

This was a cautious step into 'a new and difficult field', but the intention was to review it in the light of experience and, meanwhile, local authorities were given an open ended power to grant an allowance to *any* furnished tenant whom they judged to be in hardship.

Allowances for furnished tenants could not be based on the total rent since this included an amount for furniture (which unfurnished tenants had to pay for separately without benefit). The solution adopted was to base them on the estimated fair rent for the accommodation as if it were unfurnished but with a 'mark-up' of 25 per cent to allow for the greater management expenses of a landlord of a furnished letting. This mark-up was thought to be justified on the ground that the greater expenses would be reflected in the rent charged, and therefore properly allowable for the purpose of paying housing allowances.

This was a tortuous system which would probably have had a short life even if the Labour government of 1974 had not repealed it. Their 1974 Rent Act extended rent allowances to all furnished tenants and brought the majority of them within the fair rent system. This solved many of the existing problems but created a host of new ones to which some reference is made below.

HOUSING ALLOWANCE CONUNDRUMS

The housing allowance scheme is a complicated one – as the discussion has made painfully obvious. It gives rise to extreme difficulties in reconciling irreconcilables. For instance, it is clearly undesirable to employ a household means test not simply because of the political difficulties of introducing a test which was so hated in the interwar years, but because it gives rise to unjustifiable strains within multi-adult households, it has serious disincentive effects, it is impossible to administer fairly, and it is administratively expensive. No government could seriously contemplate such a test.

Yet, if there is to be no household means test, how is any degree of equity to be achieved between households with differing numbers of earners? Is it fair that a household with one earner should receive a housing allowance identical with that for a household with six earners? The only way of dealing with this problem is to arbitrarily determine a fixed sum to be taken into account in calculating either the income of the tenant or (what in principle amounts to the same thing) to make a standard deduction for each non-dependant from the rent rebate.

However, this then gives rise to the question of fairness between households with earners of widely differing incomes, and between those with non-dependent earners and those with non-dependent non-earners. Should the same notional contribution be assumed for a high-earning son as for one who is out of work and mentally handicapped? What should be done for non-dependants who stay at home to care for small children?

There is no satisfactory solution to conundrums of this kind – which abound in any administratively viable scheme of reasonable simplicity, comprehensible to recipients and administrators, and involving the maximum amount of rights which are certain (rather than discretionary).

The range of difficult issues (extending from students to maintenance payments, from the handicapped to the two-house owner, from wife's earnings to 'luxurious' accommodation) is illustrated in the reports of the Advisory Committee on Rent Rebates and Rent Allowances. As the first chairman used to remark: many of the questions resembled that of determining how many angels could dance on the head of a pin.

Some of the problems arise because they are intertwined with others in totally different fields which, by definition, cannot be adequately considered, let alone decided upon, by an agency concerned with housing. Students are a classic case of this. The extension of the rent allowance scheme to tenants of furnished accommodation had the incidental effect of bringing the generality of student tenants into a scheme which, when designed, assumed that they would be largely beyond its scope.

The problems which consequently arose are mind-boggling. Is a student to be assumed to be receiving the 'parental contribution' to his living costs which is assessed in calculating his grant? And what if in fact he does not receive it? How are five students sharing a flat to be treated for the purpose of a rent allowance? Should a married student with two homes – one for his wife and children who live in his home town, and one for himself in his college town – receive two allowances? There is an infinite variety of human circumstances which not even a huge tome of rules and regulations could cover.

With grant aided students, there is a strong case for channelling the whole of their rent assistance through the educational award system,[19] but this, of course, raises major issues of 'education policy' which may well clash with 'housing policy'. In any case, the difficulties to which students give rise are only illustrative of the inherent problems of a means tested scheme.

That there would be difficulties of this nature had always been anticipated, and a discretionary element was built into the scheme from the start. This enables local authorities (at their own cost) to be more generous than the national scheme provides in individual cases of hardship or in relation to a class of tenants. There is no restriction on how this discretion is to be used other than a cost ceiling of 10 per cent of the standard schemes. The particular value of this discretionary power is that it provides flexibility for dealing with unusual circumstances and cases where a strict application of the normal rules would be harsh. In a real sense, it is a 'safety net' for those whose needs cannot be adequately foreseen or catered for in a scheme designed to be of national application.

It seems, however, that the most common use of this discretion is to give higher benefits to broad groups of tenants such as the elderly or the disabled. Some authorities even use it to give an 'across the board' uplift in benefit. Such an approach has administrative advantages and is certainly less costly administratively than using the discretion to help individual tenants, but it seems a curious use of the power.[20] On the other hand, a discretionary power is precisely that, and local authorities can hardly be expected to use it in ways laid down by central government – particularly since the cost falls on the rates.

Nevertheless, it is clear that the discretion is performing a different function in the housing allowance scheme than it does in the supplementary benefit scheme. There the discretion is statutorily defined as being to give additional benefits 'where there are exceptional circumstances' to the extent that 'may be appropriate to take account of those circumstances'.[21]

HOUSING ALLOWANCES AND OTHERS

Housing allowances do not exist in isolation. Households who are eligible for them may also be eligible for family income supplement, rate rebates, social security, supplementary benefit and a host of other benefits. Though these different schemes may all be classed as income supplement benefits, each is designed for some particular need. The result is a hotch-potch of schemes which interact, overlap and sometimes conflict with each other.

Some indication of the profusion of schemes is given in Table 1. It is this profusion which makes it extremely difficult to bring about a rational and equitable reorganisation of benefits. Taxation has further complicated the position. Tax thresholds have fallen, and a household can be eligible both for tax and for an income related benefit. Moreover, the proliferation of specific benefits, coupled with tax (and social security contributions) has given rise to the so-called 'poverty trap' under which increases in income can be largely offset by changes in income-related benefits and taxes. At the extreme, this can result in an effective marginal 'tax rate' of 100 per cent or more: i.e. the combined effect of increases in tax and reductions in benefit can equal or even exceed the increase in income.

An estimate prepared by the Central Statistical Office suggested that, given an increase of £1 in earnings, 20,000 households might suffer a negative gain, 40,000 would gain up to 25 per cent, and 370,000 would gain between 25 and 50 per cent.[23] The scale of the low-income problem is indicated by another estimate which suggested that 15 per cent of all households have 'resources' at or below the level prescribed for supplementary benefits, while a further 5 per cent have resources within 20 per cent of this level. One implication of this, of course, is that relatively small increases in 'prescribed levels' can result in a large increase in the numbers eligible for benefit.

Table 1 *Some Income Support Benefits*[22]
Number of households receiving

(a) Housing allowances	1·2m.
(b) Rate rebates	2·5m.
(c) Supplementary benefit	2·9m.
(d) Family income supplement	67,500
(e) Unemployment benefit	525,000
(f) Sickness benefit	552,000
(g) Invalidity benefit	441,000
(h) Retirement pensions	8·4m.
(i) Widow's benefit	395,000
(j) Industrial disablement benefit	199,000
(k) Family allowances	4·6m.
(l) Tax relief on mortgage interest	5·5m.

Without entering into a wider discussion of these issues, it is highly relevant to point to the relationship between the housing allowance and the supplementary benefit schemes where there is a major problem which is inherent in the structure of the two schemes. In the jargon of the trade, this is the 'better off' problem. It arises from the fact that tenants who are not in full employment can obtain either a housing allowance or supplementary benefit. Unfortunately, the 'best buy' is not always easy to ascertain. 'For large numbers of people it is far from obvious whether they would be better off forgoing their entitlement to supplementary benefit and claiming a rent rebate, or vice versa. Changes in circumstances or in the details of either scheme can change the relative advantage.'[24]

The difficulty stems from the different objectives and principles of the two schemes. The supplementary benefit system is primarily concerned with the amount of disposable income which a claimant requires to meet all his day-to-day needs including accommodation. It thus provides general income support up to a certain level of net income and not beyond. The rent paid by a tenant is only one of many items of expenditure taken into account in assessing entitlement to benefit.

In contrast, the housing allowance scheme is specifically designed to provide assistance towards rent, and is based on a correlation of income, family circumstances and rent. Moreover, as income rises, rebate entitlement is reduced by 17p in the pound. This tapered reduction means that the housing allowance scheme covers a much wider range of income (up to as much as £70 a week or more in some cases where there is a large family) than does the supplementary benefit scheme which works on a pound for pound basis. Furthermore, for administrative simplicity, the housing allowance scheme is based on *gross* income (i.e. before tax and other unavoidable deductions) and has a single prescribed range of needs allowances and of non-dependant deductions, with only the very minimum of income disregards.

The two schemes are kept in as stable a relationship as possible, with supplementary benefit and 'needs allowances' being uprated together, thus minimising 'the swing of the better buy'. However, a completely stable relationship is impossible to maintain because of basic structural differences in the two schemes. For example, while the 'income disregards' in the housing allowance scheme can be increased to keep them in line with those in the supplementary benefit scheme, this does not meet the whole of the problem. The balance of advantage can still swing back to supplementary benefit since claimants on this scheme benefit from the *whole* amount of the increases, while those in the housing allowance scheme benefit by only a *part* (because of the 'taper'). And, in all cases, changes in personal circumstances, in rent, in rates, or in supplementary benefit scale rates, can affect the balance of advantage.

This is a situation which can hardly be regarded as satisfactory (and it has already led to complaints to the Parliamentary Commissioner for Administration from those who have suffered through being wrongly advised on their 'better buy'). Unfortunately, the problem is insoluble while there are two such schemes which, though different in basis, overlap for some groups of tenants. The solution has to lie in a wider review of social benefits as a whole – which is currently under way. The issue is basically one for social security policy rather than for housing policy.

Added weight is given to this view by the fact that the housing allowance scheme has no specific housing policy objectives. Though it enables households to afford good housing it is not geared to bringing this about. This is in contrast with the US Experimental Housing Allowance Program, for example, where a primary objective is to facilitate the upgrading of housing conditions.[25] Cash assistance is dependent upon 'program housing standards' being met. In the British scheme a housing allowance is payable even if a household lives in a dwelling which is statutorily unfit for human habitation.

A major reason why housing costs cannot be adequately covered by social security schemes is that they vary so widely, not only between areas but between households in the same area. Flat-rate benefits obviously cannot cope with this problem: the housing costs element will, for many, be either far too high or far too low. In the former case the benefits will be extraordinarily costly and wasteful, while in the other case they will be inadequate and result in large-scale resort to other means tested benefits. This, indeed, is the rationale for the housing allowance scheme: it meets the specific problem of the variability in housing costs.

Some of the variability is, of course, due to differences in housing quality, but much of it is the result of previous housing policies and, crucially, of inflation. The solution, if one exists, lies partly in the area of housing policy (determining a rational system of rents) and partly in the area of counter-inflation policy. How far it is possible to make progress with the former in the context of current inflationary trends is highly problematic: the immediate problems of inflation are always likely to receive higher political priority than housing policy.

If this view is correct, then attention needs to be focused on making the housing allowance scheme more effective. Above all it needs to he simplified. At least part of the difficulty of publicising the scheme is that it is complicated to explain and to communicate. It presents real problems for potential beneficiaries in determining – or even knowing of – their eligibility. These problems are shared by the administrators of the scheme and those who try to give advice on it.

Simplification can be effected, however, only by making the scheme less finely discriminating. As with supplementary benefits, 'if claimants are to understand what rights they have, and how to secure what they are entitled to, the real need is not for the Commission to publish more and more detail about a complex system, but to seek to simplify its rules'.[26]

9 Housing Policy Questions

There is not a single significant aspect of the vast, diverse, and complex housing market that is not affected by governmental action in one form or another.

US Housing Policy Review, 1974[1]

There is much to learn

English Housing Policy Review, 1977[2]

EQUITY JOUSTS POLICY

This final essay does not purport to present 'conclusions', or to provide answers to the myriad of questions which have been raised earlier. Rather it attempts to draw together some of the major threads and to give a personal interpretation of the nature of a number of crucial current housing problems.

The heavy emphasis which is laid in the housing policy review on equity is notable. This, of course, is the very stuff of politics. Playing fair – or, at least demonstrating that one is trying to play fair – is part of the politicians' stock in trade. But the problem of placing equity in the foreground is that it leads on the one hand into a philosophical and mathematical impasse and, on the other hand, into a faint-hearted conservatism where the over-riding concern becomes that of avoiding offence to anyone. Equity 'flips' into its opposite: a defence of the existing inequitability.

The inequities of the current housing situation demand a radical redirection of policy. Yet radicalism, though very much in evidence when the housing policy review was mounted, is strikingly absent from the outcome. One possible explanation lies in the difficulty of minority government, but the issue goes deeper. The fact is 'the decisions and family budgets of millions of households have been shaped by the expectation that existing arrangements will continue in broadly their present form'.[3] Given such an approach, and the politically delicate task of increasing consumer housing costs in a period of over-riding consideration for income restraint, the case for retaining the *status quo* becomes all too attractive to governments.

144   *Essays on Housing Policy*

Added support for inaction is provided by the intense political controversy which has developed in recent years on the relative financial benefits accorded to council tenants and owner-occupiers. It was not so long ago that arguments on subsidised housing were largely confined to the public sector; but now that tax reliefs (and option mortgage subsidies) have become so important, it is not easy for a government to reduce council house subsidies without at the same time reducing the parallel benefits given to owner-occupiers – particularly since they also benefit directly from inflation.

It is significant that the arguments about equity are predominantly focused on the relative advantages accruing to council tenants and owner-occupiers. These two tenures not only form the majority of the electorate: they also have strong and articulate institutional supporters (local authorities, building societies and the house-building industry). There is no similar spokesman for the privately rented sector, even though this sector presents some of the most acute problems with which housing policy should be concerned.

Against this background, it was entirely predictable that the housing policy review should conclude with minimal proposals for change in the two main sectors and for 'further studies' of the privately rented sector.

POLICIES, MARKETS AND HISTORY

Much of the difficulty attendant upon the formulation of housing policy is that housing differs from other areas of social policy (such as health or education) in the extent to which it operates within a market context. In Britain as a whole, the various private sectors constitute over two-thirds of the total and, though there have been major shifts in the balance between private renting and private owning, the public sector grows proportionately quite slowly: indeed, since 1971 it has grown by only one percentage point. The contrast with the private provision of school places or hospital beds, where there is a near public monopoly, is striking.

Thus, like it or not, governments have to have regard for market behaviour to a far greater extent than is the case with other social services (even though, as is argued later, much of this 'market behaviour' is heavily influenced by government 'interventions'). Other things being equal, an increased demand for owner-occupied housing means less demand for council housing; or (perhaps more apparent) a fall in the availability of funds for house purchase leads would-be house purchasers to turn to the public sector. Policies affecting the privately rented sector similarly can (and do) increase the demand for public sector housing. Since central government has little control over the 'allocation' of council housing, some of this demand is not met by local authorities, and so government creates or adapts other institutions (for example the Scottish Special Housing Association and the Housing Corporation) as a complement (not compliment!) to local government.

In areas where the physical housing shortage is small or non-existent (as is the case in an increasing number of areas) shifts in demand can take place from the public to the private sector, leaving local authorities with an increasing vacancy rate. Policies directed towards increasing council rents can accelerate this. (Some part of the increased demand for private housing in 1972–3 may well have stemmed from the fears of council tenants at the level of rents they would have to pay as a result of the passing of the 1972 Housing Finance Act.) Since house-building rates are slow to react to increased demand, an upsurge in demand for house purchase can result in a rapid inflation of house prices with consequential effects on land prices, land planning, policies for prices and incomes, the amount of tax relief for mortgage interest payments, option mortgage subsidies, and public sector borrowing for house purchase financing.

Changes in interest rates can affect the balance of demand for various tenures (witness the collapse of cost-rent housing association activity in the late sixties). Generous rent rebates and rent allowances may deter potential house buyers from moving into owner-occupation.

The point need be laboured no further (though the list could be lengthened considerably): given the division of housing supply into public and private sectors (not to mention the way in which each is subdivided by such things as quality, security of tenure, and cost), *any* housing policy will have differential effects through the housing system – and often of an unpredictable character.

This is one reason why 'comprehensive' housing policies are constantly being sought by governments. Yet, so far, such policies have proved elusive. Historically the reason is that (again unlike other social services) government involvement in housing has evolved slowly, unsteadily and erratically, and often in contradictory ways. This is not to imply a high degree of rationality and consistency for other areas of social policy; it is simply to point out that the nature of the involvement has been different. Moreover, while there has never been any serious question that health or education *is* a social service, with housing there has been a long-drawn-out debate as to whether it is, or the extent to which it is or should be, and what implications follow from the alternative answers.

The differences should not be exaggerated, however.[4] Actions speak louder than words and, for most of the time, successive Labour and Conservative governments have followed the same programmes (differing only in emphasis) of, for example, building council houses, encouraging owner-occupation and protecting private tenants. Typically, the approach has been incremental – gradually building upon the past and only rarely demolishing it. As a result 'housing policy' is arguably more a matter of history than of conscious design. (Again the contrast with policies in other areas – such as a comprehensive health service and 'secondary education for all' – is striking.)

It is difficult to move from positions which are historically determined, and the big battles of British housing policy have taken place only when attempts were made to do precisely this – as with the 1957 Rent Act and the 1972 Housing Finance Act. The latter can be used to illustrate the argument here being put forward.

By the end of the sixties, there was general political agreement that some major changes were needed to 'reform' housing policy. In particular, the two contending parties seemed to be in basic agreement on the need for a national scheme of housing allowances (for public and private tenants), for some recasting of public sector subsidies and, perhaps, for some 'harmonisation' of the benefits accruing to tenants and house purchasers. But the abrogation (in the English Housing Finance Act) of the longstanding power of local authorities to fix their rents and the imposition of externally determined 'fair rents' was too big a change (and arguably far too blunt an instrument for the purpose). It aroused bitter feeling and social division in a field where the trend had been towards a consensus solution. Inevitably the Labour Party immediately pledged itself to repeal the hated Act and to give back to local authorities their freedom to settle their own rents. Interim legislation in 1975 fulfilled this pledge. It was to be followed by a long-term measure which would be worked out on the basis of a comprehensive housing finance review.

Unfortunately, the review had hanging over it the long cloud of the aftermath of the 1972 Act. A precarious Labour government moved slowly and eventually (in June 1977) produced a housing *policy* review, the hallmark of which is gradualism. The change of the title of the review (from 'finance' to 'policy') underlines the modesty of the financial proposals.

There is more than one possible interpretation, but the one submitted here is that 'the lesson of Clay Cross' had been learned. British housing policy is to revert to its more traditional Fabian character. The positive advantage is that the proposals are likely to be acceptable to whatever government follows the present one, but the tragedy is that the basic weakness of the present patchwork of separately evolved policies will remain. The fundamental problems have not been solved: they have been bypassed.

The political difficulty is that a more rational and equitable system would involve gains for some and losses for others; and the present system is so complex and haphazard that it is impossible to predict who would gain and who would lose under any new arrangements.

THE LOTTERY

Indeed, so complex and haphazard is the system that it bears some of the characteristics of a lottery. The price actually paid by any particular householder can depend on the tenure of his house, the date he happened to move into it, the attitudes of the local authority, the history of house building, economic fortunes and politics in the area, and a wide range of similar factors.

For an owner-occupier the most important influence on his current costs is the date on which he purchased his house. Forty-five per cent own their houses outright and therefore have no mortgage repayments (and hence no tax relief). Mortgagors will be making repayments related to prices obtaining at the date of purchase. (In 1973 half had mortgages less than four years old.)[5] They receive option mortgage subsidy or tax relief on their interest payments, and the real cost of their repayments falls as their money incomes rise with inflation. With the normal annuity mortgage (under which the capital repayment increases each year while the interest element falls), the tax relief benefit declines.

A move to another house is easy since it can be financed in part from the sale of an existing house. Whether a 'capital gain' is thereby obtained is a highly arguable point,[6] but there is no question that once entry has been obtained to the owner-occupied sector there is a real benefit in terms of a hedge against inflation and ease of movement to another owner-occupied house.

Moves within the owner-occupied market form a significant and growing proportion of house purchase transactions (two-fifths in 1971; a half in 1976).[7] On moving, owner-occupiers finance a major part of their new purchase with the 'cash proceeds' of the previous sale, and they obtain tax relief or option mortgage subsidy on their new loan. The importance of this is that the financial benefit is transferable to a new house (and, indeed, can be increased if, for example, there is trading up).[8] On the other hand, a move involves heavy conveyance expenses,[9] stamp duty on those above £15,000 (this returned to the Exchequer some £45m. in 1975-6), and value added tax on the fees of solicitors and estate agents (producing around £20m. in 1975).[10]

It can also be argued that owner-occupiers (or at least those who own their houses outright) benefit from the absence of tax on the 'imputed income' they receive from ownership (and which, had they been tenants, they would have had to pay in rent). A further argument is that since a house purchaser obtains tax relief on mortgage interest repayments, the absence of a charge on imputed rent constitutes a benefit which is not shared by tenants (whose rent is not allowable for tax). These are highly debatable points on which strong differing opinions are held.[11]

Owner-occupiers who are not in employment are eligible (as are all households) for supplementary benefit on a test of means. In 1975 some 390,000 owner-occupiers received such benefit, of which about 100,000 were mortgagors.[12] In assessing benefit only the 'rent' element of their payments is allowed: i.e. mortgage interest, rates and an allowance for repairs; but not capital repayment.

Many of the benefits received by owner-occupiers cannot be quantified, but the total (UK) amount of option mortgage subsidy and tax relief was £957m. in 1975–6: an average of £174 per mortgagor, or £96 per owner-occupier.[13] The estimate for 1976–7 is £1,240m. (By contrast the figure for 1965–6 was £135m. in current prices and £355m. in 1976 survey prices.)[14]

As with owner-occupiers, council tenants receive some subsidies which are clearly such and others which are only arguably so. In the first class are the direct Exchequer and rate-borne housing subsidies, which in 1975–6 amounted to £1,066m.[15] These subsidies are pooled over the local authority stock and average £173 per dwelling.[16]

Additionally, local authority tenants are eligible for rent rebates and supplementary benefits. Owing to the confused position on the allocation of expenditure between the Supplementary Benefits Commission and local authorities for tenants eligible for either of these benefits, it is not always clear to what the published figures refer.[17] (This is one of the tidying-up operations proposed in the housing policy review: the rent element in supplementary benefits is to be met in full by the Supplementary Benefits Commission.) It appears that in 1975–6 the total cost of rent rebates was £256m.[18] Averaged out over *all* council tenants this amounted to £41 per household.[19] For those actually receiving rebates, however, it was £152.[20]

The actual rents paid by council tenants and the amount of rebate received by individuals varies according to the rent policy of the local authority and the history of council house building in the area.[21] Average unrebated rents (in England and Wales) rose by 107 per cent between 1970 and 1976: from £2·30 a week to £4·77 in 1976. Rebated rents rose by 85 per cent from £2·27 to £4·19.[22]

Pooling is the crucial feature of the finance of council housing. Whereas an individual owner-occupier pays for his house in terms of its historical costs, council tenants pay in terms of the pool of historical costs of all council houses in their area. Thus both pay in relation to the cost of supply, but in very different ways.

One of the effects of this is that for a long-established household the buyer has falling costs while the renter faces rising costs. The corollary is that while the first-time house purchaser pays current prices, the first-time council tenant pays a pooled historical cost.[23] Thus while (rebated) council rents rose by 85 per cent between 1970 and 1976, net outgoings of first-time purchasers (after deducting tax relief) increased by between 159 and 190 per cent.[24]

The pooling of local authority rents implies, of course, a total account (the housing revenue account) for each local authority in which rent income and subsidies balance loan charges and other costs. The larger is the injection of subsidies, the smaller are the rent increases needed to balance the account; and, of course, vice versa. Since it has been policy (in relation to prices and incomes rather than to 'housing') to restrain rent increases, while costs and interest rates have escalated, subsidies have mounted – from £401m. in 1972–3 to £1,322m. in 1975–6 (UK figures).[25] In England and Wales the proportion of costs in the housing revenue account met by unrebated rents fell from 77 per cent in 1972–3 to 57 per cent in 1975–6. (Net of rebates they fell from 69 per cent to 45 per cent.)[26]

These are all 'real' figures in the sense that no notional benefits comparable to imputed income and capital gains are included. There is an argument which holds that 'subsidies' should be defined as the difference between market prices and the prices actually paid, but this is an elusive concept which is extremely difficult to translate into actual figures.[27] There can be little doubt, however, that any calculation would produce a level of 'subsidies' considerably higher than those already quoted.

It is abundantly clear that any comparison between the financial benefits received by owner-occupiers and council tenants would be a hazardous undertaking (and to extend it to private tenants would be virtually impossible). The reasons are partly technical and partly conceptual: but, most important of all, 'any comparison involves judgements about whether or not to include in the balance sheet large and contentious items – for example, the absence of a tax on "notional income" from home ownership, and the use of historic costs rather than market values in setting council rents. There is no objective basis for deciding these questions.' So concluded the housing policy review.[28]

Nevertheless, there is extensive public debate on the current level of subsidies (and rightly so, given the huge scale of expenditure). Yet one is beset with the difficulties of comparing two unlike goods. If houses were like television sets or cars it would be possible to make a valid comparison of renting and buying: but they are not. Of particular importance is the fact that houses have a very long life and usually maintain their value (and, at least in the postwar years, have increased their value significantly). It is the *personal* right to this which owner-occupiers buy: for tenants the increased values are pooled and used to reduce rents below current supply level.

In short, valid comparisons are conceptually difficult, involve ambiguities, necessitate impossible calculations and are thoroughly suspect. Nevertheless, even though the search for equity is troublesome, it remains an important ingredient of policy; and there is certainly an important question as to whether the current level of financial aid to housing is justified. There is, however, the even more important issue of the extent to which the vast amount of aid is serving desirable objectives: questions of equity would not loom so large if it were generally felt that it was serving some good purpose.

When matters reach the complexity, confusion and haphazardness of British housing policy, it is helpful to raise simple questions. Though they may lead to complicated answers (and politically impracticable policy changes) they do have the advantage of promoting some clarity of thought and, hopefully, of pointing the directions along which incremental changes might be directed. Given the incredible confusion of the housing subsidy position, the relevant 'simple' question relates to the purpose of subsidising housing.

THE PURPOSE OF HOUSING SUBSIDIES

One common purpose of a subsidy is to promote greater consumption of the subsidised good. There are others, of course, such as to promote employment in the sector producing the subsidised good, or to protect home industries against foreign competition. So far as housing is concerned there can be additional objectives such as to encourage population to move to new towns, to retain population in areas of high land costs, to promote certain types of uneconomic building (such as stone cottages in national parks), or to restrain wage demands. All these, however, are not so much 'housing' objectives as physical or economic planning objectives.

More specific 'housing' objectives may be to secure an adequate supply of mortgage funds, or to achieve a better utilisation or maintenance of the stock, or to promote experimental building forms. These, however, are supplementary objectives which (certainly in cost terms) are of minor importance relative to the major one of enabling, encouraging or even forcing people to consume more housing. In the words of the housing policy review:

> The annual cost of a typical new house has always been high in relation to average income – currently it is equal to about one-third of average earnings of male manual workers. By meeting a proportion of housing costs, general assistance enables a larger number of households to afford houses built or improved to acceptable contemporary standards without recourse to assistance based on individual tests of income and family circumstances. It makes possible higher housing standards than would otherwise be attained. It enables the provision of houses of good standard to be maintained in the face of increases in house prices and construction costs relative to incomes, and increases in interest rates.[29]

This is the case for what the review curiously calls 'general assistance'

– assistance given 'without regard to an individual householder's ability to pay': public authority housing subsidies (other than rent rebates), tax relief on mortgage interest payments and option mortgage subsidy. In 1975–6 the total cost of this 'general assistance' was £2,023m. Of this, £1,066m. went to public sector tenants and £957m. to owner-occupiers.

Accepting for the moment the distinction between 'general' and other forms of financial aid, one is prompted to inquire whether over 2,000 million pounds a year is not rather a large sum to allocate to such a nebulous purpose in such a haphazard way. Moreover, is the *housing* objective an appropriate one in the 1970s? Would it not be more effective to transfer the resources to income support and free it from particular forms of tenure? Arthur Lewis has trenchantly commented:

> If the government simultaneously abolished housing subsidies and cut working-class taxation by an annual amount exactly equal to the subsidies the working classes would be no worse off financially; but they would then without any doubt prefer to spend the money in other ways than on housing, and would live in overcrowded and inadequately provided houses, some because they do not know the advantages of better housing, and others because they value these advantages too lightly in comparison with other ways of spending their money. That is the case, and the only case for housing subsidies, and it is put here in its crudest form because the matter is so often discussed in left-wing literature without facing reality.[30]

The extreme form in which this is put should not distract attention from the crucial issue posed; and, though it now appears somewhat dated, it is given a new relevance by the currently high rates of tax and the low tax threshold. (For a married couple with two children the starting point of income tax liability as a percentage of average weekly earnings was 210 in 1938–9 but 46 in 1976–7.[31]

Clearly this takes us into a very much broader area of taxation, social benefits and the distribution of income – which is where the basic problems now lie. The effect of the 'general assistance' has been to hold housing expenditure fairly constant as a proportion of household disposable income (around 8 per cent). Without it, the proportion would have increased by over three percentage points (to 11·3 per cent).[32]

This has been the success for the government's *incomes* policy, but it poses severe problems for *housing* policy since, by protecting households from increased costs, the gap between costs and prices widens, and it becomes increasingly difficult to reverse the trend. In Craven's words, 'the widening of the gap has been built into the system; the wider that gap, the sharper would have to be any rent increases to narrow it, and the longer it would take to effect any appreciable change. Continuing political controversy has been institutionalised.'[33] This applies equally to the owner-occupied sector though here it is inflation which has had the twofold effect of reducing the real costs to established house purchasers and increasing the tax relief and option mortgage subsidy to new buyers.

So far as council tenants are concerned, it is clear that the purpose of housing subsidies has changed. They were originally introduced as a means of enabling poorer people to live at the standard of housing which was considered to be socially desirable. Today, they play a much wider role in incomes and social security policy. They are part of the 'social wage' (which was estimated to add £20 a week to the 1975–6 wage packet); and the Labour government's 'rent freeze' was an explicit and important part of the 'social contract' with the trade unions.[34]

An equivalent issue arises in relation to owner-occupiers: it is now argued that mortgage interest tax relief cannot be considered except in the context of the tax system as a whole. In the words of the housing policy review, 'any allowance or relief that can be set against total income before tax can be criticised as "regressive" when the tax is levied on a graduated scale: but the total impact of the British system of income tax is highly progressive'.[35]

The emergence of incomes and tax policies into the field of 'housing policy' has created extraordinary confusions of means and ends. Housing policy has aimed at improving housing conditions and, by extending 'general assistance' to all classes (intentionally to the public sector, accidentally in the owner-occupied sector) standards and aspirations have risen. This stimulated demand has been continued during the period of inflation by the simple counter-inflation expedient of increasing subsidies.

This, however, is to accept the distinction between 'general assistance' and means tested assistance. The concept of 'general assistance' is a new one, introduced in the housing policy review. It excludes supplementary benefits to council tenants and owner-occupiers, and rent rebates to council tenants. Since only a very small proportion of owner-occupiers receive supplementary benefit (less than 4 per cent of the total, and less than 2 per cent of mortgagors),[36] whereas over two-fifths of local authority tenants receive either supplementary benefit or rent rebates, the inclusion of these benefits makes a major difference to any comparison between the two sectors. It is therefore of crucial importance to the 'equity' argument.

There is no profit to be gained, however, in following this line of analysis. The concept of general assistance is a phoney one. It has been concocted as a beguiling means of justifying the *status quo*. It provides governments with some apparent rationale for continuing an irrational syste r.

The conclusion is thus that housing subsidies can no longer be regarded as such: they are part of a complex assembly of income and tax benefits. Any attempt to 'rationalise' subsidies must therefore be conceived within a wider reorganisation of income, tax and social security benefits.

This of course is a horrendously difficult task, as is no doubt painfully apparent to those involved in the current review of income maintenance policies.[37] Moreover, even though inadequate incomes (and the unequal distribution of incomes) may be the basic problem, it unfortunately does not follow that income support policies can meet 'the housing problem'. Though this could sensibly be a long-term objective, in fact the designing and operating of an income support policy raises such extreme difficulties that it is highly unlikely (certainly in the foreseeable future) to be effective in disposing of even that part of the housing problem which is theoretically a function of inadequate incomes. The concept of inadequacy (like that of poverty)[38] is a relative one which is determined by the average standard of living and the distribution of incomes. The attainment of adequacy therefore implies an income redistribution policy which brings about greater equality of incomes. There is abundant experience of the practical and political problems attendant upon this.[39]

The difficulties are not solely of direct money incomes: as taxation and direct controls bite into money payments, increasingly ingenious ways are found of obtaining (and giving) benefits indirectly.[40] At the extreme, 'fringe benefits' can become more important than 'income'. Indeed, housing benefits (such as employers' low-interest loans for housing, payment of removal and legal expenses, offsetting of 'losses' and so forth), form one vehicle for the translation of earnings into fringe benefits. Of course, governments can attempt to control and tax these (as the increasingly complex taxation provisions illustrate), but the difficulties of dealing with profit-motivated human ingenuity are great if not insoluble.

Moreover, even if ways were found of tuning controls to the required degree of fineness (and of enlisting the support of a fickle electorate for their introduction and operation), one would still be left with the difficulty of coping with the huge variations in individual housing costs. If these variations simply reflected differences in housing location, quality and similar factors, there might be some theoretical way of dealing with them. But they also reflect history: the price an individual pays for his housing is greatly affected by the level of costs (and of the policies) ruling at the time when he first entered the housing market, by his luck in the housing lottery, and by the way in which his personal housing history has been affected in inflation. For an owner-occupier the crucial factor is the date when he purchased his first house. For the council tenant it is the history of local authority house building in the area. There is no way in which these differences can be ironed out, unless a viable system for indexing all housing costs could be devised.

We are thus forced to the conclusion that whatever might be done by way of income redistribution and income support policies, there would still remain a problem which can be met only by some type of housing subsidy. The aim should be to design this to achieve equity and efficiency. The fact that both equity and efficiency are elusive and controversial concepts does not detract from their importance: it merely underlines the political nature of the problem.

In the light of the housing policy review it does not need to be stressed that any policy has to be politically acceptable if it is to work. The basic weakness of that review was that the government came to the conclusion that *no* significant change would be acceptable. The practical alternative would have been to redirect policies in the direction of greater equity and efficiency. This, of course, is to submit a personal political judgement in opposition to that which carried the day. The attempt which is made in the following pages to justify the alternative in no way alters this. The objective is to assist in opening up for political debate the crucial issues which the housing policy review circumvented.

DIRECTIONS OF POLICY

Foremost among these issues is the question of the amount of resources which are to be devoted to housing. This is a fundamental political question to which discussions on housing policy should be directed. It cannot, of course, be answered solely by reference to housing matters: on the contrary, the question could be more helpfully reformulated in terms of the relative priority of resource allocation to housing as compared to other areas.

The question admits of no easy answer. If there were such a thing as a 'market' separate from the social framework within which it exists the position would be different. One could then assess market demand for housing (and all other 'goods' as well) and inflict 'distortions' on the market to the extent that these were considered necessary in order to meet 'political' objectives such as reducing the total call on resources or increasing the 'effective demand' of groups who are perceived as being unable to obtain housing of a standard considered to be socially acceptable.

The reality is different. The abstraction of the 'market' which is isolated for study by economists operates within a social framework within which 'politics' is pervasive. The multitude of ways in which governments affect housing behaviour (of demanders, suppliers and intermediaries) is manifest in the discussion in earlier essays. To take the resultant 'demand' as an indicator of the resources to be devoted to housing nationally is to indulge in circular reasoning.[41]

This is not to deny the validity of simple economic propositions, nor to suggest that governments could wield the complex of social institutions in a coherent and harmonious manner to achieve agreed objectives. The impossibility of the latter is clear from the early discussion; the reality of the former is self-evident: people will tend to consume more housing if it is cheap than they will if it is expensive. The problem facing Britain is that housing generally has become too cheap. There is therefore an enhanced demand to which governments have responded by making it even cheaper.

This was not intentional: much blame lies with inflation and with policies directed towards combating it. The result, for owner-occupiers, has been a marked decline in the costs borne by those who already have obtained housing and a widening gap between these actual costs and those facing new entrants to the owner-occupied sector. Since there has been no politically acceptable way of increasing the charges for existing owner-occupiers, the 'logical' policy has been to reduce the costs to be borne by new entrants – by reducing standards, by extending subsidies by way of option mortgages and (as proposed in the housing policy review) by new 'savings bonus and loans schemes' for first-time purchasers.

In the public sector the advantages of inflation have been pooled and, in order to keep rent increases to acceptable levels, massive subsidies have been paid to offset inflated costs. In the privately rented sector, housing costs (to tenants) have been held down by the simple mechanism of control (with some mitigation to landlords facilitated by the housing allowance scheme.

The 'housing crisis' continued nevertheless, and governments felt politically unable to accept at face value the increasing statistical evidence that the overall quantitative shortage had been met, and that more sensitive and focused policies were required both in relation to needy households and in relation to the older housing stock. Partly this was due to a justifiable scepticism about the validity of statistical calculations (and sheet disbelief that things really were getting so much better – particularly when issues such as homelessness forced themselves to the forefront of political debate). Probably of particular importance, however, was the political difficulty of selling to the articulate housing lobbies the idea that the general housing situation and the inflationary forces both pointed to less priority for housing in general, and for housing subsidies and new house building in particular.

The case for lower subsidies (to both council tenants and owner-occupiers) is that they are not needed on the present scale, that they have harmful effects in overstimulating housing demand, and that they unnecessarily increase the tax burden. There is a snowball effect here in that, if the majority of existing householders have low housing costs there is a strong political demand for subsidising new households. And so the costs borne by the housing consumer get further and further out of line with real costs. The gap is bridged by taxes which, of course, are levied on the same electorate. It is impossible to trace the redistributive effects of all this, though there have been heroic (and highly suspect) attempts to do so.[42] In truth, the system has become unmanageably complex and wasteful. Above all it fails to provide the scale of assistance required for the really needy. However successful it may have been in politically satisfying the separate interest groups (owner-occupiers, council tenants and protected private tenants) it has failed to meet housing policy objectives. Indeed, in some ways it has increased housing problems, above all by starving the privately rented sector of commensurate or even adequate support and thus diverting demand to the heavily subsidised owner-occupied and public authority housing sectors to which there is restricted access for many who were at one time served by the private landlord.

It has also concentrated attention on new building and has diverted resources from the maintenance and improvement of the existing stock. This is not to ignore improvement grants (and repair grants), but the high level of subsidies being devoted to reducing consumer housing costs has meant that very high improvement grants have been necessary to make improvement sufficiently competitive. If unimproved housing is heavily subsidised, improved housing has to be even more so.

Another implication of this is that housing is deteriorating at an unnecessarily high rate, and will continue to do so while the costs of the new are so heavily subsidised. This is one factor (though not the only one) in the growth of 'difficult to let' estates.

The very fact that the housing policy review proposes the extension of repair grants is illustrative of the point: the present system does not enable sufficient resources to be devoted to the upkeep of existing housing.

The case for a reduction in house building is essentially that demographic trends are reducing the growth in need. With a zero population increase (to be followed by a modest rate of growth) coupled with a low rate of household formation, there is simply not the need for new building on the scale of recent years.

All these arguments point to the desirability of a major shift in policy towards increasing consumer housing costs and concentrating resources on stock management and assistance to the needy. New building will still be required, of course, for (the reduced rate of) new household formation, for internal migration and for replacement; and this will be much higher in some areas than in others. It follows that 'housing policy' should be much more locally oriented in the future than it has been in the past. Hopefully, this can be achieved through the new housing plans system which is discussed later in this essay.

Local housing policies can be effective, however, only if central government establishes an appropriate framework. To reiterate, the priority must be to establish a fairer and more efficient system of housing finance; and this implies less 'general assistance' for many and more specific assistance for the needy. How far this can be done by way of housing allowances is not clear but, until wider income maintenance policies have been reformed (in a co-ordinated manner) it seems to constitute the only viable way forward – particularly if an extension (and simplification) of the system were accompanied by major increases in family allowances. The latter would provide some shield against the widespread extension of means testing. This is an explicit concern of the present government, though here again all is not clear. Given the desirability of concentrating assistance where it is most needed, is it not inevitable that there should be more means testing? And, if this is considered to be undesirable, is it not a lesser evil than the one which it can solve?

MEANS TESTING AND SOCIAL POLARISATION

The dislike of a 'much greater reliance on income testing' was one of the arguments put forward in the housing policy review against a reduction in the 'general assistance' provided by Exchequer subsidies, tax relief and option mortgage subsidy. This, however, is a political stance which, though historically understandable, is outdated. More important is the question whether increased means testing for rent rebates might eventually lead to the movement out of the public sector of the higher income groups, particulary those who are attracted by the inherent advantages of home ownership and the subsidies which are available in that sector (as well as the new benefits for first-time buyers proposed in the housing policy review – a 'savings bonus' and a five-year interest-free loan of £500).[43] Moreover, to the extent that new 'alternative forms of tenure' develop, they also may attract higher income tenants to move out of the council sector. All this could change the function of council housing into a sector which caters predominantly for the poor and disadvantaged.

Evidence is so far slender. The housing policy review concluded that 'if social polarisation between tenures has occurred then it must have happened locally not nationally, or in terms of social distinctions too fine to be picked up' by the simple five socio-economic classifications used in the analysis which was undertaken.[44] Strangely, no analysis over time was made of the changing pattern of incomes in different tenure groups, though the evidence was noted that 'the local authority sector contains a high and increasing proportion of households receiving supplementary benefit' and 'local authorities are taking into their tenancies increasing numbers of households who are vulnerable in the sense of not having the capacity to earn', particularly one-parent families and the unemployed.

Craven, however, has shown by an analysis of Family Expenditure Survey data, that 'the proportion of households in the bottom three income deciles who were council tenants rose from 26·3 per cent in 1963 to 41·1 per cent in 1972, an increase of over 50 per cent during the decade'.[45]

Quite apart from the 'social polarisation' issue, this could lead to serious financial problems in the public housing sector. Its ability to finance itself would fall to the extent that richer tenants leave and are replaced by poorer ones. The fear that this might happen (with the spectre of American public housing in the background) must act as a restraining influence on any policy directed at raising council house rents. Moreover, to quote further from Craven:

A policy of raising rents might have a number of other consequences as well. The cost of rebates to the taxpayer and ratepayers would go up significantly, so some of what they gain on rent swings would be lost on the rebates roundabout. And while it might be thought desirable that better off council tenants should buy their own homes, it is far more difficult to argue that the segregation of the poor in municipal housing estates is also desirable. This could lead to a sharpening of class divisions, which would make the further development of public housing policy even more vulnerable to irrational pressures in the future.

However, since each individual local authority must balance its own accounts, rents would rise differentially depending on the level of costs incurred in each local authority area. Costs are highest in the inner city areas, associated with costly site preparation and high land values. Yet it is in the city centres that the poorest element of the population forms the largest proportion of council tenants. Thus rents would have to increase most just in those areas where the council tenants are least able to pay them.

In short, public expenditure on housing is not as easily capable of being brought down simply by allowing council rents to rise in line with costs as is sometimes assumed.[46]

All this adds weight to the argument for a major reform of housing finance which would avoid these artificially induced problems. The fact that this is so difficult to get to grips with should not relieve governments of their responsibility to try. The housing policy review may have temporarily aborted, but it provides a base on which debate and inquiry can develop.

It could be argued that the aim should be to devise a housing finance system which is 'neutral' between tenures. In other words, there should be no 'secondary effects' which make one tenure financially more attractive than another. There are two objections to this approach.

First, since owner-occupation involves the purchase of an asset as well as the 'renting' of accommodation, it is difficult to see how a financial system could be devised which would make the two tenures 'equivalent'. Secondly, it may be desirable, as a matter of policy, to promote a particular tenure.

The case for positively promoting owner-occupation is frequently argued, though it is noteworthy that the housing policy review does not do so.[47] No doubt this was too big and sensitive a policy issue to debate at any length: the result would inevitably have given offence to too many.

The American housing policy review of 1973–4 (which makes a fascinating subject for a comparative study of the difficulties facing governments in coming to terms with housing policy) is less coy. The rationale of tax incentives to owner-occupation is argued to consist of:

the essential economics of the owner-occupancy form of tenure;
the additional real income and wealth brought into existence by homeowners;
the additional security afforded the population and the economy by a form of income – owner-occupied housing services – which
(1) does not melt or explode with ups and downs in the economy,
(2) gives individuals and families a reliable form of income with a substantial built-in inflation hedge in the face of economic change, and
(3) does not contribute to problems of escalation or stabilisation policy (as does rental tenure) in an economy which has not yet mastered the worldwide forces of inflation.[48]

To this argument can be added that of Baer who points to the comparison between the highly visible, contentious, grudgingly given, inflexible and cumbersome 'housing subsidies' to renters and the unstigmatised, backdoor, low-profile, popular and highly effective tax benefits to home buyers.[49]

The arguments are certainly not conclusive (nor comprehensive) but it would have been useful if the British housing policy review had raised such issues. At the same time there is the question of whether home ownership is of equal benefit to the poor as it appears to be to the better off, or how far its extension is even feasible. The American review is inconclusive but suggests a positive answer for many except the poorest.[50]

If this were to be the British conclusion, then a major objective of policy would be to assist lower income households in house purchase. Yet this would then raise further questions on the role of public authority housing and, eventually as in the USA, 'which of the poor shall live in public housing?' (to use the title of Roger Starr's perceptive article).[51] And so we move into wider and even more difficult areas of social stigmatisation and polarisation. As the quantitative housing shortage is transformed into a housing surplus, such more fundamental social questions become increasingly urgent (though no less difficult to tackle).

The problems can be seen most easily in the deteriorated areas of inner cities but also in relatively modern 'difficult to let' council estates. It is characterised by an increasing concentration of low-status social groups. The extent to which this aggravates problems of disadvantage is unclear;[52] and even more unclear is the direction in which policy should be directed. As the general housing position continues to improve, the difficulties are likely to increase; and the difficulties will perversely lead to additional demands for new building. Those able to move out of low-status areas will generate such an additional demand for new building. This in turn increases vacancy rates and thus adds to the forces creating neighbourhood deterioration.

The 'housing policy' failure is evident in the premature demolition of rejected and vandalised estates,[53] but social problems are not so easily 'cleared': indeed they can merely shift to another location – thus creating a new 'housing problem'.

These spatial aspects of housing are of crucial importance.[54] Increasingly, housing policy will be concerned with deterioration of neighbourhoods which, typically, will be the result of social and economic change rather than the reverse. In short, policy will need to concentrate on social and economic factors, not merely on physical structures.

That there is some awareness of this is evident from the changes in thinking on improvement policy which have been noted in an earlier essay. Yet political battles on such questions as the promotion of owner-occupation and the sale of council houses, or the pressures from local authority house-building bureaucracies, may lead to a stimulation of programmes which could exacerbate the problems of neighbourhood decline which (it is here argued) are the crucial ones with which policy should be concerned.

The small-scale community development projects initiated by the Home Office (but recently brought into the housing policy arena of the DoE) have now blossomed into *Policy for the Inner Cities* (to use the title of the 1977 White Paper). It is noteworthy that, though 'physical decay' is seen as one of the constituent problems, greater emphasis is placed on economic decline, social disadvantage and the problems of ethnic minorities.

Most of the problems are thus not 'housing' problems at all. Certainly they will not be solved by housing policies; indeed, as already suggested, housing policies may exacerbate them. It follows that housing policy should be a handmaiden of wider and more important policies. This would be nothing new: as earlier discussion has shown, housing finance policy in recent years has been a handmaiden of counter-inflation policy. The task is to change its master.

LOCAL HOUSING PLANS

It is in this context that the new system of housing plans and housing investment programmes assume particular importance.[55] In essence these require local authorities to consider the overall housing needs and resources of their areas and the contributions which can effectively be made by the various providers. On the basis of this comprehensive assessment, local authorities will decide what their particular contribution should be. This will be expressed in terms of a rolling programme of capital expenditure on new building, acquisitions, improvements, slum clearance and home loans.

This new conception of the role of local housing authorities has had a mixed reception. Some (including the present author) have seen it as a major breakthrough in a movement towards more comprehensive, flexible and sensitive local housing policies, with a minimum of central government interference.[56] Others have warned that it is likely to lead to a 'massive megabureaucratic structure', with a 'bonanza for the paper manufacturing industry, and the flight of real power to the centre'.[57]

The dangers are manifest: housing plans and housing investment programmes could degenerate into formal mechanistic presentations of data on population and household trends, housing and plumbing statistics, and forecasts of need which might be as unenlightening and as unmeaningful as many of the perfunctory analyses prepared for the old-style development plans (or the more sophisticated – but equally inadequate – analyses prepared for the new-style structure plans).[58] They could become elaborate justifications for claims on Exchequer resources with the result that much time and effort would be wasted by central and local government officials in arguing about the 'validity' of the statistics employed.

A more optimistic view would point to the character of the questions which the Scottish Development Department have listed as being relevant to housing plans. For example:

What is the effect of current allocation policy on the availability of public sector housing to different groups in the community?
What evidence is available to suggest an imbalance due to a shortage of houses in one tenure group compared to the demand, and what are the reasons for this?
To what extent is the effective demand for owner-occupation constrained by the availability of funds from private sector agencies?
What proportion of the public sector stock is proving 'difficult to

let' and abnormally unpopular, and what are the reasons for this? To what extent is there an imbalance between the location of housing and employment which generates abnormal travel-to-work journeys?[59]

It is this emphasis on the structure and operation of the various housing markets which holds out hope that the new system will prove an effective means of assessing and meeting housing needs.[60] Yet if, as is argued here, local housing policies should emanate from broader social and economic strategies this will not be enough. Nothing short of comprehensive community planning will suffice, though how far such a concept is practicable is uncertain. Indeed, so little is understood of the dynamics of social behaviour that those who grapple with the multiplicity of the inter-related problems may well despair.

What is called for is a range of local experiments, such as seems to be envisaged in the 'special partnership' arrangements heralded in *Policy for the Inner Cities*. One would have hoped, nevertheless, that there were some lessons to be learned from the earlier 'Making Towns Better' studies[61] and the three inner city studies in Birmingham, Liverpool and Lambeth,[62] not to mention the community development programme, the urban programme and the educational priority area programme.[63] Housing cannot be adequately considered in isolation: to use American terminology it is 'a bundle of commodities' of which a prime element is 'who is willing to live near whom'.[64] Social forces leading both to segregation of the poorest and to the deterioration of neighbourhoods is a result of the general easing of the housing situation, the subsidised choices for movement (particularly away from the inner cities) and the lack of service improvement in the deteriorating neighbourhoods. Here the range of jobs and the quality of the schools may be more important than any physical feature.

The problems can be exacerbated by racial prejudice, but it seems that social class is a more important determinant of segregation.[65] It follows that 'dispersal', however desirable in itself,[66] is no answer. 'Thus, if blacks felt free to exercise their legal rights in the housing market and were persuaded to integrate white neighbourhoods throughout all sections of metropolitan areas, racial isolation would obviously decline, but socio-economic isolation would increase as well-to-do blacks moved farther away from poor blacks'.[67]

Nevertheless, the implications of spatial separation and polarisation are neither self-evident nor clear.[68] The examination by the South East Joint Planning Team is illustrative.[69] It could hardly be expected that social polarisation would occur over such large areas as that of Greater London, however extreme it might be at particular places within Greater London. It is, therefore, not surprising that the team concluded that 'evidence of polarisation at the moment is either lacking or, at best, inconclusive'.[70] Hence they focused their discussion on the *concept* of polarisation.

Social polarisation is a strong force. People of similar economic position like to live near each other. In any case, the widespread desire for more space, fresher air and congenial surroundings, combined with differing income constraints inevitably leads to a degree of homogeneity. This is a positive force which both the private and the public sectors have accommodated on a large scale, with very real social benefit. This 'positive' social polarisation is, however, very different from the 'negative' polarisation which traps people in areas of cumulative disadvantage and lack of opportunity. Poor housing (by no means necessarily cheap), poor employment opportunities (with little opportunity for advancement), poor schools (or adequate schools lacking the social stimulus to educational achievement) all reinforce each other.

It is doubtful, however, how far the term 'social polarisation' is useful. Indeed, it may be positively unhelpful in that it may imply first, that there is something inherently bad about people living in socially homogeneous areas, and secondly, that the answer to the problem is some form of imposed social heterogeneity. Of course, since the concentration of disadvantage itself increases that disadvantage, the problems are compounded, but the root of these problems lies elsewhere.

Yet this is not all there is to the issue. Much of the confusion which characterises the debate on social polarisation emanates from a lack of agreement (or even clarity) on the geographical scale which is at issue. (Problems can be manufactured as well as hidden by the choice of particular boundaries.) There is a presumption – to put it no more strongly – that there is a scale of homogeneity which is problem-creating. (The problem relates, in practical terms, only to homogeneity at the lower end of the socio-economic scale. This is only to ignore – not to deny – the fact that 'too many' of the rich in a particular area may present its own problems, particularly of 'external relations': of comprehension and of willingness to contribute to the wider good.)

The threshold scale will differ: at one extreme will be 'problem families', while at the other will be 'the working classes'. In all cases, the threshold is that point at which social improvement is held back by the scale of the concentration. Put thus, it is apparent that dispersal is only part of the solution if the scale is large. Indeed, since dispersal is most probably selective it can itself lead those who are left behind to be further socially disadvantaged. To the extent that this is the case, the real answer must lie in increasing the opportunities *within* the socially homogeneous area. But can this be done without introducing more heterogeneity? If educational attainment, for example, is significantly restrained by the low-class social character of an area, is it possible to change the situation except by removing the constraints, i.e. by enticing higher social classes to move in? This is one important implication that can be drawn from the observation that 'the children of less-privileged parents have a greater chance of educational success and hence of social mobility when they go to schools which draw children from a wider range of social backgrounds than they would have if they were to go to schools which tap a segregated area'.[71] Careful determination of school catchment areas (even if democratically possible) obviously cannot be a solution where the scale of homogeneity extends beyond conceivable catchment areas. The alternative of 'bussing' (with all the social upheaval this causes) is limited in both practical and political terms, and, in any case, is a reflection of the inadequacy of earlier policies and, at best, a temporary solution.

The SEJPT report does not go so far (or at least is not so explicit) as to suggest attracting higher socio-economic groups into areas of low socio-economic status. It does, however, talk of 'social mix' and stresses the crucial importance of the future occupational structure. Logically, emphasis is also placed on the priority allocation of resources to education. But is this enough? And might it not be self-defeating? Policies (which are eminently desirable) aimed at facilitating social mobility may also (certainly on current experience) lead to geographical mobility. Those who climb the socio-economic ladder will aspire to the appropriate socio-economic areas. To the extent that they succeed, the social polarisation of the area they leave will, if anything, be increased. On the same line of argument, a 'socially improved' employment structure will hardly, *of itself*, attract higher status residents.

The alternative is housing development and environmental improvements aimed at attracting new residents. This is likely to be as popular with local authorities and their electorates as providing homes for incoming workers in areas of housing shortage. General experience of 'key workers' housing underlines the difficulty of providing houses for 'strangers' in areas where large numbers of 'locals' are in need of housing. Nevertheless, the scheme has had some success even in housing pressure areas since the employment benefits are clear. The situation is likely to be very different with a policy deliberately and explicitly designed to give some degree of priority to affluent strangers over poorer locals.

The Plowden Report underlined the complex of factors which produce seriously disadvantaged areas.[72] Of particular relevance to the argument being put forward in this essay is a reference to the need to attract teachers to live in these areas:

> Priority areas are not the kind of place where teachers normally live, yet those whose homes are near their pupils' can often do a better job than those who travel greater distances. They belong to the same community; they can understand their background better. What is more, the creation of vast one-class districts from which all pro-

fessional people are excluded is bad in itself. Sustained efforts ought to be made to diversify the social composition of the priority areas. Many professional workers feel the need to start buying a house early in their careers because mortgage terms may be more favourable, and because once they own a house it is easier for them to secure another if they move elsewhere. Their needs should be recognised by the housing and planning authorities. There should be a mixture of houses for renting, for owner occupation and for co-ownership and cost rent schemes run by housing associations . . .

The housing needs of families in badly overcrowded places are likely to be more urgent than those of teachers; but their children will not get the education they deserve if teachers are systematically excluded from the locality.[73]

The same point, in a wider context, was made in the Central Housing Advisory Committee's Report on Council Housing:[74] 'If the needs for education, health and other social and community services are to be adequately met, local authorities must ensure that those who man these services have opportunities of finding homes within the areas they serve . . . These needs must be the responsibility of local authorities, though actual provision may be met in a variety of ways.'

We must, however, heed Gans's warning that the planner has only limited influence over social action and that 'sizeable differences, especially with regard to fundamental social and economic interests, are not erased or set aside by the mere fact of living together'.[75] Nevertheless, two points need to be made. First, the experience of American cities, with their fragmented administrations and (by British standards) archaic tax systems, is not necessarily relevant to Britain. Secondly, Gans is referring particularly to social contacts and more particularly to heterogeneity at the very local ('block') level. He explicitly rejects the 'neighbourhood' both as a meaningful social unit ('since the significant face-to-face relationships occur on the block') and as a relevant unit (since 'it is not a political unit, and, thus, cannot make decisions about its population composition'). In the context of the current argument it is not this very local level which is relevant.

It is not necessary to go into the finer points of this debate to accept the major point: that a community which is so heavily *un*balanced that it is repellent to those needed for the community services of the area and to the potential local leaders suffers extreme cumulative deprivation which becomes increasingly difficult to ameliorate. Whatever the impracticability of attempting to achieve 'socially balanced' communities, there is a strong case for attempting to prevent highly *un*balanced ones.[76]

All who have wrestled with these problems have found them extremely difficult, both conceptually and pragmatically. A Marxist interpretation, laying emphasis on the impossibility of social justice in a capitalist society, provides no clue to practical programmes of reform,[77] though the analysis (when stripped of its more melodramatic embellishments) contains invaluable insights. Given the Fabian character of change in Britain and the uncertainties which abound, a more humble approach is indicated. As is the case in the USA, there is a need 'to structure ongoing programs in a way that would facilitate research and experimentation, so that it will be possible to resolve at least a few of the perplexing issues which divide those who are searching for solutions to our housing and community development problems'.[78]

INCREMENTALISM

The underlying theme of these essays is that only incremental change is practicable. It may be that an adequate housing policy review set in the proper context of a social policy review (encompassing incomes policy and questions relating to the distribution of incomes) might point to a rational and equitable future, but that is certainly beyond present horizons.

Thus one comes sadly to the conclusion that there is little alternative to something like the package of limited proposals of the nature of the 1975–7 housing policy review. This is not to support that particular package: on the contrary it is here argued that there are serious issues which the review shirked and which urgently require debate in order that incremental change can be devised in a desirable direction. The shortcoming is not that the proposals emanating from the review were modest but that they were wrongly conceived. Instead of attempting to develop policy changes appropriate to the current and emerging situation, appeasement of the largest number of relevant interests became the over-riding consideration.

The debate should now be focused on the alternative marginal changes which could be made and the objectives which they should serve. The debate must, of course, be a continuing one. Indeed, the idea of a specific housing policy review which could set the policy paths until some new crisis prompts a further review is totally inappropriate. Housing policy needs ongoing review and continuous marginal changes. The search for the holy grail should be abandoned in favour of a much more humble quest. The housing policy review was fated to disappoint because impossible expectations were raised. Rather than raise vain hopes again by the promise of an even wider review, it should be accepted that 'housing policy' cannot be a comprehensive, rational and consistent set of measures which achieve predetermined and articulated goals. The very term 'housing policy' can be misleading.

Thus, instead of seeking to attain the impossible, effort should be concentrated on experimentation and on promoting debate on achieving the possible – of identifying issues on which government policy should be concentrated, modified or abandoned, and seeking to establish the consequences (particularly those which are unintended) of current and proposed policies.

This is not to suggest that broader discussion of housing policy should be relegated to academic bywaters. On the contrary, there is a need for better informed and wider public debate. The point is that policy cannot be suspended until this debate is concluded: it will never be. It will continually evolve – and the issues which are considered as important will change as conditions and perceptions change. Today's 'agenda' will be as different from tomorrow's as it is from yesterday's.[79] In the final analysis, however, it will be broader social and economic forces which will determine the outcome of 'housing policy'.

Notes and References

References to the housing policy review volumes are abbreviated as follows:

HPC: DoE and Welsh Office, *Housing Policy: A Consultative Document*, Cmnd 6851.
HPT1: DoE and Welsh Office, *Housing Policy: Technical Volume, Part 1*.
HPT2: DoE and Welsh Office, *Housing Policy: Technical Volume, Part 2*.
HPT3: DoE and Welsh Office, *Housing Policy: Technical Volume, Part 3*.
HPCS: Scottish Office, *Scottish Housing: A Consultative Document*, Cmnd 6852.

All were published by HMSO in 1977.

INTRODUCTION

1 G. Sternlieb and J. W. Hughes, *Housing and Economic Reality: New York City 1976*, Center for Urban Policy Research, Rutgers University, 1976.
2 'Housing: roll up, roll up', *The Economist*, 25 February 1978.
3 H. Heclo and A. Wildavsky, *The Private Government of Public Money*, Macmillan, 1974, p. 361.
4 J. B. Cullingworth. *Housing in Transition*, Heinemann, 1963, p. 16.
5 M. Bowley, *Housing and the State*, Allen & Unwin, 1947, pp. 87–8.
6 E. J. Clearly, *The Building Society Movement*, Elek, 1965, and S. J. Price, *Building Societies – Their Origin and History*, Franey, 1958. For a short discussion of the lack of a comparable institution for landlords see A. A. Nevitt, *Housing, Taxrtion and Subsidies*, Nelson, 1966, ch. 3; and also M. Bowley, op. cit., pp. 88–93.
7 A. A. Nevitt, op. cit., p. 36.

1 THE INSTITUTIONAL FRAMEWORK

1 Cf. the parliamentary questions to the ministers concerned, e.g. to Defence on the housing of service families, when it was revealed that 81,228 service families were housed, in March 1977, in specially built houses and flats in Great Britain and that 12,639 service married quarters were vacant, of which 2,272 had been vacant for more than six months. (*HC Debates*, vol. 928, WA 437, 21 March 1977.)
2 In Scotland housing remained with the Department of Health until 1962 when the Scottish Development Department took this over together with town and country planning, and a number of functions from other departments – including roads, industry and electricity. A later reorganisation placed industry and electricity in the Scottish Economic Planning Department, together with certain transport functions and new towns. The object here was to organise 'economic development' policies in a co-ordinated department. The division between 'development' and 'economic planning' is a fine one but, given the size of the Scottish Office and its close internal (and informal) relationships, the precise division is of less practical significance than is the case with the much larger bureaucracies of Whitehall.
3 R. Clarke, 'The machinery of government', in W. Thornhill (ed.), *The Modernization of British Government*, Pitman, 1975, p. 85.

4 loc. cit. For further discussion of the organisation of the machinery of government see R. Clarke, *New Trends in Government*, HMSO, 1971; R. Clarke, 'The number and size of government departments', *Political Quarterly*, 1972, pp. 169-86; White Paper, *The Reorganisation of Central Government*, Cmnd 4506, 1970; and N. Johnson, 'Editorial: the reorganisation of central government', *Public Administration*, vol. 49, 1971.

5 See N. Johnson, 'Editorial: the reorganisation of central government', *Public Administration*, vol. 49, p. 5.

6 *A Joint Framework for Social Policies: Report by the Central Policy Review Staff*, HMSO, 1975.

7 See *Second Report of the Advisory Committee on Rent Rebates and Rent Allowances*, HMSO, 1977.

8 *HC Debates*, vol. 924, col. 1696, 27 January 1977.

9 Speech by R. Freeson, Minister of Housing and Construction, at the Bristol 'Save Our Cities' conference, 10 February 1977 (DoE Press Release No. 67). See also White Paper, *Policy for the Inner Cities*, Cmnd 6845, 1977.

10 For a discussion of the early history of attempts to establish a 'central planning authority' see the author's *Reconstruction and Land Use Planning 1939-1947* (Vol. I of *Environmental Planning 1939-1969*), HMSO, 1975, ch. 2.

11 See P. Draper, *Creation of the DoE: A Study of the Merger of Three Departments to form the Department of the Environment*, Civil Service Studies 4, HMSO, 1977.

12 Central Policy Review Staff, *Relations Between Central Government and Local Authorities*, HMSO, 1977, para. 5.1.

13 Cf. the attempts made by the Treasury to devise 'objective criteria' for comparing the cost of new and expanded towns and for valuing agricultural land. These are documented in the author's *New Towns Policy* (*Environmental Planning 1939-1969*, Vol. III, HMSO, forthcoming).

14 A nice illustration is the interdepartmental study on *Long Term Population Distribution in Great Britain*. This was commissioned in 1965 amid growing anxiety about the implications of the large population increase then forecast (some 20 million by the end of the century). By the time the study was published (in 1971) the population forecasts had been radically reduced and the problems to which it was addressed had changed. The introduction to the report commented that 'the study nevertheless brings together in one document a large body of data on demographic trends and the changing geographical distribution of the population . . . the government have authorised publication because of the great importance of the subject it covers and in the hope it may stimulate informed discussion'.

15 W. J. L. Plowden, 'Developing a joint approach to social policy', in K. Jones (ed.), *The Year Book of Social Policy in Britain 1976*, Routledge & Kegan Paul, 1977, pp. 39-40.

16 H. Heclo and A. Wildavsky, *The Private Government of Public Money*, Macmillan, 1974, p. 363.

17 B. Miller, 'Citadels of local power', *The Twentieth Century*, vol. 162, October 1957.

18 See the reports of the Central Housing Advisory Committee, particularly *Residential Qualifications*, HMSO, 1955 and *Council Housing: Purposes, Procedures and Priorities*, HMSO, 1969, ch. 4.

19 See J. B. Cullingworth, *Report to the Minister of Housing and Local Government on Proposals for the Transfer of GLC Housing to the London Boroughs* (2 vols), MHLG, 1970.

20 Greater London Council, *Strategic Housing Plan: Report of Studies*, GLC, 1974, p. 26.

21 HPC, para. 9.20, p. 79.

22 HPC, para. 6.04, p. 42.
23 See N. P. Hepworth, *The Finance of Local Government*, Allen & Unwin, 3rd edn, 1976, ch. VI.
24 *Local Government Finance* (Layfield Report), Cmnd 6453, 1976, p. 69.
25 op. cit., ch. 3.
26 E. Sharp, *The Ministry of Housing and Local Government*, Allen & Unwin 1969, p. 101.
27 Cf. G. W. Jones, 'Varieties of local politics', *Local Government Studies*, vol. 1, no. 2, 1975. For an extensive discussion, see D. N. Chester, *Central and Local Government*, Macmillan, 1951; West Midlands Study Group, *Local Government and Central Control*, Routledge & Kegan Paul 1956; J. A. G. Griffiths, *Central Departments and Local Authorities*, Allen & Unwin, 1966; Appendix 6 of the Layfield Report, *The Relationship Between Central and Local Government*, HMSO, 1976; R. J. Nicholson and N. Topham, 'Investment decisions and the size of local authorities', *Policy and Politics*, vol. 1, no. 1, September 1972; and N. Boaden, *Urban Policy Making*, Cambridge University Press, 1971.
28 *The Government's Expenditure Plans*, Cmnd 6721–I, 1977, para. 27. See also Layfield Report, op. cit.
29 HC 323 (1970–1), p. 86 (Q. 424).
30 White Paper, *Policy for the Inner Cities*, Cmnd 6845, 1977.
31 *The Times*, 10 February 1977.
32 *A Joint Framework for Social Policies*, op. cit., p. 5.
33 *Local Government Finance*, op. cit., p. 58.
34 See J. Stanyer, *Understanding Local Government*, Fontana, 1976, esp. ch. 10.
35 N. T. Boaden, *Urban Policy Making*, Cambridge University Press, 1971.
36 To use Anthony Crosland's term: M. Kogan, E. Boyle and A. Crosland, *The Politics of Education*, Penguin Books, 1971, p. 171.
37 Expenditure Committee, Thirteenth Report Session 1974–5, *New Towns*, Vol. I: Report, HC 616-I, para. 18.
38 Expenditure Committee, op. cit., para. 39.
39 J. B. Cullingworth, 'Some effects of planned overspill: a case study in the county borough of East Ham', *Journal of the Town Planning Institute*, vol. 46, 1959, pp. 8–13.
40 J. B. Cullingworth, 'Some administrative problems of planned overspill', *Public Administration*, vol. 37, Winter 1959, pp. 343–59.
41 J. B. Cullingworth and V. A. Karn, *The Ownership and Management of Housing in the New Towns*, HMSO, 1968.
42 Expenditure Committee, op. cit., Q. 1593 and p. 1012.
43 Regular statistics are published in the quarterly *Housing and Construction Statistics*.
44 See R. Thomas, 'Meeting minority interests', *Town and Country Planning*, January 1971; R. Thomas, *London's New Towns*, PEP, 1969; and 13th Report from the Expenditure Committee 1974–5, *New Towns*, pp. 90–2, 374–80, 408–44 and 444–73.
45 Department of the Environment, *New Towns: A Consultation Document*, DoE, 1974, para. 4.7.
46 Expenditure Committee, op. cit., *Report*, paras 43–5.
47 Greater London Council, *Report of the Town Development Committee*, 9 March 1977. A statement on the 'reappraisal' of the new towns programme was made in the House of Commons on 5 April 1977, *HC Debates*, vol. 929, col. 1110 *et seq.*
48 New Towns (Amendment) Act, 1976.
49 Department of the Environment, *Report of the Working Party on the Transfer of Rented Housing in New Towns*, DoE, April 1975, paras 5.0–5.1.
50 HPC, para. 9.29, p. 81. On the history of new town policy see the author's

New Towns Policy, Vol. III of the official history of environmental planning, HMSO, forthcoming. On the narrower housing issue, see J. B. Cullingworth and V. A. Karn, *The Ownership and Management of Housing in the New Towns*, HMSO, 1968.

51 White Paper, *Housing in England and Wales*, Cmnd 1290, 1961, para. 43.
52 Fourth Report from the Estimates Committee 1968–9, *Housing Subsidies*, Vol. II, HC 473-II, Q. 856.
53 See Central Housing Advisory Committee, *Housing Associations*, HMSO, 1971, para. 3.28.
54 Department of Health for Scotland, Circular 41/1958.
55 Fourth Report from the Estimates Committee, 1968–9, *Housing Subsidies*, HC 473-I (Report), p. 107.
56 See, for example, Socialist Commentary, 'The face of Britain: a policy for town and country planning', *Socialist Commentary*, September 1961.
57 White Paper, *A National Building Agency*, Cmnd 2228, 1963.
58 'Future activities of the National Building Agency: statement published 8th June 1967', repr. pp. 610–11 of the *Evidence to the Estimates Committee*, Fourth Report 1968–9, HC 473.
59 A nice committee example is that of the statutory Central Housing Advisory Committee which, by general agreement, had become otiose in the fifties. It staggered on until 1975 for the simple reason that governments were reluctant to expose a political flank by legislating for its abolition. By 1975, however, both political parties had had recent experience of it and it was quietly buried. (Housing Rents and Subsidies Act, 1975, section 13.) More generally the problem has given rise in the USA to a proposed 'sunset law' under which every government programme would periodically terminate unless (following an 'evaluation') Congress positively voted to continue it. On the sheer impracticability of 'this latest fad' see R. D. Behn, 'The false dawn of the sunset laws', *The Public Interest*, no. 49, Fall 1977, pp. 103–18.
60 See the Annual Reports of the Northern Ireland Housing Executive.
61 R. Greer, *Building Societies ?*, Fabian Society, 1974, p. 22
62 National Board for Prices and Incomes, Report No. 22, *Rate of Interest on Building Society Mortgages*, Cmnd 3136, 1966.
63 White Paper, *Help Towards Home Ownership*, Cmnd 3163, 1966.
64 M. Stone, 'The building societies come to terms with politics', *The Times*, 15 April 1977.
65 loc. cit.
66 But see G. Ashmore, *The Owner Occupied Housing Market*, University of Birmingham Centre for Urban and Regional Studies, Research Memorandum No. 41, 1975.
67 *Housing and Construction Statistics*, no. 19, 3rd quarter 1976, table 35.
68 HPC, para. 7.55, p. 65.
69 HPC, paras 7.62–7.64, p. 67.
70 See *Building Societies (Reorganisation and Nationalisation) Bill*, HC Bill 25, 1976; *HC Debates*, 4 March 1977; and also R. Greer, *Building Societies*, Fabian Society, 1974.
71 *Building*, 8 July 1977, p. 69.
72 Royal Institution of Chartered Surveyors, *Housing: The Chartered Surveyors' Report*, RICS, 1976.
73 British Property Federation, *Policy for Housing*, 1975.
74 M. Harloe, R. Issacharoff and R. Minns, *The Organisation of Housing: Public and Private Enterprise in London*, Heinemann 1974. p. 169.

2 HOUSING NEED AND DEMAND

1 G. Orwell, *The Road to Wigan Pier*, Secker & Warburg, uniform edn, 1959, p. 65.
2 *Housing*, Cmnd 6609, 1945.
3 L. Needleman, *The Economics of Housing*, Staples, 1965, p. 18.
4 Only a brief examination is possible (and appropriate) here. For further discussion see the author's *Housing Needs and Planning Policy*, Routledge & Kegan Paul, 1960, and 'Housing analysis' in S. C. Orr and J. B. Cullingworth, *Regional and Urban Studies*, Allen & Unwin, 1969 (on which the following section is based).
5 Census 1951, England and Wales, *Housing Report*, HMSO, 1956.
6 See D. Eversley, 'Demographic change and the demand for housing', in M. Buxton and E. Craven (eds), *Demographic Change and Social Policy: The Uncertain Future*, Centre for Studies in Social Policy, 1976.
7 See J. B. Cullingworth, *Housing Needs and Planning Policy*, Routledge & Kegan Paul, 1960, p. 17.
8 Office of Population Censuses and Surveys, *Population Projections 1975-2015*, HMSO, 1977. See also Central Policy Review Staff, *Population and the Social Services*, HMSO, 1977.
9 See e.g. D. Allnutt, R. T. S. Cox and P. J. Mullock, 'The projection of households' in *Projecting Growth Patterns in Regions (Statistics for Town and Country Planning*, series III, no. 1), Ministry of Housing and Local Government, 1970.
10 D. Allnutt et al., op. cit., p. 33.
11 See W. G. Grigsby, *Housing Markets and Public Policy*, University of Pennsylvania Press, 1963; W. E. Smith, *Filtering and Neighbourhood Change*, Center for Real Estate and Urban Economics, Institute of Urban and Regional Development, University of California, 1964; J. B. Lansing, C. W. Clifton and J. N. Morgan, *New Homes and Poor People: A Study of Chains of Moves*, Survey Research Center, Institute for Social Research, University of Michigan, 1969; C. J. Watson, *Household Movement in West Central Scotland: A Study of Housing Chains and Filtering*, University of Birmingham, Centre for Urban and Regional Studies, Occasional Paper 26, 1973. A succinct account is given in A. Murie, P. Niner and C. J. Watson, *Housing Policy and the Housing System*, Allen & Unwin, 1976, pp. 69-75. See also C. L. Leven, J. T. Little, H. O. Nourse and R. B. Read, *Neighborhood Change: Lessons in the Dynamics of Urban Decay*, Praeger, 1976.
12 A. E. Holmans, 'A forecast of the effective demand for housing in Great Britain in the 1970s', *Social Trends*, no. 1, 1970.
13 HPC, para. 3.05, p. 10.
14 *Housing and Construction Statistics*, no. 17, Table XVf, p. 80, and no. 19, table I, p. 69.
15 In the supplementary tables of *Housing and Construction Statistics*. See also HPC, p. 110.
16 See e.g. J. Greve, D. Page and S. Greve, *Homelessness in London*, Scottish Academic Press, 1971.
17 op. cit., p. 253.
18 *The Times*, 1 September 1976.
19 Greve, Page and Greve, op. cit., p. 247.
20 See R. Bailey, *The Squatters*, Penguin Books, 1973; and *The Homeless and Empty Houses*, Penguin Books, 1977.
21 See A. A. Nevitt, *Housing, Taxation and Subsidies*, Nelson, 1966; *Report of the Committee on Housing In Greater London* (Milner Holland Report), Cmnd 2605, 1965, pp. 37-43; and D. Eversley, 'Landlords' slow goodbye', *New Society*, 16 January 1975, pp. 119-21. For a brief, but useful discussion of the reasons for

the lack of investment in building for letting during the interwar years (when there was no rent control on new houses) see M. Bowley, *Housing and the State 1919–1944*, Allen & Unwin, 1945, pp. 86–93. A narrower view, which lays the blame (for this and many other things) squarely on rent control, is to be found in *Verdict on Rent Control*, Institute of Economic Affairs, 1972.

22 Society of Labour Lawyers, *The End of the Private Landlord*, Fabian Society, 1973.

23 See A. Murke, P. Niner and C. J. Watson, *Housing Policy and the Housing System*, Allen & Unwin, 1976, pp. 200–3 and 230–1.

24 Central Housing Advisory Committee, *Council Housing: Purposes, Procedures and Priorities*, HMSO, 1969, para. 444.

25 This section is a slightly amended version of pp. 49–55 of the author's *The Social Content of Planning (Problems of an Urban Society*, Vol. 2), Allen & Unwin, 1973.

26 Central Housing Advisory Committee, *Council Housing: Purposes, Procedures and Priorities*, HMSO, 1969, para. 53.

27 Op. cit., para. 118.

28 op. cit., para. 56.

29 B. Glastonbury, *Homeless Near A Thousand Homes: A Study of Homeless Families in South Wales and the West of England*, Allen & Unwin, 1971, p. 155.

30 J. Greve, D. Page and S. Greve, *Homelessness in London*, Scottish Academic Press, 1971, p. 247.

31 J. B. Cullingworth and C. J. Watson, *Housing in Clydeside 1970*, HMSO, 1971.

32 *Council Housing: Purposes, Procedures and Priorities*, op. cit., para. 96.

33 op. cit., para. 90.

34 op. cit., paras 92–5.

35 H. Street, *Freedom, the Individual and the Law*, Penguin Books, 1975, p. 295.

36 Quoted in Central Housing Advisory Committee, *Council Housing: Purposes, Procedures and Priorities*, HMSO, 1969, p. 41.

37 J. P. Macey and C. V. Baker, *Housing Management*, Estates Gazette, 2nd edn, 1973, p. 246.

38 See A. S. Hall, *The Point of Entry: A Study of Client Reception in the Social Services*, Allen & Unwin, 1974.

39 See I. Deutscher, 'The gatekeeper in public housing', in I. Deutscher and E. J. Thompson, *Among the People: Encounters with the Poor*, Basic Books, 1968.

40 See M. Harloe, *Proceedings of the Conference on Urban Change and Conflict*, Centre for Environmental Studies, Conference Paper 14, 1975; F. Gray, 'The management of local authority housing', in *Housing and Class in Britain*, Political Economy of Housing Workshop (University of Sussex School of Cultural and Community Studies), 1976; and R. E. Pahl, *Whose City?* Penguin Books, 1975.

41 See e.g. P. Griffiths, *Homes Fit for Heroes: A Shelter Report on Housing*, Shelter, 1975; and F. Gray, 'The management of local authority housing', in *Housing Class in Britain*, Political Economy of Housing Workshop of the Conference of Socialist Economists, 1976.

42 Central Housing Advisory Committee, *Council Housing: Purposes, Procedures and Priorities*, HMSO, 1969, paras 91 and 96.

43 But see the outspoken report of the Scottish Housing Advisory Committee, *Training for Tomorrow: An Action Plan for Scottish Housing* (Muir Report), HMSO, 1977.

44 E. Burney, *Housing on Trial*, Oxford University Press, 1967, p. 71.

45 Central Housing Advisory Committee, *Council Housing: Purposes, Procedures and Priorities*, HMSO, 1969, para. 90.

3 COUNCIL HOUSING FINANCE

1 *Report of the Committee on Housing in Greater London*, Cmnd 2605, 1965, p. 56.
2 See Ministry of Housing and Local Government, *Housing Revenue Accounts: Report of the Working Party on the Housing Revenue Account*, HMSO, 1969.
3 See N. P. Hepworth, 'Local government and housing finance', in Institute of Fiscal Studies, *Housing Finance*. 1975, pp. 45–6.
4 See M. Bowley, *Housing and the State*, Allen & Unwin, 1945, p. 278; Ministry of Health, *The Cost of House Building*, HMSO, 1948; and Department of Health for Scotland, *Scottish Building Costs*, HMSO, 1948.
5 National Board for Prices and Incomes, Report No. 62, *Increases in Rents of Local Authority Housing*, Cmnd 3604, 1968, para. 21.
6 Scottish Development Department, *Rents of Houses Owned by Local Authorities in Scotland 1964*. Cmnd 2598, 1965.
7 See e.g. R. A. Parker, *The Rents of Council Houses*, Occasional Papers on Social Administration No. 22, Bell, 1967; and *Report of the Committee on Housing in Greater London* (Milner Holland Report), Cmnd 2605, 1965.
8 Department of Health for Scotland, *Report on the Local Inquiry in the Matter of a Review of the Rents of Corporation Houses in Glasgow*, HMSO, 1958; *Report on the Local Inquiry in the Matter of a Review of the Rents of Council Houses in Dunbarton*, HMSO, 1961; *Report on the Local Inquiry in the Matter of a Review of the Rents of Corporation Houses in Dundee*, HMSO, 1963. See also R. D. Cramond, *Housing Policy in Scotland 1919–1964*, Oliver & Boyd, 1966; and O. A. Hartley, 'Local inquiries and council house rents in Scotland 1958–71', *Policy and Politics*, vol. 2, no. 1, September 1973.
9 A. A. Nevitt, *Housing, Taxation and Subsidies*, Nelson. 1966. p. 112.
10 See White Papers *The Housing Programme 1965 to 1970*, Cmnd 2838, 1965, and *The Scottish Housing Programme 1965 to 1970*, Cmnd 2832, 1965.
11 Central Housing Advisory Committee, *Homes for Today and Tomorrow* (Parker Morris Report), HMSO, 1961.
12 White Paper, *The Housing Programme 1965 to 1970*, Cmnd 2838, 1965, para. 41.
13 White Paper, *The Period of Severe Restraint*, Cmnd 3150, 1966.
14 White Paper, *Prices and Incomes Policy*, Cmnd 3235, 1967.
15 *Report of the Ministry of Housing and Local Government 1967 and 1968*, Cmnd 4009, 1969, p. 13.
16 *Housing and Construction Statistics*, no. 14, 2nd quarter 1975, table XXVIII.
17 *National Income and Expenditure 1965–75*, table 9.3, p. 60.
18 National Board for Prices and Incomes, Report 62, *Increases in Rents of Local Authority Housing*, Cmnd 3604, 1968. See also R. A. Parker, *The Rents of Council Houses*, Occasional Papers on Social Administration No. 22, Bell, 1967; Fourth Report from the Estimates Committee 1968–9, *Housing Subsidies*, HC 473, 1969; and Scottish Housing Advisory Committee, *Rent Rebates for Council Tenants*, HMSO, 1970.
19 See A. Crosland, *Towards a Labour Housing Policy*, Fabian Society, 1971.
20 See Fourth Report from the Estimates Committee 1968–9, *Housing Subsidies*, HC 473, 1969.
21 *Fair Deal for Housing*, Cmnd 4728, 1971, and *The Reform of Housing Finance in Scotland*, Cmnd 4727, 1971.
22 B. C. Smith and J. Stanyer, 'Administrative developments in 1971 and 1972: a survey', *Public Administration*, vol. 51, 1973, p. 397.
23 See A. Mitchell, 'Clay Cross', *Political Quarterly*, vol. 45, no. 2, April–June 1974, pp. 165–78; and, for a partisan view (which also sets the case in its historical and social context), S. Skinner and J. Langdon, *The Story of Clay Cross* (Bertrand Russell Peace Foundation), Spokesman Books, Nottingham, 1974.

24 See J. R. Jarmain, *Housing Subsidies and Rents*, Stevens, 1941.
25 Scottish Development Department, *Report for 1972*, Cmnd 5274, 1973, p. 43.
26 Ministry of Housing and Local Government, *Housing Revenue Accounts: Report of the Working Party on the Housing Revenue Account*, HMSO, 1969.
27 National Economic Development Office, *New Homes in the Cities: The Role of the Private Developer in Urban Renewal in England and Wales*, HMSO, 1971.
28 N. P. Hepworth, *The Finance of Local Government*, Allen & Unwin, 3rd edn, 1976, p. 172.
29 Central Statistical Office, *National Income and Expenditure 1965–75*, table 9.3.
30 *Housing and Construction Statistics*, no. 18, 2nd quarter 1976, table XXXV.
31 op. cit., table XXXVI.
32 *Advisory Committee on Rent Rebates and Rent Allowances, First Report 1973–1974*, HMSO, 1974.
33 A technical account is to be found in Department of the Environment, *Manual on Local Authority Housing Subsidies and Accounting*, HMSO, 1975.
34 HPT3, table VIII.31, p. 42.
35 HPC, para. 9.35, p. 83.

4 RENT CONTROL

1 W. Nickerson, *How I Turned $1000 into a Million in Real Estate – in My Spare Time*, Simon & Schuster, New York, 1959, p. 5.
2 Quoted in J. Carmichael, *Vacant Possession*, Institute of Economic Affairs, 1964.
3 Quotations are from the Debates on the Increase of Rent and Mortgage Interest (Wartime Restrictions) Bill, *HC Debates*, vol. 76, col. 420 et seq., 25 November 1915.
4 *HC Debates*, vol. 113, cols 799–800, 7 March 1919.
5 White Paper, *Rent Control: Statistical Information*, Cmnd 17, 1956.
6 See P. G. Gray and E. Parr, *Rent Act 1957: Report of Inquiry*, Cmnd 1246, 1960, p. 21.
7 J. B. Cullingworth, *English Housing Trends*, Occasional Papers on Social Administration 13, Bell, 1965.
8 P. G. Gray and E. Parr, *Rent Act 1957: Report of Inquiry*, Cmnd 1246, 1960; D. V. Donnison, C. Cockburn and T. Corlett, *Housing Since the Rent Act*, Occasional Papers on Social Administration 3, Codicote Press, Welwyn, 1961; P. G. Gray and R. Russell, *The Housing Situation in 1960*, The Social Survey, Central Office of Information, 1962; J. B. Cullingworth, *Housing in Transition*, Heineman, 1963; and J. B. Cullingworth, *English Housing Trends*, Occasional Papers on Social Administration 13, Bell, 1965.
9 J. B. Cullingworth, *Housing in Transition*, Heinemann, 1963.
10 *HC Debates*, vol. 567, col. 1472, 28 March 1957.
11 For later studies see J. Greve, *Private Landlords in England*, Bell, 1965; and P. G. Gray and J. Todd, 'Privately rented accommodation in London', published as an appendix to the Milner Holland Report, *Report of the Committee on Housing in Greater London*, Cmnd 2605, 1965.
12 For an account of Rachman, see the appendix of that title in the Milner Holland Report, op. cit., pp. 251–2.
13 See Ministry of Housing and Local Government, Circular 16/62.
14 See Ministry of Housing and Local Government, Circular 51/64.
15 White Paper, *London – Employment: Housing: Land*, Cmnd 1952, 1963. For fuller discussion see J. B. Cullingworth, *Land Values, Compensation and Betterment* (Vol. IV of *Environmental Planning 1939–1969*), HMSO, forthcoming.
16 *Report of the Committee on Housing in Greater London* (Milner Holland Report), Cmnd 2605, 1965.

17 Milner Holland Report, op. cit., p. 225.
18 White Paper, *Rents and Security of Tenure: The Rent Bill*, Cmnd 2622, 1965.
19 See J. Prophet, *Fair Rents*, Shaw, 1976; M. Partington, *Landlord and Tenant*, Weidenfeld & Nicolson, 1975, ch. 5; and *Report of the Committee on the Rent Acts* (Francis Report), Cmnd 4609, 1971.
20 F. G. Pennance, *Verdict on Rent Control*, Institute of Economic Affairs, 1972, p. xv.
21 White Paper, *Rents and Security of Tenure: The Rent Bill*, Cmnd 2622, 1965, para. 20.
22 The term was Crossman's (personal communication to the author).
23 *Report of the Committee on the Rent Acts* (Francis Report), Cmnd 4609, 1971, p. 11.
24 op. cit., p. 96.
25 op. cit., p. 97.
26 op. cit., ch. 32.
27 op. cit., pp. 233–7.
28 op. cit., p. 168.
29 See op. cit., ch. 29.
30 D. L. Evans, 'The Rent Act 1974', *Journal of Planning and Environment Law*, 1974, pp. 576–87.
31 Department of the Environment, *The Review of the Rent Acts: A Consultative Paper*, DoE, January 1977. A Scottish Paper followed in May 1977 – Scottish Development Department, *Consultation Paper on the Review of the Rent (Scotland) Acts*.
32 The objectives are reproduced in the *Scottish* housing policy review (but not in the English): see HPCS. p. 87.
33 HPC, para. 8.11, p. 71, and para. 8.23, pp. 73–4.

5 IMPROVEMENT AND SLUM CLEARANCE

1 H. Shimmin, *The Sanitary Aspects of Philanthropy*, Liverpool, 1866, quoted in M. B. Simey, *Charitable Effort in Liverpool in the Nineteenth Century*, Liverpool University Press, 1951, p. 100.
2 For a discussion of earlier policy in relation to improvement see ch. IX of the author's *Housing and Local Government*, Allen & Unwin, 1966.
3 Committee Stage Debates on the Housing Bill, 1949, *Standing Committee Debates 1948–1949*, vol. II, col. 1957.
4 See, for example, Labour Party, *The Welfare State*, Discussion Pamphlet 1952; and D. L. Munby, *The Rent Problem*, Fabian Society, 1952.
5 White Papers, *Houses – the Next Step*, Cmd 8996; and *Housing Policy in Scotland*, Cmd 8997, 1953.
6 *Report of the Committee on Housing in Greater London* (Milner Holland Report), Cmnd 2605, 1965, pp. 37–43.
7 White Paper, *Housing*, Cmnd 2050, 1963, para. 11.
8 *Report of the Ministry of Housing and Local Government 1964*, Cmnd 2668, 1965, p. 18.
9 Association of Public Health Inspectors, *Progress in Housing*, 1961; and 'Improving our houses – a plan for action', *The Sanitarian*, vol. 72, November 1963.
10 See the 'note of reservation' to the Denington Report, Central Housing Advisory Committee, *Our Older Houses: A Call for Action*, HMSO, 1966.
11 *Report of the Ministry of Housing and Local Government 1967 and 1968*, Cmnd 4009, p. 11.
12 Ministry of Housing and Local Government, Circular 53/64.
13 White Paper, *Old Houses into New Homes*, Cmnd 3602, 1968, para. 11.

14 Tenth Report from the Expenditure Committee, 1972–3, *Improvement Grants*, HC 349-II, 1973, p. 2.
15 *Public Expenditure to 1978–79*, Cmnd 5879, 1975, table 2.7, pp. 70–1.
16 For fuller discussion see K. Davies, *Law of Compulsory Purchase and Compensation*, Butterworth, 1972.
17 See e.g. E. D. Simon, *How to Abolish the Slums*, Longman, 1929.
18 See J. Clancey, 'The Housing Repairs and Rents Act 1954', *Journal of the Royal Society of Health*, vol. 76, no. 4, April 1956; and Central Housing Advisory Committee, *Report of the Standards of Fitness for Human Habitation Subcommittee* (Miles Mitchell Report), HMSO, 1946.
19 *Slum Clearance (England and Wales)*, Cmd 9593, 1955; and *Slum Clearance (Scotland)*, Cmd 9685, 1956.
20 See e.g. L. Needleman, 'A long term view of housing', *National Institute Economic Review*, no. 18, November 1961; F. T. Burnett and S. F. Scott, 'A survey of housing conditions in the urban areas of England and Wales 1960', *Sociological Review*, vol. 10, no. 1, March 1962; and P. G. Gray and R. Russell, *The Housing Situation in 1960*, The Social Survey, Central Office of Information, 1962.
21 White Papers, *Housing in England and Wales*, Cmnd 1290, 1961; and *Housing*, Cmnd 2050, 1963.
22 Ministry of Housing and Local Government, Circular 11/65; see *Report of the Ministry of Housing and Local Government 1965 and 1966*. Cmnd 3282, 1967, p. 69.
23 White Paper, *The Housing Programme 1965 to 1970*, Cmnd 2838, 1965, para. 3; and White Paper, *The Scottish Housing Programme 1965 to 1970*, 1965, para. 6.
24 Central Housing Advisory Committee, *Our Older Homes: A Call for Action* (Denington Report), HMSO, 1966.
25 See appendix to the White Paper *Old Houses into New Homes*, Cmnd 3602, 1968; 'House condition survey England and Wales 1967', *Economic Trends*, no. 175, May 1968; and Ministry of Housing and Local Government, *Housing Statistics*, no. 9, April 1968, and no. 10 July 1968.
26 Scottish Housing Advisory Committee, *Scotland's Older Houses*, HMSO, 1967.
27 op. cit., paras 104–5.
28 op. cit., para. 124.
29 See Scottish Development Department, *The New Scottish Housing Handbook*, Bulletin 2, Slum Clearance and Improvements, HMSO, 1969.
30 HPC, table 1, p. 11; and HPCS, paras 2.9–2.10, p. 6.
31 C. G. M. M'Gonigle, 'Poverty, nutrition and the public health: an investigation into some of the results of moving a slum population to modern dwellings', *Proceedings of the Royal Society of Medicine*, vol. 26, 1933, pp. 677–87; and C. G. M. M'Gonigle and J. Kirby, *Poverty and the Public Health*, Gollancz, 1936.
32 M. Young and P. Willmott, *Family and Kinship in East London*, Routledge & Kegan Paul, 1957.
33 See references quoted in ch. 3 of the author's *The Social Content of Planning* (Vol. 2 of *Problems of an Urban Society*), Allen & Unwin, 1973. Later studies include S. Jacobs, *The Right to a Decent House*, Routledge & Kegan Paul, 1976; and J. English, R. Madigan and P. Norman, *Slum Clearance: The Social and Administrative Context in England and Wales*, Croom Helm, 1976.
34 See e.g. C. Ungerson, *Moving Home*, Occasional Papers on Social Administration 44, Bell, 1971.
35 See e.g. L. Needleman, *The Economics of Housing*, Staples, 1963, ch. 10; L. Needleman, 'The comparative economics of improvement and new building', *Urban Studies*, vol. 6, 1969, pp. 196–209; and R. M. Kirwan and D. B. Martin, *The Economics of Urban Residential Renewal and Improvement*, Centre for Environmental Studies, Working Paper 77, 1972.

36 *Report of the Committee on Housing in Greater London* (Milner Holland Report, Cmnd 2605, 1965, pp. 413–29.

37 Della Nevitt, 'Prices in the housing market', *Guardian*, 17 March 1972. See also B. Nutt, B. Walker, S. Holliday and D. Sears, *Obsolescence in Housing: Theory and Applications*, Saxon House, 1976.

38 A. Stones, 'Stop slum clearance – now', *Official Architecture and Planning*, vol. 35, no. 2, pp. 107–10.

39 *Widening the Choice: The Next Steps in Housing*, Cmnd 5280; *Homes for the People: Scottish Housing Policy in the 1970s*, Cmnd 5272; *Better Homes: The Next Priorities*, Cmnd 5339; and *Towards Better Housing: Proposals for Dealing with Scotland's Older Housing*, Cmnd 5338.

40 Department of the Environment, Circular 14/75; see also Department of the Environment, Area Improvement Note 10, *The Use of Indicators for Area Action*, HMSO, 1975.

41 See ch. 5 of the author's *The Social Content of Planning* (Vol. 2 of *Problems of an Urban Society*), Allen & Unwin, 1973.

42 Tenth Report from the Expenditure Committee, 1972–3, *Improvement Grants*, HC 349-II, p. xvii.

43 T. Roberts, *General Improvement Areas*, Saxon House, 1976, p. 34.

44 See evidence to the Expenditure Committee on *House Improvement Grants*, op. cit.

45 op. cit., pp. 6, 286, 317 and xxiii.

46 op. cit., p. 235.

47 op. cit., p. 304.

48 White Paper, *Towards Better Homes*, Cmnd 5338, 1973, paras 14–15.

49 *House Improvement Grants: Government Observations on the Tenth Report from the Expenditure Committee*, Cmnd 5529, 1974, p. 2.

50 Scottish Development Department, Circular 67/1975.

51 See 'Housing rehabilitation – Assist', *Architects' Journal*, 10 November 1976, 8 December 1976 and 9 February 1977. For a wider discussion of *Housing Action Areas in Scotland* see the report so entitled by T. L. C. Duncan and R. H. Cowan, The Planning Exchange, Scotland, 1976.

52 Department of the Environment, Circular 160/74.

53 Department of the Environment, Circular 13/75.

54 White Paper, *Development and Compensation–Putting People First*, Cmnd 5124, 1972. The proposals were enacted in the Land Compensation Act, 1973 (see Department of the Environment, Circular 73/73).

55 T. L. C. Duncan, 'Housing action areas in Scotland', *Housing Review*, January–February 1977, p. 20.

56 P. Graham, 'Are action areas a mistake?', *Municipal and Public Services Journal*, vol. 82, no. 27, 5 July 1974, pp. 809–11.

57 P. Graham, op. cit.; see also T. L. C. Duncan and R. H. Cowan, *Housing Action Areas in Scotland*, The Planning Exchange, Scotland, 1976.

58 T. Mason, 'Intention and implication in housing policy; a study of recent developments in urban renewal', *Journal of Social Policy*, vol. 6, pt I, January 1977, p. 27.

59 op. cit.

60 HPC, para. 10.19, p. 94.

61 See ch. 5 of the author's *The Social Content of Planning* (Vol. 2 of *Problems of an Urban Society*), Allen & Unwin, 1973.

62 W. G. Grigsby et al., *Rethinking Housing and Community Development Policy*, University of Pennsylvania, Department of City and Regional Planning, 1977, p. 28.

6 OWNER-OCCUPATION

1 Quoted in C. K. Meek, *Land Law and Custom in the Colonies*, Oxford University Press, 1946, p. 243.
2 HPT1, table 1.24, p. 39.
3 HPT3, table B1, p. 145.
4 See e.g. *Housing Problems, Priorities and Preferences*, Opinion Research Centre, 1967; F. G. Pennance and H. Gray, *Choice in Housing*, Institute of Economic Affairs, 1968; J. B. Cullingworth and V. A. Karn, *The Ownership and Management of Housing in New Towns*, HMSO, 1968; B. Ineichen, *A Place of Our Own*, Housing Research Foundation, 1974; J. Madge, *The Housing Experience of Newly Married Couples*, Centre for Studies in Social Policy, 1976; North Region Strategy Team, *Housing in the Northern Region*, 1976 (especially Vol. 2, Appendix M); and National Economic Development Office, *A Survey of Attitudes Towards Current and Alternative Housing Policies*, HMSO, 1977. A convenient summary (from a not unbiased source) of a range of studies is to be found in Building Societies Association, *Facts and Figures*, no. 12, October 1977.
5 See Ministry of Health, *Private Enterprise Housing* (Pole Report), HMSO, 1944, Appendix IV; and Department of Health for Scotland, *The Provision of Houses for Owner Occupation in Scotland* (Laidlaw Report), Cmd 6741, 1946, p. 10.
6 See the Pole and Laidlaw Reports, op. cit.
7 White Paper, *Housing*, Cmd 6609, 1945, para. 26.
8 White Paper, *Housing Programme for 1947*, Cmd 7021, 1947.
9 White Paper, *Houses – The Next Step*, Cmd 8996, 1953, para. 7.
10 White Paper, *Housing Policy – Scotland*, Cmd 8997, 1953, para. 39.
11 See White Paper, *House Purchase: Proposed Government Scheme*, Cmnd 571, 1958.
12 Central Statistical Office, *Social Trends*, no. 1, 1970, table 90.
13 F. Field, M. Meacher and C. Pond, *To Him Who Hath: A Study of Poverty and Taxation*, Penguin Books, 1977, p. 10.
14 White Paper, *The Housing Programme 1967 to 1970*, Cmnd 2838, 1965.
15 White Paper, *The Land Commission*, Cmnd 2771, 1965.
16 White Paper, *Leasehold Reform in England and Wales*, Cmnd 2916, 1966.
17 White Paper, *Help Towards Home Ownership*, Cmnd 3163, 1966.
18 op. cit.
19 *Report of the Ministry of Housing and Local Government 1969 and 1970*, Cmnd 4753, 1971, pp. 10–11.
20 *Housing and Construction Statistics*, no. 18, 2nd quarter 1976, table 39, and no. 19, 3rd quarter 1976, table 41. See also no. 16, 4th quarter 1975, tables XIX and XX.
21 HPT2, p. 61, para. 77.
22 HPT2, table VI.26, p. 60.
23 See note 4 above.
24 *Housing and Construction Statistics*, no. 20, 4th quarter 1976, table X. See also A. W. Evans, *The Five Per Cent Sample Survey of Building Society Mortgages*, Central Statistical Office Studies in Official Statistics No. 26, HMSO, 1975, pp. 12–14.
25 J. Madge, *The Housing Experience of Newly Married Couples*, Centre for Studies in Social Policy, 1976.
26 See M. Bowley, *Housing and the State*, Allen & Unwin, 1945, pp. 177–8.
27 As is abundantly illustrated in 'Fairness between tenants and home owners', HPT2, ch. 5.
28 HPC, para. 7.14, p. 52.
29 HPC, ch. 7.

30 HPC, para. 7.03, p. 50.
31 Northern Region Strategy Team, Technical Report No. 15, *Housing in the Northern Region*, Vol. I, 1976, p. 76, A much earlier statement of the importance of housing in regional economy was made in the Toothill Report, *Report on the Scottish Economy*, Scottish Council (Development and Industry), 1961.
32 White Paper, *The North East: A Programme for Regional Development and Growth*, Cmnd 2006, 1963, p. 79.
33 For a discussion of 'trading up' see HPT2, pp. 35–47.
34 HPT2, table B1, p. 69.
35 P. G. Gray, *The British Household*, The Social Survey 1947, table 24.
36 R. D. Cramond, *Housing Policy in Scotland 1919–1964*. University of Glasgow Social and Economic Studies, Research Paper 1, Oliver & Boyd, 1966, ch. IV.
37 Scottish Housing Advisory Committee, *The Demand for Private Houses in Scotland*, HMSO, 1972, p. 63.
38 Scottish Housing Advisory Committee, *The Cost of Private House Building in Scotland*, HMSO, 1970, p. 48.
39 HPCS, para. 2.28, p. 13, and Fig. 2K, p. 15.
40 'Building societies and the Scottish housing market', Building Societies Association, *Facts and Figures Quarterly Bulletin*, 6, April 1976, p. 16.
41 HPCS, pp. 74–5.
42 See e.g. A. Murie, *The Sale of Council Houses*, University of Birmingham, Centre for Urban and Regional Studies, Occasional Paper 35, 1975; R. Forrest and A. Murie, *Social Segregation, Housing Needs, and the Sale of Council Houses*, University of Birmingham, Centre for Urban and Regional Studies, Research Memorandum 53, 1976; and J. English and C. Jones, *The Sale of Council Houses*, University of Glasgow, Discussion Papers in Social Research 18, 1977.
43 F. Field, *Do We Need Council Houses?*, Catholic Housing Aid Society, Occasional Paper 2, 1975.
44 See J. English and C. Jones, *The Sale of Council Houses*, University of Glasgow, Discussion Papers in Social Research 18, pp. 61 and 65 *et seq.*
45 *HC Debates*, vol. 931, col. 1804, 13 May 1975.
46 P. Niner, *Local Authority Housing Policy and Practice*, University of Birmingham, Centre for Urban and Regional Studies, Occasional Paper 31, 1975; A. Murie, *The Sale of Council Houses*, University of Birmingham, Centre for Urban and Regional Studies, Occasional Paper 35, 1975; R. Forrest and A. Murie, *Social Segregation, Housing Need and the Sale of Council Houses*, University of Birmingham, Centre for Urban and Regional Studies, Research Memorandum 53, 1976.
47 J. English and C. Jones, op. cit., p. 10.
48 A. Murie, op. cit., p. 126 and p. 149; note the qualification on p. 128.
49 R. Forrest and A. Murie, op. cit., p. 17.
50 R. Forrest and A. Murie, op. cit., p. 33.
51 D. Harvey, *Social Justice and the City*, Edward Arnold, 1973.
52 A. Murie, op. cit., p. 93.
53 See the stimulating, disturbing yet unsatisfying papers of the 'Political Economy of Housing Workshop of the Conference of Socialist Economists', *Political Economy and the Housing Question*, 1975, and *Housing and Class in Britain*, 1976. The unsatisfying nature of all this type of discussion is that it provides little by way of politically practicable programmes for new policies.
54 A. Murie, op. cit., p. 150.
55 A. Gilmour, *The Sale of Council Housing in Oslo*, University of Edinburgh, Architecture Research Unit, 1971, p. xi.
56 This section is based in large part on the account given in the author's *The Social Content of Planning*, Allen & Unwin, 1973, ch. 3.
57 National Economic Development Office, *New Homes in the Cities: The Role*

of the Private Developer in Urban Renewal in England and Wales, HMSO, 1971.
58 The fifteen towns were Birmingham, Bradford, Bristol, Cardiff, Coventry, Kingston upon Hull, Leeds, Leicester, Liverpool, Manchester, Newcastle upon Tyne, Nottingham, Sheffield, Stoke on Trent and Wolverhampton.
59 *New Homes in the Cities*, op. cit., p. 19.
60 Department of the Environment, *Report of Working Party on Local Authority/Private Enterprise Partnership Schemes*, HMSO, 1972.
61 D. R. Denman, 'Should we put our cities out to grass?', *New Society*, 30 June 1977. See now the report on *Urban Wasteland*, Civic Trust, 1977; and J. Burrows, 'Vacant urban land: a continuing crisis', *The Planner*, January 1978.

7 ALTERNATIVE TENURES

1   W. A. Lewis, *Development Planning*, Harper & Row, 1966, p. 112.
2   J. B. Cullingworth, *Housing in Transition: A Case Study in the City of Lancester*, Heinemann, 1963, p. 30.
3   M. Bowley, *Housing and the State*, Allen & Unwin, 1945, pp. 139 and 176.
4   Central Housing Advisory Committee, *Private Enterprise Housing*, HMSO, 1944, para. 113.
5   W. Ashworth, *The Genesis of Modern British Town Planning*, Routledge & Kegan Paul, 1954, p. 85.
6   For a succinct history see Central Housing Advisory Committee, *The Operation of Housing Associations*, HMSO, 1939.
7   White Paper, *Housing in England and Wales*, Cmnd 1290, 1961, para. 43.
8   *Report of the Ministry of Housing and Local Government 1963*, Cmnd 2338, p. 14.
9   White Paper, *Housing*, Cmnd 2050, 1963, para. 41.
10 Department of the Environment, *Housing Associations: A Working Paper of the Central Housing Advisory Committee*, HMSO, 1971, para. 3.40.
11 op. cit., para. 3.7.
12 *Report of the Ministry of Housing and Local Government 1969 and 1970*, Cmnd 4753, p. 5.
13 Department of the Environment, *Housing Associations: A Working Paper of the Central Housing Advisory Committee*, HMSO, 1971.
14 op. cit., Foreword by Julian Amery, Minister for Housing and Construction.
15 White Paper, *Fair Deal for Housing*, Cmnd 4728, 1971.
16 White Papers, *Widening the Choice: The Next Steps in Housing*, Cmnd 5280, and *Homes for the People: Scottish Housing Policy in the 1970s*, Cmnd 5272, 1973.
17 For a detailed account of the post-1974 Act provisions see C. V. Baker, *Housing Associations*, Estates Gazette, 1976.
18 *HC Debates*, vol. 873, cols 48–9, 6 May 1974.
19 *Housing Corporation Annual Report 1975–76*, p. 4.
20 J. Baker, 'Housing associations – their place in housing', *Journal of the Institute of Rent Officers*, vol. 8, no. 1, April 1977, p. 9. See also the annual reports of the National Federation of Housing Associations.
21 Ninth Report from the Expenditure Committee, 1976–7, *Selected Public Expenditure Programmes, Chapter III: Housing*, HC 466-III, 1977.
22 *Housing Corporation Annual Report 1976–77*.
23 Department of the Environment, Circular 8/76.
24 J. Hands, *Housing Co-operatives*, Society for Co-operative Dwellings, 1975.
25 Department of the Environment, *Final Report of the Working Party on Housing Co-operatives* (Campbell Report), HMSO, 1975.
26 Campbell Report, op. cit., p. 5, para. 1.22.
27 See ch. 10 of J. Hands, op. cit.

28 The arguments are set out and discussed in both J. Hands, op. cit., and the Campbell Report, op. cit.
29 See Campbell Report, op. cit., e.g., pp. 26, 29 and 8, para. 1.37.
30 *Housing Corporation Annual Report 1976–77.*
31 Department of the Environment, Circular 170/74.
32 National Federation of Housing Associations, *Federation News*, January 1976, p. 7.
33 T. Collison, 'Democracy in housing', *Labour Weekly*, 4 June 1976.
34 HPC, paras 9.59–9.60, p. 88.
35 See e.g. J. F. C. Turner and R. Fichter, *Freedom to Build*, Macmillan, 1973; J. F. C. Turner, *Housing by People*, Marion Boyars, 1976; C. Ward, *Housing: An Anarchist Approach*, Freedom Press, 1976; C. Ward (ed.), *Vandalism*, Architectural Press, 1973; Architectural Association, *Alternatives in Housing?*, Architectural Association Printshop, 1976; Docklands Joint Committee, *Housing: A Working Paper for Consultation*, Docklands Development Team, 1975; National Consumer Council, *Tenancy Agreements*, NCC, 1976; Association of London Housing Estates, *Tenants Participation in Housing Management*, ALHE, 1975; A. Gilmour and S. Musgrave, *Alternative Patterns of Housing Tenure within the Public Sector*, Lambeth Borough Council, 1974. See also the papers of the Political Economy of Housing Workshop of the Conference of Socialist Economists, *Political Economy and the Housing Question* (1975) and *Housing and Class in Britain* (1976), School of Cultural and Community Studies, University of Sussex; and various reports of the Community Development Project, for example, Southwark Community Development Project, *Housing for the Poor?*, 1975 and *Alternative Forms of Tenure: Preferences and Costs*, 1976.
36 S. Clarke and N. Ginsburg, 'The political economy of housing', in *Political Economy and the Housing Question*, Housing Workshop of the Conference of Socialist Economists, 1975, p. 31.
37 D. Page (ed.), *Housing Associations: Three Surveys*, Centre for Urban and Regional Studies, University of Birmingham, 1971.
38 Minority Report in Architectural Association, *Alternatives in Housing? A Report on Self-Build in Britain*, Arhictectural Association Printshop, 1976, p. 27.

8   HOUSING ALLOWANCES

1 P. H. Leven, 'Discrimination in housing policy', in K. Jones (ed.), *The Year Book of Social Policy in Britain 1976*, Routledge & Kegan Paul, 1977, p. 145.
2 White Paper, *Fair Deal for Housing*, Cmnd 4728, 1971 (from which all the unidentified quotations are taken).
3 *Advisory Committee on Rent Rebates and Rent Allowances, Report No. 2, July 1974 to December 1976*, HMSO, 1977, p. vii. Hereafter this will be referred to as *ACRRRA Report No. 2*. Similarly their first report, covering the period March 1973 to June 1974, will be referred to as *ACRRRA Report No. 1*.
4 For a discussion of administrative aspects see C. Legg and M. Brion, *The Administration of the Rent Rebate and Rent Allowance Schemes*, Department of the Environment, 1976. On the wider issue of means testing see *Means Tested Benefits: A Discussion Paper*, National Consumer Council, 1976.
5 *ACRRRA Report No. 2*, p. 31; see also D. Page and B. Weinberger, *Birmingham Rent Rebate and Allowances Study*, University of Birmingham, Centre for Urban and Regional Studies, Research Memorandum 44, 1975; and P. F. Taylor-Gooby, 'Rent benefits and tenants' attitudes', *Journal of Social Policy*, vol. 5, pt 1, January 1976, pp. 33–48.
6 loc. cit., and Department of the the Environment, *Haringey Rent Allowance Project: Interim Report*, 1975.

7   C. Legg and M. Brion, op. cit., p. 78.
8   C. Legg and M. Brion, op. cit., ch. 11.
9   Personal communication from the Director of Housing, London Borough of Hammersmith.
10 But see C. Legg and M. Brion, op. cit., pp. 67–8.
11 *Supplementary Benefits Commission Annual Report 1975*, Cmnd 6615, 1976, p. 57. (The figures were 11,000 private tenants and 2,000 owner-occupiers – whose 'rent' is mortgage interest payments; there were no local authority tenants whose rent was not met in full.)
12 *ACRRRA Report No. 2*, p. 23.
13 *ACRRRA Report No. 1*, p. 14, para. 18.2.
14 loc. cit.
15 *ACRRRA Report No. 2*, pp. 24–5 and 32.
16 See e.g. M. Wicks, *Rent Allowances: The Exclusion of Furnished Tenancies*, Child Poverty Action Group, 1972; and D. Bebb, *Rent Rebates and the Furnished Tenant*, Shelter, 1972.
17 *ACRRRA Report No. 1*, p. 7.
18 loc. cit. and Department of the Environment, Circular 48/73.
19 *ACRRRA Report No. 2*, p. 18.
20 See C. Legg and M. Brion, op. cit., ch. 5, and *ACRRRA Report No. 2*, p. 25.
21 See *Supplementary Benefits Commission Annual Report 1975*, Cmnd 6615, 1976, ch. 8.
22 (a) England and Wales, October 1976. Source: *ACRRRA Report No. 2*, pp. 30–1.
    (*b*) England and Wales, 1975. Source: *Local Government Finance* (Layfield Report), Cmnd 6453, p. 161.
    (*c*) Great Britain, 1976. Source: *Supplementary Benefits Commission Annual Report 1976*, Cmnd 6910, p. 20.
    (*d*) United Kingdom, 1975. Source: *Social Trends*, no. 7, 1976, table 5.26, p. 121.
    (*e*)–(*j*) United Kingdom, December 1975. Source: *Social Trends*, no. 7, 1976, table 5.22, p. 120.
    (*k*) United Kingdom, December 1975. Source: *Social Trends*, no. 7, 1976, table 5.30, p. 123.
    (*l*) United Kingdom, 1976–7. Source: HPT2, p. 4, para. 14.
23 *Social Trends*, no. 7, 1976, table 5.28, p. 123.
24 *ACRRRA Report No. 2*, pp. 4–5.
25 J. J. Valenza, *Program Housing Standards in the Experimental Housing Allowance Program*, The Urban Institute, 1977. See also US Department of Housing and Urban Development, *Housing Allowances: The 1976 Report to Congress*, US Government Printing Office, 1976.
26 *Supplementary Benefits Commission Annual Report 1975*, Cmnd 6615, 1976, p. 13.

9   HOUSING POLICY QUESTIONS

1   US Department of Housing and Urban Development, *Housing in the Seventies: A Report of the National Housing Policy Review*, US Government Printing Office,1974, p. 1.
2   HPC, para. 9.09, p. 77.
3   HPC, para. 2.14, p. 6.
4   The British differences are small compared with those in the United States. On this, see the illuminating discussion on 'Housing as a social service', in H. L. Wolman, *Housing and Housing Policy in the US and the UK*, Lexington Books, 1975. See also T. H. Marshall, *Social Policy*, Hutchinson, 1970, p. 166.
5   HPT2, table VII.25, p. 120.
6   HPT2, p. 14.

7 HPT2, table A1, p. 67.
8 Little is known about trading up, but see HPT2, pp. 42–9.
9 There has been a long debate on the complexities and costs of conveyancing; see, for example, K. Weetch and C. Prestige, *Debate: Who Does Conveyancing on Your House?*, Aims for Freedom Enterprise, 1976; and Consumers' Association, *Evidence to the Royal Commission on Legal Services*, 1977. See also HPT1, pp. 225–30.
10 HPT2, pp. 64–5.
11 See HPT2, chs. 5 and 6.
12 HPT1, table II.33, p. 88; and HPT2, table VI.27, p. 64.
13 HPT2, table V.1, p. 19 and para. 14, p. 4.
14 HPT2, table VI.26, p. 60.
15 HPT2, table V.1, p. 19.
16 HPT2, para. 14, p. 4.
17 See HPT1, pp. 184–5.
18 HPT2, table V.1, p. 19.
19 HPT2, para. 14, p. 4.
20 The figure is for England and Wales (April 1976) and excludes those on supplementary benefit: see *Housing and Construction Statistics*, no. 20, 4th quarter 1976, table XXI.
21 See 'Local authority housing in England and Wales: financial arrangements', HPT3, ch. 8.
22 HPT1, table IV.15, p. 187.
23 See P. H. Hare, 'Comparing the costs of owning and renting in Scotland', *Housing Review*, May–June 1973, pp. 113–17.
24 HPT1, table IV.15, p. 187; and HPT2, table VI.22, p. 54.
25 HPT1, table IV.7, p. 176.
26 HPT1, table IV.12, p. 185 (but note the technical difficulty which arises over rebates which is explained on p. 184, op. cit.).
27 See the brave yet unconvincing attempt by J. C. Odling-Smee, 'The impact of the fiscal system on different tenure sectors', in *Housing Finance*, Institute of Fiscal Studies, 1975.
28 HPC, para. 5.39, p. 39.
29 HPC, para. 5.07, p. 32.
30 W. A. Lewis, *The Principles of Economic Planning*, Allen & Unwin, 3rd edn, 1969, p. 32.
31 HPT2, table VI.24, p. 58.
32 HPT1, table IV.26, p. 204.
33 E. Craven, 'Housing' in R. Klein (ed.), *Social Policy and Public Expenditure 1975: Inflation and Priorities*, Centre for Studies in Social Policy, 1975, p. 117.
34 See S. Clark, *The Distribution of Public Expenditure on Housing: Who Benefits?*, (Evidence to the Expenditure Committee on behalf of Shelter), Shelter, 1977.
35 HPC, para. 5.37(iii), p. 39.
36 HPT1, p. 88; and HPT2, pp. 63–4.
37 For a sketch of some of the issues see ch. 1 of *Supplementary Benefits Commission Annual Report 1976*, Cmnd 6910, 1977.
38 See P. Townsend (ed.), *The Concept of Poverty*, Heinemann, 1970.
39 See, for example, D. Wedderburn (ed.), *Poverty, Inequality and Class Structure*, Cambridge University Press, 1974. A recent attempt to measure trends in the nature and extent of poverty is G. C. Fiegehen *et al.*, *Poverty and Progress in Britain 1953–73*, Cambridge University Press, 1977. For a recent spirited discussion of poverty and taxation see F. Field, M. Meacher and C. Pond, *To Him That Hath*, Penguin Books, 1977.
40 See R. M. Titmuss, *Income Redistribution and Social Change*, Allen & Unwin, 1962.

41 For a more theoretical discussion than is appropriate here see, for example, E. Gellner, 'A social contract in search of an idiom: the demise of the Dangeld state?', *Political Quarterly*, vol. 46, no. 2, April–June 1975, pp. 127–52.

42 A recent example is G. A. Stephenson and R. P. Harris, 'The redistributive effect of subsidies of households', *Economic Trends*, November 1977.

43 HPC, paras 7.33–7.42.

44 HPT1, pp. 84–5.

45 E. Craven, 'Housing', in R. Klein (ed.), *Social Policy and Public Expenditure 1975: Inflation and Priorities*, Centre for Studies in Social Policy, 1975, pp. 119–20.

46 E. Craven, op. cit., p. 120.

47 See HPC, paras 7.01–7.03, p. 50; and HPCS, paras 8.1–8.2, p. 66.

48 R. E. Slitor, 'Rationale of the present tax benefits for homeowners', *National Housing Policy Review, Housing in the Seventies, Working Papers 2*, US Government Printing Office, 1976, p. 942.

49 W. C. Baer, 'On the making of perfect and beautiful social programs', *The Public Interest*, no. 39, Spring 1975, pp. 80–98.

50 *Housing in the Seventies: A Report of the National Housing Policy Review*, USGPO, 1974, pp. 136–7; and G. Vernez and R. K. Yin, 'Social aspects of federal low income housing programs', *Working Papers 2*, op. cit., pp. 857–93.

51 R. Starr, 'Which of the poor shall live in public housing?', *The Public Interest*, no. 23, Spring 1971, pp. 116–24.

52 For a thorough discussion of the problems of 'disadvantage' see M. Rutter and N. Madge, *Cycles of Disadvantage: A Review of Research*, Heinemann, 1976.

53 For a detailed study of one such estate see *Bowhouse Alloa: Feasibility Study of Improvement Potential*, Scottish Development Department, 1974.

54 On this see particularly W. G. Grigsby *et al.*, *Rethinking Housing and Community Development Policy*, University of Pennsylvania Department of City and Regional Planning, 1977.

55 See Scottish Housing Advisory Committee, *Planning for Housing Needs*, HMSO, 1972; Scottish Development Department, *Local Housing Needs and Strategies: A Case Study of the Dundee Subregion*, HMSO, 1976; *SDD Circular 6/77*, and Scottish Housing Handbook I: *Assessing Housing Needs: A Manual of Guidance*, HMSO, 1977. There is much less material (and rethinking) on the English housing plans, but their very title ('housing investment plans') suggests a narrower concept – though much of the background is similar: see HPC, pp. 42–5, and Housing Services Advisory Group, *The Assessment of Housing Requirements*, DoE, 1977.

56 J. B. Cullingworth, 'Housing priorities and inflation', *Housing Review*, vol. 25, no. 1, January–February 1976, and 'New responses to new scarcities', *Housing Review*, vol. 25, no. 4, July–September 1976.

57 'Shore's housing plan turned inside out'. *Municipal Engineering*, vol. 154, no. 20, 24 May 1977.

58 For an example of an analysis which attempts to break away from the standard rituals, see North Region Strategy Team, Technical Report No. 15, *Housing in the Northern Region*, 1976.

59 SDD, Circular 6/77. See also SDD, *Assessing Housing Needs*, op. cit., pp. 7–9.

60 For further discussion of housing plans see A. S. Murie, 'Estimating housing need: technique or mystique', *Housing Review*, May–June 1976; the conference papers published in *Housing Review*, July–August 1977; and A. S. Murie and P. Leather, 'Developments in housing strategies', *The Planner*, November 1977.

61 Department of the Environment, *The Oldham Study*, *The Rotherham Study* (2 vols), and *The Sunderland Study*, HMSO, 1973.

62 Department of the Environment, *Unequal City* (Birmingham), *Inner London* (Lambeth) and *Change or Decay* (Liverpool), HMSO, 1977. See also *Inner Area Studies: Summaries of Consultants' Final Reports*, HMSO, 1977.

63 See the chapter on 'social planning' and the references quoted in the author's *The Social Content of Planning* (Vol. 3 of *Problems of an Urban Society*), Allen & Unwin, 1973.

64 C. L. Leven *et al.*, *Neighbourhood Change: Lessons in the Dynamics of Urban Decay*, Praeger, 1976, p. 6.

65 T. R. Lee, *Race and Residence: The Concentration and Dispersal of Immigrants in London*, Clarendon Press, 1977; and Greater London Council, *Colour and the Allocation of GLC Housing*, GLC Research Report 21, 1976. See also E. C. Banfield, *The Unheavenly City*, Little, Brown, 1968, ch. 4.

66 See Central Housing Advisory Committee, *Council Housing: Purposes, Procedures and Priorities*, HMSO, 1969, ch. 9.

67 W. G. Grigsby *et al.*, *Rethinking Housing and Community Development Policy*, University of Pennsylvania Department of City and Regional Planning, 1977, p. 59.

68 This section is a slightly edited version of pages 145–8 of the author's *The Social Content of Planning*, op. cit.

69 South East Joint Planning Team, *Strategic Plan for the South East, Studies Vol. 2: Social and Environmental Aspects*, HMSO, 1971.

70 op. cit., para. 1.98.

71 op. cit., para. 1.99(iv).

72 Central Advisory Council for Education (England), *Children and their Primary Schools*, HMSO, 1967.

73 op. cit., para. 162.

74 Central Housing Advisory Committee, *Council Housing: Purposes, Procedures and Priorities*, HMSO, 1969, para. 63. (See also Seebohm Report, *Report of the Committee on Local Authority and Allied Personal Social Services*, Cmnd 3703, HMSO, 1968, para. 490.)

75 H. Gans, *People and Planning*, Basic Books, 1968, p. 170.

76 For additional evidence see A. McGregor, 'Intra urban variations in unemployment duration: a case study', *Urban Studies*, vol. 14, 1977, pp. 303–13; and R. Murray and R. Osborne, 'Segregation on Horn Drive – a cautionary tale', *New Society*, 21 April 1977. Two literature reviews are to be found in W. Etherington, *The Idea of Social Mix: A Critical Bibliography*, Centre for Environmental Studies, Research Paper 7, 1974; and W. Sarkissian, 'The idea of social mix in town planning: a historical review', *Urban Studies*, vol. 13, 1976, pp. 231–46. See also M. Rutter and N. Madge, *Cycles of Disadvantage: A Review of Research*, Heinemann, 1976.

77 In *Social Justice and the City* (Edward Arnold, 1973), David Harvey concludes that 'it remains for revolutionary theory to chart the path from an urbanism based in exploitation to an urbanism appropriate for the human species. And it remains for revolutionary practice to accomplish such a transformation' (p. 314).

78 W. G. Grigsby *et al.*, *Rethinking Housing and Community Development Policy*, University of Pennsylvania Department of City and Regional Planning, 1977, p. 114.

79 On the concept of 'agenda' of issues of public and political concern, see W. Solesbury, 'The environmental agenda: an illustration of how situations become political issues and issues may demand responses from government: or how they may not', *Public Administration*, vol. 54, 1976, pp. 379–97. See also R. W. Cobb and C. D. Elder, *Participation in American Politics: The Dynamics of Agenda-building*, Allyn & Bacon, 1972; and D. A. Schon, *Beyond the Stable State*, Temple Smith, 1971, and Penguin Books, 1973.

Index